YELLOW ARROW F

The Grumpy Pilgrim's Guide to Santiago

Rudy Noriega

Copyright

Dedication

To Margriet and Anouk, without whom this may never have happened.

9th September: Prologue Bayonne to Saint-Jean-Pied-de-Port

The town is familiar but the feeling isn't. I have been coming to Bayonne for ten years and this is the first time I have ever woken up clear-headed. Six weeks ago, surfacing from my bed in the same hotel was almost done to the sound of someone drawing a chalk outline around my body. I wasn't the only one who felt terrible that morning but the town was a very different place then. It was the time of the annual fête - France's largest - when hundreds of thousands of people took to the streets over the course of five days to celebrate their region by eating and drinking themselves into oblivion. It was obligatory to wear the Basque uniform of white trousers, a white t-shirt, a red neckerchief and a red scarf worn around the waist. If you wanted to go the whole hog, you could wear a red beret as well. Under normal circumstances, I think the only people who should be allowed to wear white trousers are cricketers and members of Abba tribute bands, but you stand out if you don't when it's the party season. Over the course of several years, I have acquired the full costume though I haven't quite come to terms with how I look in it.

Stages were dotted around the town, but if you stood still long enough, the music would come and find you: small marching bands forced their way through the heaving streets, stopping now and again to give a prolonged show to those assembled nearby. Bars and restaurants added to the crowd congestion by placing tables and chairs outside to try to attract customers with special fête menus. Everywhere was a place of constant noise and movement, and it continued well after I had run out of steam and weaved back to my hotel in the small hours. I was lucky to have a room; several of my fellow partygoers spent the night passed out on one of the town's roundabouts.

It is not just that the days of the fête are well and truly over - it's much more than that. For a midweek morning, there's an air of Sunday lethargy that hangs over Bayonne. There is no commuter

1

buzz, no sense of urgency nor indeed any real sense of activity at all. It is unnervingly quiet as if the town has completely closed down. There are barely any cars about and the streets are virtually deserted. The revelry finished at the end of July but the civic hangover is still going on. In fairness, it was one hell of a party.

There is some life at the railway station but not much. At least there are other people around but they are conspicuous by their lack of movement, which is odd when you consider what they are wearing. It's a sort of uniform too; this time it's rucksacks, walking boots and poles, and alcohol-fuelled jollity is noticeably absent. I really thought I would be the only one here but there's about twenty of us taking up what little seating is available, or nervously standing around. As there is a train that is about to leave for Saint-Jean-Pied-de-Port in a few minutes, it's clear that we all have the same thing in mind. We are not just usual walkers; for whatever personal reasons, we are all heading west – a long way west. We have mentally signed up for an 800km long walk that is likely to take between five and six weeks and which traditionally ends at the alleged final resting place of St James.

Information about the patron saint of pilgrims is sketchy, to say the least. According to the Bible, St James was an early disciple of Jesus and legend has it that he headed to "Finisterre" - the end of the Earth - to preach the Gospel. Finisterre is identified as being part of what is now the north-west Spanish region of Galicia. After negligible evangelical success, he returned to Jerusalem and was beheaded for his efforts. Now things start to get a bit weird. His bones were gathered up by a couple of disciples and were returned to Galicia by means of a stone boat that had no sails or oars. His body was brought inland and buried at what is now the city of Santiago de Compostela and was forgotten about for the best part of a thousand years.

He was rediscovered, conveniently some might say, by a man named Pelayo who reported seeing a star over his grave. The word "Compostela" may be derived from this incident - "campus stellae" meaning field of stars. A church was built and St James became a figurehead in the battle against the Moors. The site became a place of pilgrimage from the tenth century onwards and the route became the subject of one of the first guidebooks, the *Codex Calixtus*, named after Pope Calixtus II. The final chapter gives descriptions of the

2

road to Santiago, the countryside, the places to stay and the peoples along the way. A millennium later the guidebooks may have been updated but the route has stayed pretty much the same.

As an excuse for a walk, the excursion to see the bones of a bloke who may or may not have been transported several hundred miles in a stone boat ranks alongside somebody pointing to the end of a rainbow and saying "If we head there, there might be a bit of cash in it for us". However, despite the dubious foundations, you can't fault a thousand years of success. Despite fluctuations in its popularity, the Camino still attracts a steady stream of pilgrims who are seeking a challenge, looking for spiritual renewal or just determined to put a further 500 miles between them and their problems. Now at Bayonne station, we are the latest in a long line of people to follow in the footsteps. Statistics are on completing the Camino are vague but according to one source, one in five don't make it, at least in the year they set out.

We exchange "I know where you're going" looks but nobody appears to be in a particularly talkative mood; hardly surprising given the hour of the day and the thoughts that are probably circulating. We may be strangers but we all look rather boringly similar in dark coloured fleeces and trousers. Despite the accidentally coordinated outfits, it's also clear that we're a solitary bunch. There are no groups, no pairs. Clearly, no one's fallen for the "Come on, it's only 800km. It'll be a laugh!" line.

I have to admit to being scared. I'm not a seasoned walker. My idea of fun is not being stuck on a fell, hunched over a flask of lukewarm tea while rain falls around me in slanting sheets of iciness. I like my walking urban, preferably punctuated by pubs and with easy access to cake and fully plumbed toilets. I haven't attempted anything like this before. I have been in training though and during my practice walks, I've managed to carry my kit for 35km without any major problems, and that is a lot longer than I intend to walk on any given day. That's the good news; unfortunately, my exertions were confined to the Thames Path in London. It does reach the dizzying heights of 2m above sea level just outside "The Black Lion" in Chiswick but it's hardly the best preparation for a stage that will take me higher than Ben Nevis tomorrow.

It's not the most glamorous of trains that takes you to Saint-Jean-Pied-de-Port. It's a single carriage effort that travels relentlessly

3

uphill on a single track with no great urgency and with a certain amount of strain. I travelled down yesterday using the Eurostar and a French high-speed TGV and this is very much the poor relation. On this particular morning, it's catering solely for walkers. It initially passes through tree-lined valleys barely wider than the track itself and it takes a good forty minutes for the scenery to open out and bring the mountains into view. Then it is another twenty minutes before they develop into a truly frightening size. It's easy to talk about the majesty and beauty of the Pyrenees but opinions change when you're facing the scary proposition of walking over them. At this point, they look dark, intimidating, and frankly, terrifying.

I sit opposite a woman in her fifties who is in full hiking gear and has a headband keeping her vivid red hair out of her eyes. She spends most of the journey assembling and reassembling her walking poles with a reverential amount of care, like Edward Fox putting together his sniper's rifle in *The Day of the Jackal*. I half expect her to blow down the tube and point it at me. This is followed by a long period of calibration, twisting gently to make sure that her poles are of equal length. Every so often, she stands up and takes a couple of steps with them to test them out, before sitting down again and making barely perceptible adjustments. Her attention to detail is admirable but I can't understand why this process is taking place on a train rather than on a path or road. If it's an attempt to show her fellow walkers how serious she is about the whole Camino, it's totally wasted on me. I'll regard it as a result if my socks match in the morning. I have walking poles too but can't say I've ever spent more than a few seconds adjusting them. She eventually decides that she can't do anymore and sits down with an over-loud sigh and a big smile, which demands to invite conversation.

Despite the clear warning signs that this woman has attention-seeking tendencies and should be ignored at all costs, she's a pilgrim and I want to have my first pilgrimage conversation. I want to know all about the motivations of my fellow walkers, hear their stories, and find out why they're doing this. I want to feel inspired and moved. Unfortunately, appearances aren't deceptive. Her name is Monica from Austria and within a few minutes, I'm aware that she was married for thirteen years, her husband ran off with the next-door neighbour a few months ago and she only decided to do the walk just after her dog died. It's a breathless monologue of misery

4

delivered in fluent English and I get the feeling it will be repeated rather a lot over the next month or so. She keeps punctuating her story with the mantra "but I'm OK now", though she certainly doesn't sound it. I nod my head sympathetically while inside I'm thinking, "You stupid bugger, you knew something like this was going to happen". I would be a bit more sympathetic if she wasn't so relentless. She barely stops for breath, and by the time the train reaches its destination I'm wondering if she's had her tonsils replaced by a fan-belt. It could have been worse, though; at least she didn't mention spirituality. I overdosed on that in my pre-Camino book reading and have no desire at all to return to that dark crystal-lit place ever again. The other bright side is that she's starting her walk immediately whereas I'm resting up and beginning tomorrow.

Saint-Jean-Pied-de-Port is a lot bigger than I thought it was going to be. I expected little more than an old, picturesque street and a railway station, but it's a good-sized place of about 1,500 people. It is situated on a plateau 180m above sea level and it takes the train an hour and twenty minutes of constant climbing and noticeable effort to get here. The walk goes to a height eight times greater tomorrow so you can imagine the personal trepidation. While the town feels welcoming, the surrounding mountains continue to look daunting and unfriendly.

We march in a loose line from the station past newish looking housing with the traditional Basque red and white decoration before edging into the old part of the town, which largely consists of one dangerously sloping cobbled street, the Rue de la Citadelle. This is the site of the pilgrimage bureau and is the first stopping point for anyone who wants to start their Camino from here.

There is no one specific starting place for the pilgrimage. There are routes that begin in Paris and Switzerland and there's no reason why you can't start from your own house and join the Camino along the way; many people do. There are also several pilgrimage routes that cross Spain at different angles but Saint-Jean-Pied-de-Port is perhaps the best known starting point for the most popular way to Santiago, the Camino Francés.

The bureau is already busy when I get there. There are five helpers, or *hospitaleros* sitting behind tables talking to prospective pilgrims and there's a short wait before I'm able to take my place opposite a friendly-looking bearded man who presses his hands together as if he's about to start praying.

I am expecting to hear a well-rehearsed speech about the Camino and what it involves, but I'm a bit taken aback when his first words are, "How can I help you?"

I inquire about the weather tomorrow. Part of me wants to hear bad news so I can take the alternative low-lying route and not have to bother with the 25km long "Route de Napoléon" which goes over the Pyrenees. He tells me that all is looking good and that I have nothing to worry about. He can smell my fear. He gives me a list of hostels or *refugios* along the way and a rather terrifying sheet of paper that has a list of stages to Santiago plotted on graphs showing altitude against distance. If it's given to alarm people, it certainly works with me. Tomorrow is not so much a learning curve as a line that strays far too close to the vertical for my liking.

Exactly a week ago, I was in the office of the British branch of the Confraternity of St James in London. I went there to pick up the latest guide to food and shelter and to have a talk to someone who has done the walk for some advice. While I was drinking tea, a retired couple came in who were seeking information on walking to Rome. When they found out I was taking on the Camino their reaction was incredibly buoyant.

"Oh I'm so jealous," enthused the woman, "I wish I was going to Santiago for the first time again."

"It's an amazing experience," added the man that I assumed was her husband, "we've done it a few times."

The woman's words made no sense to me at all but their enthusiasm was infectious. They laughed politely about my fear of not even making it over the Pyrenees and their optimism was based on experience. My worry is based on cold hard numbers: no matter how you disguise it, it's 20km of walking uphill to reach an altitude greater than anything found in Britain, followed by a dangerous 4km of heading down the other side.

"Take each day as it comes," was the message from the retired couple. The advice hasn't sunk in properly yet but I take my first step by folding away the sheet showing the stage profiles and putting it in my rucksack with the aim of never looking at it again.

I pick up a scallop shell, the badge of identity for all pilgrims and attach it to my rucksack. It's a strange emblem for a walk that

6

goes nowhere near the sea but it can be traced back to St James' arrival in Spain. As his stone boat approached the shore, a man rode into the sea on top of a panicking horse. Instead of being devoured by the waves, both horse and rider came to the surface unscathed and covered in scallop shells. St James had notched up his first miracle and Christianity got another easily recognisable logo into the bargain.

There's also a bit of paperwork to be done. I am asked to fill in my name, address, and nationality and tick a box to give my reason for doing the Camino. They're very general consisting of one-word subjects covering "personal", "spiritual" and "religious". They all apply to some extent so I tick each one. Finally, I receive my *credencial*. This is a pilgrimage passport that allows me to stay in the hostels along the route. It has to be stamped at each one I visit in order to receive my certificate of pilgrimage, or *compostela*, at the end of it all.

I am now a fully badged up Santiago pilgrim. I have my *credencial*, the world is my scallop, and I'm going to use it to find somewhere to stay. The Confraternity of St James told me that you just turn up at *refugios* in Spain and places are allocated on a first come, first served basis. You can book in France though I was told it probably wouldn't be necessary at this time of year. However, one of the places here is already full and a couple more don't open until the afternoon. I don't particularly want to carry my backpack for the rest of the morning so I'm pointed in the direction of the newer part of town and a building that looks more like a private house than a hostel.

I know I'm in the right place after a few minutes when the front door opens suddenly and several pilgrims are decanted none too gently onto the street. Behind them is a woman screaming ferociously at them in French. She looks like she's wearing a large baby-grow which was probably white once, has holes in and it's not exactly lacking in calories either; at least I hope they're food stains. She has a cigarette in one hand and, given the performance I'm witnessing, possibly a meat cleaver in the other. The pilgrims appear to be smirking. She raises her arm in a gesture of aggression and they walk down the street giggling. It's an impressive display but perhaps not the best advert for hospitality that I've ever. Her face changes when she sees me. I wouldn't call it a smile but she does approach looking vaguely human. Her voice softens and drops several dozen decibels.

"Are you a pilgrim? Would you like a bed for the night?" she asks.

After the show I've just witnessed the honest answer is "I'd rather dip my genitals in bleach", but one of the things I've decided to do on the walk is to say "yes" more often and to see what new experiences this may bring. Immediately and at the first opportunity, this feels like a really bad idea. I hadn't factored in a potential night at the Basil Fawlty memorial *refugio*.

I think about it briefly and decide I'm too scared to refuse. I go no more than a couple of steps into the house before she manages to suppress a shout to tell me to take my boots off. I'm then taken to a desk in a back room and she switches back to what I imagine she thinks is charm and takes my details. This is her part of the house; there is a living room and a kitchen behind her which both look a bit disordered. There are two dormitories in the building and I opt for the one on the first floor. She then opens a file that contains a list of house rules in various languages. It's basically a list of "don'ts and more don'ts", but in fairness, none of them sound unreasonable. There are no shoes of any kind to be worn in the building and it's forbidden to dry clothes in a dormitory. There's a 10pm curfew and quietness has to be maintained between then and 6am when you're allowed to leave. The quietness rule interests me because it's clear this woman has a couple of dogs and cats. She may even own a cockerel; I can certainly hear one.

While all this is being explained to me, the front door opens and in walks one of the pilgrims whom had previously been thrown out. The pilgrim has an uneasy smile on her face; my new landlady quite definitely doesn't. The pilgrim, who appears to be German has left something behind and wants to get it back. The *hospitalero* screams and the pilgrim rushes into the downstairs dormitory, grabs something and runs like a rabbit out of the door again. It's going to be an interesting night.

I get to my dormitory via a wooden spiral staircase. There are four bunk beds crammed into it; the dormitory downstairs has a similar arrangement. I leave my rucksack on a bottom bunk and when I'm putting my boots on to go back out again, I notice that the hallway is decorated with posters extolling the virtue of calmness and being Zen-like. Obviously, I don't know the owner at all but on first impressions, she strikes me as being one of the least Zen-like people I've ever come across. I have stayed in various types of hotels for work, places where you stay in sterile, featureless rooms and where you are overwhelmed by insincere corporate friendliness, but this is something completely new. I've never spent a night in a firetrap run by a mad woman with no people skills. Look where saying "Yes" gets you.

It's now around eleven o'clock and I have the rest of the day to kill in St Jean. Rather oddly, there are not many fellow walkers about though compared to early morning Bayonne it looks like chucking out time at Wembley. I walk up the Rue de la Citadelle as far as the entry arch, the Porte St Jacques and then head upwards to the Citadelle itself. I'm hesitant about the wisdom of this as it's accompanied by some very heavy breathing, which takes over the body very quickly. After only a couple of minutes, I feel absolutely knackered and fear flows through the mind. What if I twist an ankle or do myself another injury? Anxiety now accompanies every step, particularly those that take me back down to the town. I decide to be a bit more careful with my physical exertions for the moment and take advantage of the shade provided by some trees to drift off to sleep on a bench.

My peace is rudely shattered minutes later by the staccato sound of stones rattling the seat back like machine gun fire. I jump to my feet and see about half a dozen teenagers running away laughing. I want to say something suitably abusive but the French obscenities won't come so I just stand there open mouthed and indignant. I settle down again and doze off, only to be disturbed ten minutes later when the shelling starts again. I'm supposed to be undertaking a spiritual walk where, as a couple of books have pointed out, "every step is a prayer" but any feelings of spirituality go on hold for a few seconds as I get coordinated enough to sit up and direct some anger.

"Bugger off you little bastards!"

A pointless thing to shout in the direction of people who are already well advanced in the process of buggering off. I see them disappearing into the distance and any feelings of pilgrimage guilt are softened by the fact that I don't start walking until tomorrow, meaning there are still several hours left of guilt-free grumpiness.

There are a good few cafés and restaurants in the town and I walk around expecting to see pilgrims congregating together, rucksacks leaning against outside tables but there doesn't seem to be anything like that happening at all. There are a lot of coach parties here and the main street seems geared up for the casual tourist rather than the walker, with shops selling traditional crafts and postcards. There are also Santiago-related things for sale including a t-shirt depicting an image of a badly bruised foot and the slogan "Santiago – No Pain No Glory". It makes me look at my walking boots with a new sense of fear and for an instant, I have a vision of dozens of people limping battered and bruised across the finish line, propped up by fellow walkers and looking like they've survived the long trek away from an earthquake.

I edge into the newer part of Saint-Jean-Pied-de-Port and eat an unremarkable meal among the coach parties in the main square, the Place du Gaulle, before finding a big supermarket and stocking up on supplies for the next day. I also have a look at the route out of town tomorrow morning. Time drags slowly and painfully indeed and I can't help wondering where all the walkers are.

In the evening, I seek out a church and go to a service, expecting this to be a gathering point for pilgrims. There are only a handful of people here and I appear to be the only non-resident of the town. It is still early but I have exhausted the possibilities of Saint-Jean-Pied-de-Port. It's time to head back to the *refugio* and think about tomorrow.

The dormitory is full when I return and shared equally by men and women. We all have the same idea of laying out our clothes for the next day and there is multi-lingual chatter as curfew approaches. Most of us are starting our Camino here but there is a bloke from Quebec who started his walk at Narbonne and there's a battle-hardened look about him that the rest of us just don't have. His clothes are a bit scruffier, and when he speaks, there's a certain weariness attached to it. His voice lacks the sense of excitement and expectation of those around him. He's not lording his experience over the novices but is just matter-of-factly different. He's been broken in.

Just as we're all settling down in a shared atmosphere of eagerness, the proprietor decides to launch a pre-lights-out raid.

"What's this?" she screams in English, as she picks up a pair of sandals. "I said no shoes!"

She moves towards the window and for one second it looks like she's going to throw them onto the street. There is a woman by her bunk trying to protest and retrieve her footwear but is unable to get a word in. The hausfrau also spots a shirt dangling from the edge of a bed. She rubs her hand on it and shouts again.

"This is wet! No drying!" before whipping the shirt off the hanger and shoving it under her arm.

Her eyes skirt around the room again looking for more evidence of flagrant rule breaking. We all stay frozen in our poses; the woman whose shoes have been taken looks like she's been nailed to the floor. The *hospitalero* takes the offending items of clothing with her, announcing that they can be collected in the morning. Her eyes are absolutely blazing. It's one of the scariest performances I've ever seen and it's all over in less than two minutes. When she leaves, the dormitory is silent as we all stare at each other before smiles break out and turn into laughter. In fairness to her, the rules were made very clear when I signed in but maybe she shouldn't apply for the job at the Samaritans just yet. I'm not sure she should be in the hospitality business either. As I'm drifting off to sleep, it occurs to me that I've got over a month's worth of stays in *refugios* ahead of me. They can't all be like this one, surely?

10th September: Stage 1 - Saint-Jean-Pied-de-Port to Roncesvalles

Surprisingly, the night isn't disturbed by the owner coming in every fifteen minutes and waving a torch about in search of illicit footwear. I actually sleep quite well until the cockerel kicks off at about 4.30am and then it all gets a bit fractured. Everything I've read about the Camino suggests that getting an early start on the first day is important. Of course, in this particular establishment there are house rules which dictate when we can leave, and after last night's performance, I'm not going to put them to the test. My alarm goes off at six but nobody else in the dorm appears to be stirring. I manage to put a stop to this contented restfulness by getting up and banging my head on the bunk above, sending out audible vibrations and barely suppressed obscenities. There then follows a master class in how not to get ready in silence. Folding a sleeping bag, something I've done dozens of times before, suddenly sounds as if I'm rolling marbles around in a biscuit tin while jumping on crisps at the same time. Co-ordination deserts me. I couldn't make more racket if I was playing a Motörhead album for accompaniment. I somehow manage to get dressed, though with more concern given to speed than appearance. I pack as best as I can under the thin beam of my torch and then take my rucksack in my hand and edge delicately out of the dormitory.

There is no sign of any life in the house and all is pitch black. There's a temptation to turn on a light but I'm terrified of the consequences, and anyway, I can't find the switch. The agony isn't over and I tiptoe my way towards the wooden spiral staircase. It wasn't easy to negotiate in daylight yesterday, but it's even worse now as it appears that the steps have been polished. My stockinged foot slips alarmingly as I find the first step. There's only a banister on one side and I cling onto it as best I can while my other hand carries my backpack. Each step is a major focus of concentration and I can feel my feet slide forward a little every time I head downwards. It's a dicey journey and just as I approach the bottom, the bloody cockerel crows again, shredding my nerves to pieces. I

12

nearly slip over in fright and narrowly avoid some very loud swearing. I can't get out of the house fast enough now. I pick up my boots, slip out of the door and finish getting dressed in the street.

It has taken about forty minutes between getting up and actually being in a fit state to walk. Having already proved that I'm not as quiet as a mouse, I rather get the feeling that I'm going to spend the rest of the day showing I'm not as agile as a mountain goat either. It's been estimated that it's about a million steps to Santiago from here and I take my first ones down the Rue de Citadelle, stopping outside the church to fill up my water bottles at a fountain. There's another walker already there and he doesn't appear to be in the mood to exchange pleasantries. Once his bottle is filled, he heads off at a brisk pace and is soon lost in the darkness. I'm in less of a hurry and linger on the stone bridge over the River Nive for a minute or two, watching it flow beneath me, appreciating the significance of the moment; this is the lowest altitude I'll be at for the entire walk. I feel a bit anxious but that's not because of what's to come. It's more about whether I've left anything behind because I have absolutely no desire at all to retrace my steps. Given the choice of having to face the *hospitalero* again or taking on the mountains, show me which way is up. If what they say about footsteps is true, it really is time to start praying.

The first part of the walk isn't particularly difficult - that's assuming I'm going the right way. It's hard to make anything out in the rural darkness and while I can't see any other pilgrims, I can hear the scraping sounds of walking poles on tarmac, which is reassuring. If we're getting lost, we're doing it together in the Camino spirit. Sound is the most reliable of the senses, as it's extremely difficult to discern anything else with accuracy. I'm heading softly uphill on a road that is devoid of street-lighting. There are houses, as I can just about make out their shadowy, fuzzy outlines but anything beyond that is invisible. Even the mountains are obscured but you can sense their presence.

Dawn doesn't so much break as bend, as darkness slowly gives way to very heavy mist just before I get to the first landmark of the journey - the hostel at Huntto. Although visibility isn't brilliant, there's enough murky light to see fellow pilgrims and swap "Buen Caminos". A few are enjoying a coffee outside and I'm tempted but somehow it feels wrong to have a break after only an hour's walking.

A hot drink has to be earned and I think I'm made of sterner stuff. Then again, I could be just really stupid. Ignoring the chance of a catered rest may be a luxury I pay for later.

There's a path a bit further on which cuts out a curve in the road and, according to my guidebook, there are commanding views to be had across the mountains. I can't confirm this as visibility is about 5m at best. In fact, it's considerably less for me because my glasses keep steaming up. At one point, I'm nearly sent flying by an avalanche of sheep which descends at speed and which I catch sight of very late. Then, just as the path is about to rejoin the road, a large digger appears and evasive action is needed once again. The weather conditions get more and more claustrophobic with height, and soon it's as bad as the darkness of the early morning. The fear kicks in again as I think I've failed to spot a water fountain. Now, not having a break at Huntto seems like a very bad decision indeed.

The shortcut marks a definite change in the nature of the walk: the slopes are no longer gentle, and I'm sliding into territory that ranges from difficult to brutal. The gradients are getting steeper and longer, and the ankles are starting to throb. Each climb is punctuated with pauses for heavy breathing. I'm ready for a rest now and right on cue, I'm saved by the next hostel at Orison. It can't be said that it's a welcome sight because the fog is so thick that I nearly walk past it without noticing. I order a hot chocolate and sit on a bench outside with two German women. I'm still convinced that in my hurry to leave this morning, I have left something behind so I unpack and repack my bag while I'm resting, much to the amusement of my new friends; they probably stayed somewhere sane last night. With everything present and correct, it's only now that the sense of anxiety disappears and I can think of actually enjoying the day. While I swap names with the Germans, there appears to be a bit of a Camino schism going on. More walkers arrive but when a cyclist emerges through the mist, they join another table with fellow biking pilgrims. The cyclists look absolutely battered and it's not over yet. In terms of height, we're not even halfway there.

It's a good twenty minutes before I set off again, having refilled my water bottles. It's a steep start, but then the whole aspect of the walk changes radically in the space of about 200m. The mist thins out as the road breaks through the cloud line and the world shifts rapidly from a dull monochrome to glorious high definition

14

technicolour. It's a truly spectacular contrast, like arriving in the land of Oz, having blown in from Kansas. Mountain peaks float above the clouds all around me, their outlines clearly and precisely defined, rocky islands in a sea of white. The pastureland alongside the road has become an intense green and the sky above is totally cloudless and shiny blue with the sun blazing down. It's an amazing moment and it's perhaps one of the most exhilarating feelings I've ever had. All of a sudden, this feels like the adventure that it's supposed to be. The spirit soars like the eagles that now fly above me. I don't feel the need to utter expletives every time the gradient increases anymore. The rucksack feels lighter than air, and life feels incredibly good.

You can sense similar feelings in the other pilgrims. A couple of cyclists that I saw at Orison creep past me as the cloud thins out and you can sense the joy in their faces. They shout "Buen Camino" through big smiles and I reply with enthusiasm. The road is still pointing uphill, and if anything, it's steeper than it was, but everything feels easier now. There are pilgrims strung out in front and behind me. There are dozens of us as far as the eye can see, and I know I'm not alone. There are friendly nods between us and groups form and disband over the course of the morning as we all start to get to know each other. I talk to an Italian couple, Guido and Pia, who have both taken early retirement and have wanted to do the walk for several years. They don't cite any particular reason for it, apart from the urge to have a different sort of holiday. We talk about our previous lives, but mostly it's all about the scenery around us, and how good it is to be able to enjoy it in an unhurried way.

We reach the Pic d'Orisson, which is the next landmark, and it also means we're above the 1000m mark. There's a statue here of the Virgin Mary and a backdrop of majestic mountains (I'm not scared anymore; mountains can be classified as beautiful again), and rocky valleys descending into the feathery clouds; it is truly magnificent. There are sheep grazing all around, unperturbed by the numbers of walkers who take advantage of the surroundings and improvise picnics and share food with their fellow pilgrims.

A big wayside cross indicates where the Route de Napoléon leaves the road and heads onto a good path which leads towards the Spanish border. For a few hundred metres, all that separates the two countries is a simple wire fence, and for a while, the path runs parallel to it. As frontier crossings go, it's hardly Panmunjeom or Checkpoint Charlie – Spain's entered via a cattle grid - but all the same, it's deeply symbolic for me.

I'm not Spanish. I don't speak the language in any meaningful way, and despite my surname, I've never felt part of the land that produced Cervantes, Dali and Real Madrid. Admittedly, nobody in Valencia or Malaga cheered as loudly as I did when Andreas Iniesta thumped the ball past the Dutch goalkeeper Maarten Stekelenburg to win the 2010 World Cup for Spain, but that was largely because I had placed a tenner on them before the competition began to win at odds of 10-1.

The thing is I have a legitimate right to support Spain, and indeed, if I was any good at sport, play for them. I'm entitled to the passport because my father was Spanish. I grew up eating and drinking Spanish things and sprinkling Spanish words into conversations. In our house not only did we eat chorizo in the 1970s, we knew how to pronounce it too. Holidays were spent away from the Costas in the northern region of Cantabria, which nobody seemed to have heard of. None of this felt strange to me, though it did to my friends. My dad's obvious foreignness meant we were given a sort of "exotic" tag by our Merseyside neighbours - something that usually only applied to people who didn't have Irish grandparents.

My father died when I was 14 and since then all of my Spanish-ness has ebbed away. As an adult, Spain became associated with football, forgettable ditties to the Eurovision Song Contest and people who had a disturbing interest in torturing animals in the name of sport or religious holidays. I didn't care that much, to be honest. I didn't think I was very British either until a former girlfriend who was Belgian burst out laughing when I told her how European I thought I was. When the mirth subsided - and it took a disturbingly long time - she pointed out my love of tea-drinking and watching cricket, before adding that the only time she'd ever seen me get angry was when somebody pushed past me in a queue. Within a couple of sentences, I'd been reduced to a British cliché.

I'm more than that, I know I am and I'm at an age when I feel the need to reconnect with my past. What better way to get back to my Spanish roots than by walking across the country, taking in the landscapes and reactivating my language skills? To eat the food and drink the wine? The problem is that I quite definitely feel more at home in France. I speak the language enough to argue, visit often and I've had a couple of French speaking girlfriends. The only words of Spanish I can successfully deploy are the ones you don't find in pilgrimage handbooks. Despite the family history, everything on the other side of the cattle grid represents the unfamiliar. Time to fill up my water bottles with French water for the last time and negotiate my way across the metal bars into the unfamiliar homeland.

One big difference about the path now is that it passes through woodland which provides welcome protection from what has become an unrelenting sun. A couple of pilgrims have taken to Spanish culture straightaway by having a siesta and I can't say that I blame them, though I have no desire to join in. Last time I fell asleep in the Spanish sunshine, I woke up looking like someone had gone over me with a blow-lamp. Like at Huntto earlier, there's a need to need to keep walking and after one hour I reach the Col de Lepoeder, the highest point of today's stage. The views are glorious but it's nothing compared to the feeling of achievement in getting here; I really do feel like celebrating.

The day's not over yet, though. There is the matter of getting down to my destination for tonight, Roncesvalles, which is about 5km away and 500m lower down. The walking books and websites tell you that you're more likely to be injured heading downhill than uphill, but here at least there are two options; a straight descent down a path, or an easier but longer route which involves following a wavy road. I'm joined in my deliberations by an Irishman; another man who's just retired and is ticking off the first thing on his "to do" list. We both decide to take what looks like the safer alternative; I'm still wary of getting injured on my first day and the straight path looks like a risk too far. Compared to negotiating a polished wooden spiral staircase in stockinged feet in the dark, it's probably a piece of cake, but I don't really want to push my luck, especially when I don't have to.

There's nothing complicated about the alternative route, which just involves following one road down to another, but about halfway through the descent the Irish pilgrim stops. He looks to his left and points with his stick to some trees, "I think we may be able to take a short cut through there. Shall we give it a try?"

If only he hadn't said the last bit. I'm back to my saying yes policy and once again, I've got severe doubts. If a path's overgrown, I'm inclined to believe there's probably a good reason for its non-use. Equally, common sense would also suggest that if a route has been in existence for a thousand years, the chances are that all the shortcuts will have been found by now. Even if there is a quicker way, it would involve only saving about 200m and this gain would be negated by leaving a tarmac surface to pursue an uneven track. There is absolutely no sensible argument for following this man, none at all, but I decide for the sake of the "yes" rule I have to do it. We eventually enter into woodland where quite frankly everything looks like a path, and none of them looks as if they lead anywhere.

"My sense of direction rarely lets me down. I'm sure we should be heading this way", he says, pointing his stick with confidence.

I've got no problems with his sense of direction. I do have a major issue with the lack of a recognisable route to follow. After much scrabbling about on our hands and knees under low branches, followed by the realisation that any further progress would involve a vertical drop of about 8m, we double back and return to the road to continue our descent with some ease. I decide now that I'm never going to deviate from the marked route ever again. A millennium's worth of pilgrims can't be wrong. I'm also contemplating a serious re-think of saying yes to everything.

We're soon back on the flat again and following a path that will take us to Roncesvalles. My Irish navigator points up beyond a natural wall on the left. "That's where we were. I knew I was on the right track". Yes, and if you'd had a rope we could have bloody abseiled down.

We get to the complex of buildings at Roncesvalles just before 3pm. My Irish friend doesn't feel tired so he's carrying on, but despite feeling rather buoyant, I don't want to push it any further and so decide to stop here. The pilgrimage office isn't open until 4pm and there are about a dozen people sitting on the floor outside it with their backpacks next to them. You can sense the shared tiredness. While every new pilgrim that arrives is greeted with a nod and a smile, there is very little talking going on. The focus of my practice walks was to get over the Pyrenees and as far as I'm concerned, I'm just pleased to be here. I've beaten Napoléon. Everything else now will feel like a bonus.

When the office finally opens, we are invited in a few at a time to sit at a long table and fill in a form with our nationality details. This is then handed in and the *credencial* is stamped. We're then directed to an austere looking stone building situated on what passes for the main road. It's all a lot different to yesterday's *refugio* experience: it's friendly for a start. There are about half a dozen *hospitaleros* to greet us and point out the facilities. The whole ground floor is a dormitory and looks like the dining room at Hogwarts, with the long tables replaced by one hundred and twenty beds, all in bunks. The bathroom facilities are in the basement and they are spotlessly clean and modern. However, there are exactly four showers, two for each sex, to service us all. I'm sure there are people complaining about it, but I'm not, I'm in the second wave of shower users and the wait is minimal. I wouldn't fancy being at the back of the queue of about forty that are lining up as I get out. It's then time to wash the clothes I've been walking in, in one of the sinks and hang them outside to dry on a rather crowded washing line outside.

Roncesvalles feels like the real start of the Camino. The concentration of pilgrims more than doubles the village's population, and gives an unadulterated sense of excitement and shared purpose that was totally lacking back in St Jean. There are no bus parties nor casual tourists to dilute the experience. We're on our way. To emphasise this there's a rather daunting road sign which announces that Santiago is a mere 790km away. Again, it's the hard numbers that have the ability to unsettle. I think of this time yesterday and my fears of crossing the Pyrenees, and here I am with no ill effects. I didn't think about getting to Santiago yesterday or today and I won't think about it tomorrow. From my limited Camino experience, the things to worry about are mad *hospitaleros*, and Irish pilgrims with a keen sense of direction but no other sense at all.

There's not a lot to the village itself. There are two restaurants though, and if you flash your *credencial* beforehand, you can book a place for a three-course pilgrimage meal. The place I choose has a rather surly barman who seems reluctant to take any reservations at all, or indeed sell drinks. Eventually, we all gather outside the door of the *comedor,* or dining room, before we are all let in and told to fill each space up one at a time. I end up on a round table with seven other people who are all French speaking, and it takes some time to

19

realise who's with whom. Next to me is an elegant woman in her 50s with immaculate blonde hair, who looks as far removed from being a walker as I can imagine. Her name's Francine and she's doing the walk with a couple of her friends and, contrary to all appearances, has just walked over the Pyrenees too. For the first few minutes, she and her friends think I'm German until I finally convince them that I'm not. I would like to say that I'm half-Spanish but it's only day one of my re-acclimatisation, and I still have the county cricket scores on my mind. Of course, we volunteer information and ask questions of each other, but rather oddly, the question of why any of us are doing the walk never really crops up. I don't feel comfortable asking it, and I don't honestly feel like answering it either. We're all doing the Camino and maybe that's all we need to know. The company is delightful, but the food is forgettable and comes with a choice of take it or leave it.

We are fed and watered in under an hour, and afterwards most of us head in the direction of the monastery for a multi-lingual blessing at the church of Santa María. The people who dined elsewhere join us, and we all are looking at each other rather than the surroundings as the blessing is given. We may be sick of the sight of each other by the end of the week, but for the moment, there's goodwill and optimism in the air. Guido and Pia and the two German women from earlier in the day are here, and we greet each other after the service with big smiles and hugs like long lost friends. Day one and mission accomplished; the Pyrenees have been crossed and, as the sign outside says, only 790km to go.

It's a peculiar and novel experience being in a huge dormitory. The last time I slept with that many people was when I went to watch Tranmere at Leyton Orient. Obviously snoring is an issue but not as much as the bastard with the mobile phone who carries out his conversation in Japanese at about 4.30am. Unlike yesterday, the dormitory all gets up at the same time due to the house policy of switching on the lights at 6am. This results in a Le Mans start to get to the bathroom facilities, as people leap out of their sleeping bags and scurry like mad to get to a toilet, shower and a wash basin.

I'm up and out by 6.30am but I wonder what I gain by doing so. I go past the Santiago sign and then enter some woods which are enveloped by the total darkness of the hour. There are a couple of people ahead of me - I can see their torch lights darting around - but I'm attempting the same paths in the dark. After kicking tree roots for several minutes, common sense comes into play and there's a rummage in the rucksack for my torch. By doing this I lose visual contact with those ahead and by the time the pack is reattached there's only darkness and silence. The only sounds I can hear are produced by me walking, and things are starting to get a little creepy, to say the least. With the torch beam bouncing off the trees, there's an uncomfortable reminder of the *Blair Witch Project*. What would look friendly by day has a menacing quality to it when it's glimpsed in a brief shaft of light. Branches look like twisted limbs, and faces seem to appear in the undergrowth. The senses are heightened and I can't wait to get back on a road. After what feels like ages but must be considerably less than five minutes, I'm grateful to see that the path leads to tarmac, and the village of Burguete. As luck would have it, there's a café open and I order a hot chocolate and a pastry.

There's a young Spanish walker already there whom I recognise as being the first person out of the door this morning. We introduce ourselves and from my limited knowledge of Spanish, I gather she felt the fear in the woods and got worried when she noticed that I'd stopped and wasn't a few metres behind her anymore. It has been an edgy start to the day but things are going to get better, at least weather-wise. The television is on in the bar and the forecast is encouraging with a big sun over this part of the country. There'll be no more fear of the dark, and nature can be benevolent again.

There are the first shimmerings of daylight when I leave. The Pyrenees are in the rear-view mirror but the foothills are all around. There's no need for a map to go on the Camino as the route is way-marked all the way by painted yellow arrows which can be found on the pavement, buildings, stones, and trees. On this particular morning, they point through farmland, past fields of unconcerned cattle and across stepping-stones. There are more pilgrims about and the smiles are big on all of us. It really is a glorious day for hiking, with the way passing through pristine villages with the Basque red and white decoration to them. Most walking appears to be done as individuals or in small groups, but there's an uncanny sort of party atmosphere when you get to a café. Outside tables fill up quickly and pilgrimage bonding takes place over hot drinks. After last night's meals and blessing, there's a lot more recognition and sociability. I catch up with Francine and her friends over a *bocadillo* or sandwich, and we're joined by a rather boisterous and friendly Italian man from L'Aquilia called Marco. Although it's only just after 10am Marco has decided to have a beer to keep his spirits up, and he looks like he may be staying for a couple more.

So much of my pre-Camino time was spent worrying about getting over the Pyrenees that it never occurred to me that the day after would be more difficult. There are no major climbs it's true, but it's a couple of kilometres longer than yesterday and, as the day progresses, the undulating landscape with steep ascents and descents on loose rock through woods and fields makes its impact felt. There is a particularly evil descent of 5km into the town of Zubiri, which takes about an hour, and a quarter of careful negotiating. Walking poles are not seen as essential but on a hill like this, it's good to have them to pick out a route through the stones and uneven ground. I don't think I've ever been so glad to see a place as I do this lunchtime when the town finally comes into view.

The Camino doesn't actually pass through Zubiri, but it's only a short detour over the Puente de la Rabia. This is a medieval bridge over the Río Arga and it was believed that if animals crossed it three times they would be cured of rabies. If it does anything for swollen ankles I'll give it a go. I join Guido and Pia sitting outside a café. All the talk is about the descent into town and it's clear we're all feeling it a bit. There's a British woman who's also suffering and she is determined not to do it in silence. She's actually in a neighbouring bar and doesn't appear to be talking to anyone in particular. She's just making sure we can hear her pain. She asks a waiter if she can get a taxi to Larrasoaña because she doesn't think she will be able to manage it on foot.

There is no reason why she can't stay here. There are a couple of hostels and it looks like a friendly place to be, but the taxi monologue is constant, loud and rather bloody annoying. Guido nods his head sympathetically at her plight and suggests that as I'm British I should go and talk to her, possibly in the form of taking one for the team. To be honest, the only things I can think of to say are "Why don't you stay in Zubiri tonight?" followed by "Have you considered the possibility of shutting up?" I haven't quite grasped the charitable side of pilgrimage yet. I rather get the feeling that if I did engage with her I may never get away. Apart from anything else, what happens if she makes some kind of invitation? If that happens the "saying yes" scheme gets abandoned here and now. I've decided that no good can result in spending time with an attention-seeking pilgrim. Eventually, interest shifts elsewhere as the tables at our café fill up with fellow walkers who all look happy that they've survived the plunge into town. There is relief among the broad smiles and laughter and when I look over to the other café a few minutes later the British woman has gone.

Larrasoaña is another ninety minutes away and the route follows the Arga, which makes it sound a lot more beautiful than it is. Rather than clinging to the riverbank, a large part of the walk goes through a magnetite mine, making it the ugliest bit so far. As well as the yellow arrows, small signs with a yellow scallop shell on a blue background occasionally appear, advertising how far away certain places are. I'm sure the ones featuring Larrasoaña have been tampered with as the last couple of kilometres drag painfully despite being the flattest part of the day's course. It's a small place with a lengthy pilgrimage history which it's particularly proud of, and a disproportionally large village hall where you go to get the *credencial* stamped. There's only one place to stay here but there are two buildings; I am recognised for being the riff-raff I am by being shunted into an outhouse across the square.

It's a white structure with about fifteen bunks crammed into one room on the first floor, and it's busy with the sounds of everyone in different stages of showering, getting dressed and washing clothes. With somewhere smaller comes more intimacy and friendliness. There is consideration too, and we all tidy up after ourselves while doing our best not to get in each other's way as we do our washing. There are nods, smiles and snippets of multilingual conversation as everybody does their best to accommodate everyone else. I've been living in London; I'm not used to this at all.

Although lacking in shops, the village does support two bars and I spend a leisurely hour or so in the garden of one of them. At the moment, I don't feel like I'm in Spain at all. All around me, people are speaking French and Italian, and architecturally I could still be in the familiar surroundings of South West France. I'm joined by an intense looking Frenchman who is another one who thinks I'm German and wants me to call him Steve. He's got piercing grey eyes which almost burst through his glasses, and has short white hair. Eventually, I convince him that I'm British which displeases him for some reason, though sadly not enough for him to go away. He has a notebook with him and it appears that he's going to time each stage to Santiago and fill in the readings from his pedometer. I hope I can sit next to him at dinner, I can tell already that he's going to be loads of fun. He chastises me for not being able to remember what make my rucksack is and then talks about the problems he had choosing the boots for his walk. He's clearly confusing me with someone who gives a toss.

He is touching a bit of a nerve, though. For the past few months, equipment choice completely took over my life and turned me into the most tedious pub companion ever. I had a mental map of every camping shop within five miles of Piccadilly Circus and could quote the web addresses of rucksack comparison websites by heart. Things that had never bothered me before, like the weight of trousers, were committed to my memory like F.A. Cup Final winners and European capital cities. I knew about compression straps, back systems, smooth toe seams and anti-pilling micro fleeces – all things I'd never heard of six months ago. I could bore for England on the subject, and for the last six weeks, my friends informed me of this on a daily basis.

The websites proved particularly useful but you did have to sift the good advice from the postings made by a strange breed of cyber walkers who were obsessed with boasting about how they'd made it to Santiago carrying next to nothing and in the shortest possible time. It was the first time I'd been in the (cyber) presence of men (and they were all men) who were boasting about who had had the smallest and who'd finished the quickest. I'm sure if I'd looked hard enough I could have found somebody who'd done it in a week wearing flip-flops and carrying a shopping bag.

When you finally wade through the tedious boasting, there is some useful advice to be gleaned, principally that you should aim to carry about 10% of your bodyweight with a maximum threshold of 10kg. My bag weighs exactly 10kg and what is inside it doesn't feel like enough to me. Clothing-wise, there are a couple of shirts, a spare pair of trousers, a t-shirt, an Irish rugby jersey, two pairs of underpants and three pairs of socks. There is also my sleeping bag, a pair of sandals, a first aid kit and a limited amount of toiletries. I'm going to be away for the best part of two months and I'm carrying a lot less than I would if I were visiting a friend for a long weekend. Despite the information overload, there has always been a worry that the whole plan could flounder if I don't have the right gear. I've waited years to do this and I've had nightmares about the whole thing going wrong because of an abrasive toe seam.

Steve strikes me as being one of those people who inhabit these websites, and it could be a long afternoon. Sitting here with a beer in my hand and my eyes glazing over, I now completely understand what I put my pub companions through. Then again, they were friends and it goes with the territory. Anyway, my obsession with walking equipment disappeared the moment I'd bought it all and at this moment, I really don't care.

I am saved from death by tedium by a Canadian couple whom I don't think I've seen before. It doesn't matter; I greet them with unearned familiarity because quite frankly, any conversation is going to be better than the one that I'm already having. They're called Tony and Margaret and, like many of the walkers overnighting in Larrasoaña, they are retired. Both are highly entertaining and good fun. Tony was a pilot, first in the Canadian Air Force and then with Air Canada. In his air-force days, he was stationed in Germany where he flew Starfighters, a plane I know as being synonymous with an appalling safety record.

He concurs, "You were pretty much guaranteed a funeral every month." Then there was a pause before he added, "and one was for my brother."

A silence hangs in the air and starts to become obvious. I'm mentally scrambling for something diplomatic to say, but nothing comes to mind. Just as things start to become unbearable, I'm saved by Steve who seizes his moment with both feet.

"What type of rucksack do you have?" he asks Tony intently.

The bar provides a meal and the arrangement is similar to the night before, in that you have to book in advance and queue up at the appropriate time. The head barman makes a big effort for us and the food is served with warmth and a big smile. I'm particularly enthusiastic as Steve is on another table, but so are Tony and Margaret, and Guido and Pia. I'm with a small Swiss-Italian woman who recognises me from Bayonne railway station, a French couple and two people from Brazil who are confused by what's going on. The Brazilians only speak Portuguese but the Swiss-Italian woman goes to great lengths to try to include them in all the conversations. It gets to the stage where we are all speaking in an improvised sign language. Unlike last night, the barman is in no rush to chuck us out, so another bottle of wine is ordered and we continue to develop our own version of visual Esperanto before heading back to our respective buildings.

After the exertions of the previous forty-eight hours, today's plan is a short 16km effort to the first major city on the Camino, Pamplona. I leave at 6.30am and am joined at the door by a Hungarian man of about thirty. Like me, he has given up his job to do this and sees the walk as providing him with some thinking time. Right from the start, he attacks the path with a determination and speed that I struggle to match. He surefootedly negotiates the darkness while I find myself stumbling on tree roots and stubbing my toes. I soon realise that I can't keep up with him and don't really have the desire to. After tripping over a couple of times and getting worried that I could injure myself on what on paper looks like a very straightforward stage, I let him forge ahead, or rather I recognise the sheer madness in trying to keep up with him.

The Camino continues to follow loosely the course of the Río Arga and criss-crosses over it a couple of times before slowly shedding its rural serenity and heading towards the big city. There are no villages of note and there are no obvious stopping points along the way in the form of cafés or water fountains until you cross a beautiful stone bridge to get to Trinidad de Arre, which marks the beginning of the Pamplona's suburbs.

The Swiss-Italian woman and Guido and Pia are in a café on the edge of the town and are refuelling for the push onto Cizur Menor, which is about 5km beyond the city limits. I'm tempted to join them but I'm taken in by urban excitement. I've been looking forward to visiting Pamplona though I have to confess that apart from the bull-running at the festival of San Fermín and the Ernest Hemingway connections, I know very little about it.

It's a great walk into the city as the Camino edges around the old walls and crosses a drawbridge. There's a real sense of arriving somewhere special and stirring. I've made a bit of a misjudgement of timing, though, possibly due to the enthusiastic pace-making of my earlier walking companion. I've got here at 11.30am which is ninety minutes before the *refugio* actually opens. Still, there's a

27

whole city to explore and it's a good excuse to have a bit of a walk around and get my bearings.

I get to the Plaza del Castillo, the heart of the city, at the height of the tobacco and lottery ticket-buying rush hour. The shop I visit to get a phone card has a queue coming out of the door and there are signs of frustration filtering along it. There's tutting and arm gestures a-plenty and I'm asked my opinion by a short grey-haired man in a cardigan who seems agitated with those in front of him. Despite this, the line moves quickly and I'm served in a few minutes. I'm greeted with a surprised look when I ask for a phone card. I don't know if this is because this is the first request for such an item for several months or because, despite my best efforts, the words that come out of mouth are Italian. I can sense more impatience from those behind me who need their nicotine considerably sooner rather than later and I suddenly grasp that I'm not used to this kind of behaviour. After a couple of days in a cocoon of total pilgrimage sociability (which obviously started after I'd left the hostel in St Jean), I'm now exposed to the petty frustrations of urban life.

If you have a low tolerance for Ernest Hemingway, Pamplona is perhaps not the city for you. They milk the connection for all they're worth. There's a street named after him, as well as a bar and a hotel. There's a statue too (at the bullring, naturally), and my personal favourite, the Ernest Hemingway kebab shop. In Plaza del Castillo, they point out about ten places which have a connection with the writer including the hotel he used to stay in and various cafés he used to frequent. Some connections are more tenuous and speculative at best and consist of the "he was seen here after a bullfight in 1953" or "he may have looked into a shop window here in 1927." In terms of tourism, the city has a lot to thank Hemingway for, though he had mixed feelings about how the city changed during his lifetime. When he first came to the San Fermín festival in the 1920s, it was rare to hear a non-Spanish voice. Now thanks to his writing, the city has an international profile based on its dangerous and let's face it, mind-blowingly stupid, tradition.

My concession to the writer is to have a beer on an outside table of the Café Iruña which features in his book, *The Sun Also Rises*. Despite being tied to Hemingway, it feels Spanish even if I don't. In no other situation does the difference between my father and I stand out more than when it comes to getting the attention of barmen and waiters. I have strong childhood memories of being on holiday in various parts of Spain and with one shout of "jefe", he could have waiters falling over chairs and competing to get to him in the quickest possible time. It's a talent I've never inherited and my ability to be largely ignored in similar circumstances crosses national boundaries rather easily. I am made aware of this genetic defect once again as I try to pay. I shout "jefe" several times at different volumes but the waiter makes no attempt to deviate his movements. The farce continues for ten minutes, increasingly accompanied by less voluble phrases such as "You blind pillock". It's not as if the waiter is rushed off his feet either. There are about six occupied tables out of dozens and you'd think that he would notice a bit of random shouting. Not even a glance in my direction. I try a compromise solution which involves bellowing "jefe" while waving a five-Euro note. It gets me exactly nowhere and the frustration is starting to build. In the end, I stand up, walk up to the waiter myself, and pay him. I actually feel really upset and humiliated by having to do this - it genuinely does feel that my would-be Spanishness has taken a major kicking.

Another thing that has been getting a battering is my earlier feeling of urban enthusiasm. There's nothing wrong with Pamplona. I have a good look round and it strikes me as being a lovely place; it's clean, busy and lively. The thing is that after a couple days of walking across mountains and through small villages, being back in a city is becoming a massive and unexpected shock to the system. I see my first bus for three days and it looks out of place in my life. The situation gets worse as the day progresses. I feel overwhelmed by the number of people and it becomes more and more difficult to relax.

Over the past couple of days on the Camino, café and bar owners have welcomed us with great enthusiasm. Of course, pilgrims would account for most of their clientele and they have an interest in being pleasant but it goes beyond that. Here in the big city, you are almost invisible. You are one of a very big crowd and not different at all. From my visit to the tobacconist earlier to sitting in a bar, there has been either an attitude of inconvenience or indifference. I was a bit sceptical of the idea of a "Camino Spirit" before I started the walk but something feels like it has been lost in Pamplona. Right now staying in a big city seems alien and wrong.

The cathedral is round the corner from the *refugio* and there's a pilgrimage blessing in the early evening. It's a calming and moving experience and brings the Camino back into focus, but immediately afterwards it's back into the sunshine and the noise of a city gearing up for a Saturday night. Any lingering positive feelings are doused by a visit to another café where I go to eat. After the ticketing arrangement for dining of the past couple of days, my plan for the weeks ahead is to have one big meal a day in the evening selected from the *menú del dia* or a similar Pilgrims' menu. This is the standard three-course meal in cafés which allows you a choice of about half a dozen different starters, main courses, and desserts, and comes in at around €10. I order the *menú del dia* here only to be told when the bill arrives that I am expected to pay double. I am told that the special menu doesn't apply on a Saturday though this was the page that was presented to me on arrival and was referenced by the waitress who had served me. The waiter gets agitated and my lack of ability to argue leads to frustration. And swearing. My knowledge of Spanish is limited but I can swear and I do. I slam the money I think I should pay down, tell the waiter to go and play with himself, and leave in irritation.

Pamplona never recovers after that. The centre of the city is crowded and people are pouring in and out of bars and onto the narrow streets. I find it all very disaffecting after a couple of days of village tranquillity. I really don't want to be here at all and make the easy decision to head back to the hostel. I'm tucked up in my bed by 9pm. There's a glass ceiling above my top bunk, which means I can hear and see some of my fellow pilgrims pacing around like that scene from Alfred Hitchcock's version of *The Lodger,* but it's more friendly and comforting than the sounds of the city partying outside.

Getting out of Pamplona in the dark isn't particularly straightforward as, not surprisingly, the yellow arrows are difficult to spot. They are on the back of signs or painted on the pavements and, even with street lighting, it's not an easy path to follow. It's hugely disorientating as well, and I have absolutely no idea in which direction I'm heading. I start off walking with Jean-Paul who was one of the wine drinkers from Larrasoaña, and together we try to spot the clues that will lead us out of town. He soon gets derailed by the smell of fresh bread just as we get to the outskirts, and goes off in search of the bakery. I decide to press on to Cizur Menor in the hope of finding a bar and settling down for some breakfast.

The village is situated on a hill just outside Pamplona, and has been looking after pilgrims since the twelfth century. Despite its long Camino tradition, most of it looks impressively new and has been built to provide housing for some of the city's work-force. It looks nice enough and, even in the dark, it possesses more charm than any planned settlement has the right to. All that remains of the early days of pilgrimage is the rather splendid Romanesque church of St Michael, which is, not unexpectedly, shut when I walk past it. The policy of catering for pilgrims continues and there are two shelters here now. I pass one of them and then look back to the distant lights of a slowly waking Pamplona. There's a twinge of regret that I didn't follow Guido and Pia and stay here. It feels cosy, safe and, above all, friendly. It also has the potential for a serious and intimate pilgrimage wine-drinking session that neither an inattentive nor hostile waiter can spoil.

I get here after about an hour on the road and find an open bar. It doesn't look promising from the outside, but the door pushes open and I am greeted with a friendly smile from the barman. I know at once I'm back on what feels like the proper Camino. He rustles up some bread and jam, and a cup of hot chocolate, which happily takes away the bad taste that Pamplona had left me with. As is now becoming traditional, I leave the bar just as day is overtaking night.

An orange sun pierces the early morning mist, and launches like a fireball to light up the way ahead.

Most of my walking so far has been on narrow paths through scrubland, woods, and fields but this is the first time since the Pyrenees that there are 360-degree views. The track heads through fields of fading sunflowers and harvested grain, until the looming shadow of Alto del Perdón, the "Hill of Forgiveness", comes into view. This is the major feature of today's walk, and an intimidating and foreboding prospect it looks too. There are other hills around but this one lies isolated on a plain, which gives it a portentous appearance, even in the soft morning light. It's just short of 800m high and along its ridge are around fifty large wind turbines. You can't miss it no matter how much you want to.

The Camino takes a diagonal direction up the hill. There's a whole line of pilgrims who have concertina-ed together as we attack the slope, and soon there's enough heavy breathing to keep a wind turbine going on its own. It's an attritional climb on perhaps the most difficult surface so far. The path is barely wide enough to take walking poles and is extremely rocky in places, so we're all picking our way carefully. Above and below, pilgrims are stopping to catch their breaths. This feels far more difficult than anything on the Route Napoléon and looks like it's going to take a one or two stop strategy to get over it. If this is the hill of forgiveness, we all must have done something noriously bad in our lives to deserve it. It really hurts. The path seems to be attacking the soles of the feet and each step jars, sending uncomfortable vibrations through the body. My lungs are bursting in agony with every metre climbed. I'm not alone. The pain is carved into the faces of those who finally make it to the summit and, true to form, nobody is in a rush to make their way down the other side.

When you get to the top, you're left in no doubt why there are turbines here in the first place. There's a metal sculpture here depicting pilgrims and animals all heading to Santiago, and the gusts make it whistle and clang disturbingly, as if it's about to fall over. The views over the rolling hills are beautiful and full of colour, but the vista is disfigured by wind turbines in every direction – possibly hundreds of them. Don Quixote could have a field day if he fancied a tilt here. There's a grim sense of accomplishment in getting up here, but possibly the best news is that as soon as I make my descent, I won't have to see Pamplona again.

The path on the other side is more direct and tackles the slope head on. As I carefully negotiate my way downhill, prodding slowly with my sticks, the more reckless gallop past me. One of them is Marco who promises me a beer at the next bar, as he hurtles downwards. I'm not even slightly tempted to join them in a quick descent and I find this part of the journey a lot more treacherous than the way up. My lungs hurt going up the other side of the hill; here it's my calves, and I can feel the muscles tightening. It's a whole different layer of agony on a body that's already suffering.

After spending the last few hours admiring and cursing the stubborn beauty of the Alto de Perdón, I find another reason to swear when I get to the bottom of it. Once the path levels out a bit, the edge of it is strewn with rubbish that other pilgrims have tossed aside. There is a staggering amount of litter here, from food waste to discarded bags and bottles. It's concentrated in an area which makes it look like small-scale landfill, a blemish amidst the greenery. The fact that pilgrims are responsible for it somehow makes it a lot worse.

The bar and hostel at Uterga is about half an hour away from the lower slopes of the Alto de Perdón, but is perfectly located for catching up with fellow walkers. There's nothing like a bit of adversity to bond pilgrims and the garden is filled with groups celebrating the fact that they've survived, though there are a few who look absolutely haunted by the experience. Marco is true to his word and is sitting outside with two cans of beer in front of him, and he hands one to me as I approach. It's a bit early in the day for me, but it does feel like it's been earned. He must have got here a good quarter of an hour before me, but the sweat is still pouring into his white headband. He looks in remarkably good condition, considering he's just run down a sizeable hill. He's in his thirties, and has the weather-beaten look of someone who once did a lot of outdoor sports but has let himself go a bit. We talk about his love of cycling, and he becomes the first Italian I've ever met who freely admits to voting for Silvio Berlusconi. He necks his beer and puts his backpack on. He doesn't have a target destination for tonight, and intends to keep going until he feels it's time to stop.

I'm aiming for Puente la Reina, though I am tempted to stop before then at Obanos, which looks really rather lovely and is apparently home to the skull of St William, a figure I know absolutely nothing about. As saints go, he has a particularly low profile; not for him the honour of a city named after him, or a walk devoted to his relics. I can't think of any churches dedicated to him either. Or railway stations, or hospitals. Please let him be the patron saint of shyness.

The body feels good though, so I press on, and an hour and a half after leaving Uterga, I arrive at my destination. It's another place that's been catering for pilgrims for the best part of a thousand years, but the place I'm staying in isn't "olde worlde" at all. It's situated underneath a hotel for a start, and there's very much a hotel feel to it. It has more communal areas than any other hostel I've stayed in so far – there's a good-sized kitchen, a garden, and the novelty of a lounge. Beds are situated in a couple of windowless dormitories, but there are also individual rooms if you feel like splashing out.

I should mention the differences between the different types of *refugios*, *albergues* and hostels along the way. They have their own classifications, with some being run by the local authority, which means they have a warden or *hospitalero* on site. They tend to be at the more basic end of the scale, and the price charged reflects that. If the one at Larrasoaña is anything to go by, you're just as well off there as anywhere else. Others are run by religious groups or associations, while many are owned by the local diocese and have a connection to the local church. There's a choice of three different types here. The place I'm staying at tonight is privately run and, at €7 a night, it's at the upper end of the price bracket for the average pilgrim. Private ones tend to have more amenities, but I'm doubtful anyone cares too much. I don't really have any preferences about where I stay and I'm here quite simply because it's the first place I came to.

It is located just outside Puente la Reina itself, so I head over there for the afternoon and walk across the bridge that gives the place its name. It's one of the most famous sights on the whole Camino and I take the time to admire it from all angles as I'll be walking across it in darkness tomorrow morning. There's one beautiful cobbled street which leads arrow straight towards it.

34

Beyond this things are considerably more modern, but certainly not unattractive. It does give the impression though, that the old part looks a bit like a film set. It's not a particularly big place, but it is of some importance for pilgrims because it's where the less fashionable route over the Pyrenees, the Camino Aragonés, and the Camino Francés meet. As a result, there are several bars, three churches and a choice of places to stay. It's a sleepy place on this warm Sunday afternoon and just the place to unwind with a beer after a challenging 24 hours. Pamplona now feels like a world away and thankfully, there's now several kilometres and a bloody big hill between us.

I don't have to risk searching for a *menú del dia* as my billet provides an evening meal. The bad news is that it's a pilgrimage-expensive €11. The good news is that it's an all-you-eat-buffet and this extends to the ice-cream. Even better than that, I meet Tony and Margaret again and we now feel it's safe enough to talk, or to be brutally honest, laugh about Steve whom it transpires none of us has seen since the night in Larrasoaña. Conversation covers today's walk, the class system in Britain, and how Tony comes to be a member of Dornoch golf club in Scotland even though he lives in Canada. They are extremely good company with many a good anecdote, and with the food trough being filled at regular intervals, the evening absolutely flies past. Tony and I disappear upstairs to the bar for a post-meal beer and more confidences are exchanged. He is incredibly grateful for the life he's lead and speaks lovingly about his wife and two daughters. He chuckles when I ask him if Margaret was cabin crew on one of his planes.

"Lots of people ask me that. No. She was a teacher at the air force base I was stationed at. I knew straightaway that she was the woman for me."

There is absolute certainty in his voice and I want to know more.

"It's because she didn't need me. I had to wait nearly three weeks for a second date. She wasn't playing hard to get. It's just that she had a genuinely busy life."

He can sense he has a little bit more explaining to do, and takes another sip of his beer. "When I worked on airlines, cabin crew and others would throw themselves at pilots because 'they came with a life'. There's a sense of status and money attached to the job. Nothing's likely to change and the situation is an attractive one. Margaret never cared about my job and certainly didn't need me to fill in any gaps in her life. She went out with me because she liked me. Does this make any sense?"

Actually, it does. Several years ago, a girlfriend left me rather abruptly to go back out with an ex. He quite definitely 'came with a life', while I quite definitely didn't and still don't. I've given up my job as a radio producer and my flat in London to do the Camino. My post-walk future is uncertain and I'm as far away as "coming with a life" as I have ever been. At this moment, it's debatable if this is a good thing or not.

"I don't quite know why we're doing the walk," Tony confesses before adding that it was his wife's idea.

"Maybe it's to say thank you," I venture.

He raises his beer to his lips and pauses and then adds, "I think you might be right," before emptying his glass and placing it heavily on the table.

I could happily talk to him all night. Sadly, private hostels have curfews too, even if the legwork only involves going down the stairs. He's not stupid. He and Margaret are staying in a private room with a window. They're lucky: my dormitory feels like a sauna and there's no natural light.

14th September: Stage 5 - Puente la Reina to Estella

Few stages on the Camino can have such a beautiful start as this one. The main street of Puente la Reina and the bridge are beautifully moody in the ghostly darkness. After crossing the Arga again there's a bit of a hill climb and I can look back to see the light emerging over yesterday's nemesis – Alto de Perdón. Then I go on auto-pilot for an hour or so as the walk passes through vineyards and a steep ravine near the ruins of an eleventh-century monastery. Gradually my thoughts turn to breakfast. There was nowhere open in Puente La Reina this morning and I have high hopes for the village of Mañeru, but nothing is stirring when I arrive. Mercifully, it's not too far on to Cirauqui and the spirits lift when I see it. It's situated on a hilltop and it looks gorgeous on this particularly luminous morning. It also looks big enough to support a couple of bars at least, and provide all the help a knackered and hungry pilgrim needs.

However, on arrival, you could be forgiven for believing that nobody lives here at all. It's worryingly silent and decidedly lacking in population. It's only when I hear the unmistakable sound of someone sweeping up broken glass that I appreciate that there hasn't been a natural disaster or an outbreak of disease. If anyone is suffering in Cirauqui this morning it's almost certainly their own fault. There was obviously some kind of fiesta the night before. There are half-drunk bottles of beer and wine lying about, and the town's solitary active human being is sweeping up the carnage around a temporary stage. The stench of urine and alcohol lies heavy in the air, which takes a bit of dealing with on an empty stomach. There's absolutely nowhere open: no bars, cafés or shops. The whole place appears to be suffering from the after effects and I've got no sympathy at all. I've been on the go for a couple of hours and the lack of food is an issue now. There's no option but to head onto Lorca, the next village, but it's 5km and a further hour away.

Apart from the hunger, I didn't sleep particularly well last night either. There were about a dozen of us bunked together in a relatively small room, and the heat was decidedly oppressive. So much so in fact that I had that unpleasant feeling that I was slowly sticking to the inside of my sleeping bag. My good humour, which had started to run out on the far side of the bridge at Puente la Reina, is running on empty and I'm now a fully formed grumpy bastard.

The path to Lorca follows a Roman road but its joys are wasted on me. It takes in a timeworn stone bridge over the Río Saldo and flirts with a major highway, but for all I care or notice I could be walking on tarmac, glass or yellow bricks. All I know is that the horizon looks to be a bloody long way away when you're hungry. I can't wait until Lorca comes into view and I'm sure the sight of Santiago won't be as lifting to the spirits as the open bar is when I get there.

It's a busy place full of hungry and desperate souls like myself, and there's much pilgrimage chit-chat among the mouthfuls of *bocadillos*. A Scottish man and his Norwegian girlfriend are here. Like me, they started on the same day at Saint-Jean-Pied-de-Port, but they are very much walking to a timetable. They have a flight to catch on October 15th from Santiago and they are very aware of their deadline. They have planned where they are going to stay every night, and every part of their Camino is rigidly timetabled. I am doing it in an open-ended way. I have no plans for when I get to Santiago, nor does it really matter when I arrive. I've got nothing immediate to go back to Britain for either. Agitated is probably the wrong word, but they are mindful of what they have to do and this impinges on how they're approaching the Camino. There will always be a background element of rush to their proceedings and it appears that they're walking to schedule now. They invite me to join them but I'm not rushing anywhere. It's taken me three hours to get here in the first place and I need a sensible break to stuff my face and calm down a bit. This is quite definitely a "two *bocadillos*" pit stop.

I really hoped that the food and rest would revive the spirits. It doesn't work. I bowl into today's destination, Estella, at about 12.30pm in a truly foul mood and I can't really give you a good reason why. I felt it almost immediately after I had left the pleasant surroundings of the bar and I decided to keep talking to a minimum. "Buen Caminos" to my fellow pilgrims have been uttered through much gritted teeth. I was hungry before I got to Lorca and now it seems that I'm well and truly fed up.

The large municipal hostel here doesn't open until 1pm and I'm too impatient to hang about waiting. Estella has other options though, so I decide to head across the town in search for one of the parish-run affairs. I'm loitering outside an unlikely looking doorway on the ground floor of an apartment block, which is apparently the way in, when a man appears in the entrance.

"Well, hello there. Come on in!"

The voice is American and full of natural warmth. There's nothing this British bloke hates more when he is in a bad mood than to be treated with total kindness by strangers. When I cross the threshold, I'm confronted with a double act. They are Michael and Barbara, and they seem to be completely overcome by the sheer joy of life. They have just received a food order and are putting things away with such an air of good humour and laughter that it would make Mary Poppins vomit.

"We have so much yo-gort Michael. We'll be eating it all night!"

"We sure will dear", replied Michael, following this up with a hefty chuckle.

I hate to break up this wholesomeness; actually, that's not true: I revel in it, and Michael leaves his shelf-stacking behind to sign me in and to show me into a room with nine bunks aligned along the perimeter. It looks clean and pleasant but given the nature of the *hospitaleros*, I can't see how it could be anything else. Every bed has probably been sprinkled with fairy dust.

After the traditional washing rituals, I lie down on my bed for a few minutes but the sound of undiluted happiness from the other side of the doorway is just too much to bear, and I have to go out and find some pigeons to kick. As I'm leaving, Barbara informs me that the cook has just left and that she will be taking on the food duties tonight. There's a sheet of paper on the back of the door if I want to sign up for the evening meal and "we can eat together as a big family." If she even mentions the words "Apple Pie", there's going to be trouble. Today is the day the "say yes" policy gets binned. I'm straight out of the door and on a mission to find nosebag opportunities elsewhere. I am grumpy, proud and I refuse to be killed with kindness.

Estella comes highly regarded as a stopover because of its interesting history, but in my irritated state, I can't see why. It's a medium sized town with a river going through the middle of it.

Apparently, the must-see is the church of San Pedro de la Rúa which is where former kings of Navarre swore allegiance. It dates from the twelfth century and it's quite definitely closed when I get there. There's also a monastery and an old pilgrimage bridge, the Puente Picudo, with steps going across the top of it but to my cantankerous eyes at least, it has sod all else going for it. I find a café in the triangular Plaza Santiago and order a beer to be miserable with.

I'm forced to go back to the Disneyworld *refugio* as it's getting breezy and I need the extra layer of the rugby jersey. To my absolute horror, it has now filled up with other pilgrims and cheeriness has reached epidemic proportions. Thankfully, I've been inoculated. The pilgrims who have signed in after me have formed a plan to cook dinner for everyone and spare Barbara the aggravation. An Argentinian couple and a Spanish pairing have initiated this scheme and are waxing enthusiastically about what they are going to put together. I hear them as I pass through the kitchen area to my dormitory. There are few things that can have me legging it in search of a Pizza Hut, but having dinner with an Anglo-Hispanic version of *The Waltons* is fast becoming a strong contender.

As it turns out, everyone else - about 25 in total - has signed up to the evening meal and the notable exception is the unfriendly British git. Not only am I being exposed for the grouchy individual I am, I feel like I'm being press-ganged into trying to enjoy myself. I reluctantly add my name to the bottom of the eating list with all the enthusiasm of somebody signing their own death warrant. The only advantage I can see to all of this is that I don't have to wander round a rather cold and windy Estella in search of grub.

As we are rearranging the furniture and placing tables and benches into a cramped C-shape to get everyone accommodated, I get talking to Michael and Barbara. They come every year to Estella for two weeks to run the hostel before handing over to another group of volunteers. They have done the Camino and they see it as their way of giving something back. There are several places along the way that are run along similar lines and I can see how it makes some kind of sense. I start to feel really guilty about my own attitude towards them earlier in the day. They are giving up their time to make pilgrims feel welcome (even the antisocial ones) and extend a tradition that has gone on for centuries. It works for them. They are actually leaving tomorrow and are obviously very sad to go.

My frostiness continues to melt as a very pleasing evening unfolds. The food is excellent and we are treated to vegetable soup followed by meatballs and salad. Predictably, there's yoghurt for dessert, as there are at least three shelves of the stuff in one of the fridges. In Larrasoaña, I was one of the youngest people there but here I'm at the upper range. I find myself sitting with two American couples – one of whom is delightfully called Janet and John. The wine flows easily and endlessly, and my mood switches around completely, to such an extent that it becomes one of the happiest evenings I've ever spent. There is a lot of laughter and freewheeling good will with truly lovely people. There are no egos and no-one talking about personal problems. And not once does anyone ask why they are doing the Camino. It's my first experience of staying in a *donativo* – a pilgrimage hostel where you decide how much to pay for your stay: the money being ploughed back into food and upkeep. I retire to bed at 9.30pm a happy man and somehow feel that I've learned a lesson of sorts today.

I am rewarded with the best night's sleep I've had so far and I wake up feeling totally refreshed and ready for anything. One of the first places on today's itinerary is Irache. There's a monastery that dates from the tenth century, and later on a pilgrim hospital was sited here. However, its most famous feature is situated on the wall of the former convent winery. Someone knows exactly what the average pilgrim needs and has installed a tap that dispenses free wine. Although it's just after 7am and barely daylight, I think I should have a glass for research purposes, and I fill the top of my water bottle with some of the local red. It may be the time of day, or the vintage that is on offer, but it tastes like there's a rotting carcass in the barrel. To be honest, I know I've drunk worse and paid for the privilege, and I'm certainly not going to argue about the price here. After a few sips, I decide to carry on my slightly more merry way but vow to stick to water and hot chocolate until the evening.

First light brings up a corrugated landscape of cornfields and vineyards and there are the early signs of another sunny day. There is also the sight of the hilltop castle at Monjardín which dominates the view for the next couple of hours. I actually stop in the village which is a couple of hundred metres below the castle itself. There is a café here, but pilgrims are ignoring it and instead are congregating at a few tables where biscuits and cakes plus tea and coffee have been laid out. I ask about prices and am told that there aren't any; the idea is that you make a donation for what you consume. After staying in a *donativo* hostel last night, I'm now eating at an improvised *donativo* café. Apparently, this kind of stopping point crops up all over the Camino but you're never sure where they're going to occur. It's certainly the first time I've come across one and it makes me feel like I'm taking part in some kind of orienteering competition. It's a great idea though, and it's staffed by enthusiastic helpers. It's also where I see my first Camino casualty and rather unluckily, it's Marco. Yesterday evening he felt a twinge in his leg and the warden at his *refugio* called a doctor. He thinks he can continue but there is doubt in his voice, and I'm not going to put money on it. He's limping markedly and there is disappointment written all over his face. He must be suffering as this is the first time I've seen him at rest without a beer in his hand.

For the next hour or so, I walk with Paco, a Spanish lawyer, and he represents another truly positive result of saying yes. He is doing the Camino a week at a time over several years. This is his first day of this year's section and he's in a suitably buoyant mood. We walk slowly, taking detours into the vineyards to loot handfuls of grapes, which then spend a lot of time in our hands before we can find a water fountain to wash them. The other significant agricultural features of the day are huge haystacks, two or three storeys high, shaped into large cubes. A few pilgrims are taking advantage of the shade they provide for a bit of rest or as a picnic spot. It is a truly beautiful day to be out. The sun is shining, but a gentle breeze takes away the worst excesses of the heat, and it's shaping up to be the best day's walking so far.

After Paco, I pair up with Jean from Quebec, the battle-hardened pilgrim from my first night who had started his pilgrimage in Narbonne. We've been on "Buen Camino" terms for several days now, having stayed together in St Jean and Pamplona, but we haven't really spoken before. I notice that he now doesn't look any scruffier than anyone else, or sound any different. We've reached his level with the early naïve enthusiasm being swapped for slightly less animated reality. We communicate the best we can in my broken French and his rusty English, and it soon becomes clear that he's slightly deaf which doesn't help. The rural tranquillity is shattered on a couple of occasions as I try to repeat something in a louder voice while fellow walkers look on amused. My destination for today, Los Arcos, is approaching and I ask him if he's staying there too.

"Municipal zoo? What municipal zoo?" he replies.

Los Arcos doesn't seem like a promising destination at first sight. It looks little more than a handful of stone buildings and a drinks machine, but the main road slopes downhill to reveal a significant sandy-coloured village with a crumbly but pleasant appearance. It's not as picturesque or as well preserved as Puente La Reina but, with the sun bouncing magically off the adobe buildings, it has a delightful feeling of timelessness about it.

43

Although a place that's been embedded in pilgrimage culture for hundreds of years - even now there are three other hostels here - there's a bit of modernity on display. The town is passed on two sides by major roads and, by Camino standards, there's a substantial amount of traffic when you move out of the village confines. It's also evident in the place I'm staying in. It's back to a large municipal hostel – this time in what looks like a converted school building. It's white with big windows and looks several hundred years newer than pretty much everything I walked past on the way in. It advertises pilgrimage massages but perhaps the biggest pulls are a lengthy washing line and a working mangle.

Los Arcos also has a grocery shop on its main street and I venture in for supplies. After yesterday's long march to Lorca on an empty stomach, there's no desire to repeat the experience tomorrow. You can tell by the service that the shop caters for the locals as well as passing pilgrims. The service is unapologetically brusque and unsmiling and, just as I'm reaching out to test the freshness of the apples I'm pointed to a large sign written in English warning against touching the food. To make me like the place even less, my €10 banknote is held up to the light for scrutiny when I pay for my unmolested fruit and some chocolate and bread. This annoys me immensely so I do the same with the €5 note that comes in my change. The shopkeeper is unamused, to say the least, and I'm on the end of minor rant. I've probably not done my fellow pilgrims any favours here but the stunt makes me feel happier - well for a couple of seconds at least.

I can't remember when I first heard about the Camino but I certainly remember the first person I met who had done it. She was a Peruvian student in my class when I was a TEFL teacher in Bournemouth. I think about her as I walk back to the hostel. She gave a short talk on it, having completed the walk a matter of weeks before. She inspired the other students as the question and answer session lasted longer than the speech did. It impressed me too, and I asked her all about it afterwards over tea. I was inspired and headed home via the library to try to find a book on the subject. The only one I discovered was by a couple who had covered the distance on horseback with their son. Most of the narrative revolved around the state of the horses at the end of the day, but there was enough there to keep me interested. I think I decided there and then that I would do the walk one day.

As I'm thinking back and watching the ducks on the river, I hear a shout of "There's a proud Irishman!" which seems to be hurled in my general direction.

I don't realise the comment is aimed at me until I feel a tap on the shoulder. I turn around and see a couple in their twenties. He is another one who looks like he's lived the outdoor life and has a tanned stubbly face and black wavy hair. She looks slight with porcelain features and worried-looking green eyes. They are called Rod and Cassie and they're from South Africa.

The source of the confusion is that I'm wearing an Irish rugby jersey, as it's another blowy afternoon. It was a present, and the sole reason I've brought it with me is because it takes up less space folded up than the other jumper alternatives I considered.

"Are you from Dublin?" Rod asks enthusiastically. "I was in Dublin a couple of years ago and had a great time there."

"I'm not Irish, I'm British". I decide it's not worth adding the tag, "and possibly Spanish as well" for reasons of confusion and the fact that I feel a long way from full rehabilitation.

Rod looks disappointed, and his face falls even more when I tell him I'm not a big fan of rugby union either. He does have the sense to comprehend though that this conversation is best continued in a bar and so we sit in the main square facing the rather oversized church of Santa María with beers in our hands. We're out of the wind and so can take in the gorgeous sunshine and talk about the Camino experience so far. It is Cassie who is the more experienced walker, and this is her idea of a holiday. She's taken a break from her career in publishing and this is what she wanted to do.

We are joined by another woman who announces her presence by being delighted to "finally find somebody else who's Irish". Her accent is more Catford than Waterford and her name's Caitlin. She professes to be the genuine article but equally admits that she's spent most of her life in London. She's loud, persistent and talks non-stop.

"Guess how old I am. Go on. You wouldn't believe I've got a 21-year-old daughter, would you? Everyone's surprised when I say that. People always say how young I look. Go on, how old am I?"

We're not allowed to guess because the monologue hasn't finished yet and there's no sign of the batteries running out. Rod

45

catches my eye and raises his eyebrows. I certainly think she looks old enough to have a 21-year-old daughter. I'd put her at around 40. Rod diplomatically suggests that she's 35, which seems to annoy Caitlin. Clearly, the estimate isn't young enough.

"I'm only 39. Can you believe it?"

Well to be perfectly frank, yes. Meanwhile, Cassie, who has been knitting her eyebrows and listening intently looks at her and expresses a thought that might have been best left unvoiced.

"39? I would have put you in your early 40s."

There's no malice intended and Cassie seems blissfully unaware of what she's said. I'm getting the idea that she's quite an intense and serious person. A cloud passes across Caitlin's face but it's not enough for her to move away. I'm sure she's harmless but she talks unceasingly and is very tiring in the afternoon heat.

The evening entertainment comes in the form of a mass at the church, which is attended by about fifty of us. It's followed by a rather moving and personal pilgrimage blessing. The priest takes his time to shake everybody's hand and asks us where we come from. He also encourages us to have a glass of wine for him in Santiago - he thinks he's had enough prayers said for him there - and he finishes off by stamping our *credencial*s. It's only taken me eight years from being inspired by a student to actually getting on the Camino, and all is going well so far. Then again, I've only just met Caitlin.

I have a disturbed sleep caused mainly by an enormous Spaniard who snores like a buffalo all bloody night. He was in situ when I came in yesterday evening and is still unconscious when I leave. He was thrashing about a bit as well. God knows what he was dreaming about, but judging by the sound effects a ménage-a-trois involving a horse and an owl can't be ruled out.

At about 1.30am, when the people in my part of the dormitory were coming to the conclusion that sleep was going to be tricky at best, an Australian woman in a bunk opposite me let her annoyance show by shouting, "Oh for fuck's sake won't somebody smother that bastard?"

From the laughter, you could tell that the noise was affecting a lot of us. However, the perpetrator slept on regardless, leaving the rest of us to struggle. Generally waking up time on the Camino tends to be around 6am but, because of the noise, most of us were up, about and annoyed half an hour earlier.

It had to come, I suppose. The first drops of rain fall on the Camino a few minutes after I get underway, and it causes several problems. The first of these is when my poncho splits after about twenty minutes of use. It's the first time I've had to put it on, and I struggle to use what bits of it that are serviceable to provide some kind of protection. I would have done better trying to wear a crisp packet. The only way I can get some purpose out of it is to wrap what is left of it around my shoulders and hold it together at chest level. This means I can't use my walking poles. I'm not actually sure it's worth the effort. It's not as if it's really biblically lashing it down. It's a persistent and annoying downpour, but there is that cricket feeling that if the rain stops, play would get underway in an hour or so.

Another problem is that I underestimate how cold it is. There are precious few stopping places during the early part of the walk and I find myself trying to put my rugby jersey on in a small bus shelter while trying to make sure that what was left of my poncho doesn't blow away. Another reason for staying undercover is that I got lost in the darkness of the morning. I am not alone in this; there are about half a dozen other people in the same predicament, and we are hunched together for warmth while studying our guides. We know that if we stay on this particular road we can reach a place called Sansol and rejoin the Camino properly there. I join an escape party that decides to double back and take advantage of the greater daylight to find out where we went wrong. Fortunately, the terrain is flat and featureless, so all we have to do is look for fellow pilgrims to get back on track.

It's difficult to walk properly because of my need to cling on to my poncho. There's no shade at all and the rain, if not torrential, is certainly unrelenting. It's not even slightly pleasant to be out, as I can't really concentrate on the scenery. I drip helplessly into a bar at the next available stopping point, Torres del Río, and I'm not the first because the wooden floor is soaking. It's dark and gloomy and there's only one other pilgrim around, but it's a hell of a lot better than being outside. I'm hoping a leisurely half-hour nursing a hot chocolate might mean that the rain passes over, but I'm wrong. The weather has stayed the same and doesn't look like it's going to change in the next hour or so. I contort what is left of my poncho around my body, and head back out again.

The Camino snakes across the N-111 road, and many pilgrims abandon the path and stick to the road instead, their blue and yellow ponchos vivid against an intolerant sky, heads down to protect against the elements. There's sense in sticking to the road but it twists and turns a lot and I'm not sure how considerate the motorists may be. It's not a particularly busy stretch of highway but it's hardly deserted either and, due to the corners and weather, visibility won't be brilliant for drivers, no matter how bright your rain protection is. It's all a big change after the sunlit pastoral beauty of yesterday.

I stay on the path and feel the mud sucking upwards to cling to my boots, increasing the effort expended. Every step brings more soil out of the ground and I feel a couple of inches taller and considerably heavier. It's not a flat path either, and includes a 100m climb up the hill of Nuestra Señora del Poyo, and from it I can just about make out the buildings of Viana against a gunmetal sky. It's still a fair distance away but it brings optimism and it looks like most of the rest of the journey will be on the flat.

I get there just as the sky is lightening up. There is a temptation to carry on to the city of Logroño, if only to get a new poncho, but Viana sounded interesting when I read about it before and it looks promising now, and not only because I feel wretched. Logroño is still about 8km and a couple of hours away and, even though the weather is improving, I don't want to take the risk. Equally, I'm not sure if I'm ready for another night in a big city after the Pamplona experience.

There's another improvised refreshment stop on the modern outskirts of the town and, even though the water from the flasks on the tables is luke-warm, it feels like one of the best drinks I've ever had and it couldn't have come at a better time. I assume the sites of these impromptu cafés are chosen from experience, and on a day like today the help is particularly gratefully received and appreciated. There are a few pilgrims gathering in the slowly fading rain, and no one looks like they have enjoyed today. There are smiles but they are smiles of relief and shared hardship. Tony and Margaret are here but we just have time to exchange hellos before they head off again. They're pressing on to Logroño but there's no way I'm going further than the other end of town.

Having missed a couple of fiestas by the odd day, I walk headlong into Viana's celebrations. Along the main street of the old part of town, there is a procession of musicians and flag carriers heading towards me. It's a narrow road and there's no way to go past it, so I'm shunted into a small square next to the church. Unfortunately, so is the oncoming parade as this is where it's going to finish. The end of the pageant is greeted with loud bangs, and small objects are launched into the sky with considerable velocity. It's only when one connects violently with the top of my head on its way back down, that I notice that they are sweets. While I'm rubbing away the pain in stunned confusion and dealing with mint-ball-induced concussion, there are children scrabbling at my feet, gathering up as many as they can.

I'm in the shadow of the church tower that I had first seen from Nuestra Señora del Poyo. Just like the churches in Roncesvalles and Los Arcos, this one is dedicated to Santa María (and poor St William still doesn't get a mention). It's a glorious structure with an ornate recessed doorway and an elaborate but unoppressive exterior. It's also the final resting place of Cesare Borgia who was killed nearby

49

while making a right mess of besieging the local castle. When provisions were smuggled into the stronghold one night, he chased after the rebel leader, Luis de Beaumonte, who supplied them. In his enthusiasm for revenge, Borgia outdistanced his supporting troops and was ambushed when he was pretty much on his own. He's actually buried outside the church, as his original mausoleum was vandalised. It's not every day that you stumble across a grave belonging to the son of a Pope. I don't how many there are. Oddly enough, the Catholic Church is reluctant to grasp the huge money-grabbing potential of this novelty, but maybe it's only a matter of time.

Tonight's place of rest is a converted monastery which consists of several dormitories made up of triple bunk beds. It also has a terrace where you can see the buildings of Logroño in the distance. It must be gorgeous when the sun's out, but I can't see many people taking advantage of it today and nobody's taking the risk of hanging their clothing outside either. With the rain, there is much activity in the hostel laundry room, as fellow pilgrims seek space to dry their boots. There are washing machines here but not a lot of space to hang clothes and, for the first time, there is a dent in the spirit of the Camino. There are several sniping quarrels as people fight for a bit of washing line in this tiny dark room that feels only marginally warmer than the world outside. After a week of brotherly and sisterly love, things have snapped over cleaning facilities.

When I return blinking into the daylight, one of the town's roads has been gated off for some bull-running. Viana may not be particularly big but it can support its own bullring. Unfortunately, it struggles a bit when it comes to bulls, as one of the animals on display is clearly sporting udders. As I noticed earlier with the procession, there's not a huge amount of room to manoeuvre on the main street, nor is it particularly long. Space has been created at either end by fencing off a couple of roads to provide a small square which just about accommodates the turning circle of agitated cattle. It is also where the animals are taunted by some of the local men who jump at them and stamp their feet in the hope of provoking a chase. If a bull makes a move, the men rush to the sanctuary of the wooden gate and leap onto it. It's all a bit of a farce really, as the road isn't long enough for a bull (or cow) to pick up speed, and there's little chance of anyone getting gored. I do live in hope, though. I'm sure there's a valid reason for the tradition but if I ask someone, the answer will almost certainly be "We've always done it like this."

I watched this spectacle in the company of Rod and Cassie behind one of the gates. While Viana-man is taking on the Bovril, I have my own internal Spanish-British conflict going on inside my head. At first, I'm undecided if I like the spectacle or not. It's certainly an event, it's different and it's very non-British. I'm no great animal lover but as the afternoon progresses there is no doubt that my allegiances lie with the four-legged team. Mind you, my frequent shouts of "Gore the stupid bastard!" every time somebody jumps into the square in front of me, probably don't make me popular with the locals.

Cassie is an animal lover and she winces when a bull slips as it turns around. There are tears in her eyes when it gets up again and is subsequently taunted. She's unhappy about what's going on so we decide that we've had enough and go in search of food. The nearest restaurant has to be entered via the back way because of the bull-running, and there's no respite for Cassie. The front door is open but there is a metal gate in front of it, so that the bull-run can still be witnessed. Conversation takes place to a soundtrack of the inelegant galloping of hooves on cobbles outside. It's an offbeat feeling sitting down in a restaurant when you can see and hear the main course charging up and down outside.

We're joined by Caitlin who it turns out has been travelling around Central America for the past few months and has presumably come back to Europe as it's another continent she can bore.

"You'd love Costa Rica, Rod. You really would. I see you Rudy as more El Salvador. Cassie, you're definitely Belize and I'll tell you why..."

Oh, please don't. Normally I love listening to travellers' tales, but hers are a whistle-stop list of place names and people, delivered at breakneck speed with only a passing nod to interest. She barely pauses for breath but does stop for wine, which she can clearly consume in huge amounts. After several minutes in her company, Rod, Cassie and I realise that the best evasive action we can come up with is to match her drink for drink. Due to the fiesta, we're pretty much locked in, so we stay for several hours, knocking back bottles of red as afternoon merges into evening. There's a brief interlude between bull runs when we can sit outside, but that's the limit to our physical activity. It becomes one of those occasions when you look up and notice that it's suddenly dark outside. It is a rather sheepish walk back as curfew approaches. I even manage to lose Caitlin in the two minutes it takes to get back. I fear the worst after dedicating over a quarter of the day to wine consumption and sit in the kitchen space drinking water to minimize any potential after-effects. I also try to make sense of a hostel sign which reads "To leave all cleared one and gathered in the closets". Even sober and without the bleary eyes, I doubt if I could understand it.

Somehow I manage to avoid the hangover which the previous day's drinking had seriously deserved. The pain comes from elsewhere. A fair amount of co-ordination and flexibility is needed to negotiate the middle bed of a triple bunk. These are two qualities I don't tend to have when I'm drunk, and yesterday evening it took a couple of goes to get into position. Neither of them was particularly quiet. I was the last person in the dorm too and I entered to the gentle sound of rustling sleeping bags and low key snoring. I climbed the bunk ladder and tried to swing my body into the appropriate space but my knee connected forcefully with the bed frame, sending vibrations akin to an earthquake to the people above and below. The accompanying "Fuck me that hurt!" probably didn't ingratiate me to the rest of the sleepers either. And that was before I banged my head. I suspect I am not the most popular man in the dormitory so I decide to get up and get out before the ructions start. Should anyone mention the previous night's events later in the day, I'm going to say that it was Caitlin.

My immediate destination is Logroño, and I head off in the darkness towards its distant lights and I have the paths to myself. The walk passes through what look like allotments and then into an area of greenery known as the Pantano de las Canas. Looking back, I can see the silhouettes of Viana under a silvery and slight crescent moon. It's one of those beautiful moments when you feel you're the only person around and the silence is intoxicating. I stay there staring for a few minutes taking deep breaths and thinking how beautiful the world looks just as night turns into day. I can hear the footsteps of some fellow walkers, and scared that it may be a lynching party from my dorm, I head through the parkland and around a lake before leaving rural pleasure behind and heading into the city.

After a week in Navarra, it's time to enter the new region of La Rioja. This border crossing is achieved by way of a rickety bridge over a muddy ditch in the middle of an industrial estate on the outskirts of Logroño. It's an idiosyncratic introduction to an area famous for its vineyards. The walk then takes me around the side of a hill and before long, the full city skyline emerges. On the descent, I pass through a village that has been swallowed up by the spread of the suburbs but where a Camino family tradition still takes place. For years, a woman called Doña Felisa opened up her living room and put out bread, cakes, and coffee which each pilgrim could take advantage of in return for a donation. She died several years ago but her daughter keeps up the custom. She even has her own special stamp for the *credencial*, which has the slogan, "Higos – agua y amor"; figs – water and love. It's a perfectly timed breakfast stop for me and I am the first walker of the day to indulge in the gorgeous cakes and a hot drink. I'd love to talk to the daughter but my language skills just aren't up to it at all. I can't thank her enough – it is easily the best breakfast so far.

I have a bit of a loiter in Logroño, not because it is particularly beautiful, but rather because I need to buy a new poncho. Although today's walk has been a return to the sunshine, I should be prepared for anything. It looks like a busy and pleasant enough place but it doesn't make me regret not staying there. I kill time by having a tea in a metallic, featureless city bar which has a huge television fixed onto a wall. It's tuned to a music channel that is hell-bent on reliving some of the musical nightmares from the 1980s. Relief isn't that far away - it's only about twenty minutes before a nearby shop opens and I can escape from New Romantic hell and buy a new, improved and slightly over-priced bit of rain protection gear. If it lasts more than the last one did, it might just be worth it.

Like Pamplona before it, the city is difficult to navigate your way out of, even though this time at least I'm doing it in daylight. Getting in was awkward enough but leaving takes an eternity, with one busy road looking very much like another and the chances of getting lost seeming to magnify. I also start to feel very light headed and this morphs into a real fear of fainting. It may not be the most beautiful place in the world but I'm seriously glad to be in an urban environment where I can easily find a bar to rest in, and take in more food and drink. The light-headedness is scary and I've got no idea what has brought it on.

A lot of my friends and colleagues knew about my desire to walk across Spain. For a long time, it was only an idea and I didn't know how or even if I was going to achieve it. The only way it seemed to make sense – as many pilgrims I've met on the walk can verify - was after retirement when the time would be available to commit to a multi-week walk. And so it remained a vague dream that was occasionally revisited over cups of tea and pints of beer. A few months ago one of the Camino guidebooks appeared in my pigeonhole at work. In my job I used to be sent a lot of books for reviewing, and for potential author interviews but this particular one wasn't mailed by a publisher or agent – it wasn't in an envelope for a start. One of my colleagues (and I have never found out who) was giving me the hint to stop talking about Santiago and actually go out and do it. The idea morphed from pipe dream to solid reality in months and I'm now a hundred miles into it with no regrets. The same guidebook, slightly more dog-eared, is now being studied in some detail as I decide what may be an achievable destination for tonight.

After a pilgrimage record hour-long break, I decide it's time to continue, with Navarrete being the target. It's still a significant 12km away and walking is now done with a certain amount of trepidation, and more effort than usual goes into making sure that I take in as much water as possible. The speed is reduced and I try to keep other pilgrims in sight both in front and behind. If I'm going to pass out, I want people to know about it.

The walk out of Logroño echoes the way in. It involves a park and edging past a lake before heading through more fields and finally into the famous La Rioja vineyards. There are a few fig trees along the way too, brought viciously to my attention when some fruit falls on my head. At one point, the route runs parallel to a main road and across a motorway. We're separated by a crosswire fence which has been decorated by literally hundreds of improvised crosses. They have been made with twigs, bits of bush and grass – anything that happens to be lying about - and are woven in and out of the wire. The fence is several hundred metres long and there are crosses for the entire length of it, to the point where it's almost impossible to find any space at all. I've got no idea why they are there in one of the most unspiritual locations you can ever hope to come across. Decorative or symbolic, it's still a striking display.

It's also a good day for the impromptu cairn. I've seen several of these precarious looking pyramids of stones resting on top of signs or flat rock. They're another improvised sign of pilgrimage intent, with the idea being that the stone you add represents the emotional burden you're carrying. The ones I've seen look so delicate that any further addition could bring the whole lot crashing down. There's no way of knowing if they've been here for days or decades.

I get to Navarrete, about a quarter of an hour before the hostel opens and with no further signs of light-headedness. There are already about a dozen backpacks lined up outside the door and we wait under a stone vaulted roof which covers the pavement. When we sign in there is a delay, as an argument develops. The *hospitalero* doesn't believe that the couple in front of me has walked all the way from Los Arcos and is rather angry about it.

"You didn't begin in Los Arcos. It's impossible."

The couple are French and they show their *credencial*s with the appropriate stamps which show they were in Los Arcos last night. The *hospitalero* is not letting go though and smells a rat.

"You walked 40km and you are here now? I don't believe you!"

Quite frankly, neither do the rest of us. If they got here just before me at about 1.45pm, they must have been going at one hell of a rate and they don't even look slightly tired. There's no hint of pilgrimage attrition, or resigned wariness. The couple still refuse to budge and the *hospitalero* actually refuses them entry. The rest of us in the queue look at each other in stunned silence. They then decide to come clean and say that they got a bus part of the way to avoid walking through Logroño. He's still not happy about this and they have to wait while the rest of us sign in and get stamped, and then see if there's any room left. It's the first time I've seen an incident like this, and indeed witnessed a *hospitalero* getting angry (excluding my first night of course which is now seeming more and more like a never-to-be-repeated experience). Normally signing in is a pretty uneventful experience and just involves filling in your name, nationality and starting point, and finding out what the rules are.

It's a good hostel to stay in. There are a few dormitories spread over a couple of floors. There are four bunks in my room though they could easily squeeze in more beds if they want to. After staying in a few places where space is at a premium, it's great to be able to spread out a bit. There's a large kitchen and dining area, which pleases Rod and Cassie who are also staying here. They are doing the Camino as cheaply as possible and they tend to make their own food – yesterday in Viana was very much an exception. They're certainly not in the minority here, and for the first time, I feel as if I'm missing out by not doing the same. There's a lot of noise and general goodwill in the kitchen as people come back from the shops and get together to cook. The smells are also alluring and I'm hoping for an invite to dine so I can say yes to it.

I don't recognise any of the people in my dorm. Half of them appear to be Scandinavian so I'm subject to hearty amounts of Nordic cheer. I'm also sharing with Brian who is a rarity among pilgrims in that he's also British. They are all cooking for themselves too, so I go out in search of a bar to sample the local food and find one close by. There's only one other couple in the *comedor* and so the atmosphere is woefully lacking; the only sounds to be heard here are provided by the television in the main bar area. The food from the *menú del dia* however, is excellent and features the usual line up of pork, chicken or meatballs followed by rice pudding or *flan*. It's all aided by a bottle of the local wine, but somehow I think those back at the hostel have got a better deal in terms of ambience and experience. The weather is closing in as I walk back, and my washing is retrieved from the line outside the window just before it starts to belt down with rain. The sky is looking very evil indeed but hopefully, things will be different in the morning. At least it's not going to be difficult to climb into a bunk tonight.

When I awake, it's throwing it down with extreme ferocity. The water is bouncing off the roads to knee height and it's unpleasant from the moment I leave. Once again, I pay the penalty of being one of the first out by finding it difficult to navigate my way out of the town. My head is bowed to avoid the worst excesses of the weather and I do the first part of the journey from the memory of the reconnaissance walk of the previous evening. The occasional car headlights penetrate the darkness and illuminate just how heavy the downpour is. Even when daylight comes, the cloud cover is enough to reinforce the air of gloominess. The rain is so unyielding that it is difficult to follow the yellow arrows and there are enough places where a wrong path could easily be taken. This is certainly not a day to get lost and have to retrace your steps. On the plus side, my new poncho is working but my legs are exposed to the slanting sheets of rain, and after 2km my trousers are sticking to them like a second skin. I can feel the water draining into my socks and it's an uncomfortable 8km and a couple of hours until a suitable stopping point can be found.

This comes in the shape of the first available bar of the morning at Ventosa. Hanging about outside are about half a dozen walkers looking like refugee smokers, wringing out their socks and generally looking despondent. I take my backpack inside and join in with the cleansing ritual outside, my bare feet cold on the steps. It is the first time I've had to change my socks mid walk and there's a feeling that today is going to be endured rather than enjoyed. There is no optimism to be gained from looking at the sky either. If ever there is a moment for a hot chocolate then it's this one and I share a table with a jovial, bearded German called Michael. He speaks excellent English having lived in Ireland for a couple of years. He seems to be in the habit of attempting marathon walks and once hiked to Macchu Picchu, but even he confesses that he's never had to go through a day like this one.

I'm hoping that the weather may relent during my break but it isn't going to. It's still threateningly dark and wet and after a couple of minutes of further walking, I just want it all to be over. Anything has to be better than this – even staying in that futuristic looking café in Logroño and being subject to Visage videos. There's a main road nearby and you can see and hear wheels splashing through the considerable amount of surface water. Even in a car, it doesn't look like much fun.

Progress continues to be slow and what could be a beautiful part of the walk through vineyards is made treacherous as the terracotta paths turn to mud which leeches the rivers and streams red. Motion is more sideways than forwards and once again each footstep takes appreciable effort and brings up a sizeable amount of soil. There's that feeling of being taller and heavier again but this is far worse than the road to Viana. The paths are more exposed and the rain falls like bullets. The walking poles come into their own again as trying to stay vertical is incredibly difficult. It doesn't bother some people though. Rod and Cassie hare past me effortlessly without the need of sticks, and with enviable displays of balance and determination, and soon disappear into the soggy distance.

I stop in the modern looking town of Nájera. It wasn't my target for the day, but with the weather the way it is there is no way on Earth that I am going to make it to Azofra. It's a further 5km and ninety odd minutes away which is a bloody long time to keep going in sodden socks and boots that are a couple of inches higher than when I set off. Anyway, I quite like the look of Nájera. There's nothing particularly charming or ageless about it and the rain hardly adds to its attractiveness but it looks friendly enough.

It is also another place that appears to be in the throes of a fiesta when I arrive. No bull-running this time; it looks more like the type of place where the fattest boy in the school gets to sit on the town cat – it gives off that sort of impression. There are no obvious parades or sweets flying through the air, and on first evidence, celebrations seem to be confined to wearing silly colourful trousers and setting off bangers.

I find a small grocers and decide to enter in search of chocolate and fruit: a simple task which ends up being highly embarrassing. The chocolate is situated in a narrow aisle with a dead end and when I get there it dawns on me that if I attempt to turn around with my rucksack still on, I'm going to take out a couple of shelves. I size up the task in hand and evaluate that even attempting to take off my backpack will result in some collateral damage to the displays. A shop assistant appraises the situation and comes to reverse me out. She isn't exactly laughing but I can sense the vibrations in her hands, and now know what grinning loudly feels like. I don't mind; I am served by someone with a smile on their face and I get to feel the fruit before buying it.

A river flows through the centre of Nájera and the hostel is on the opposite bank under a looming sandstone cliff. There is a small queue of people waiting for it to open and it's clear that we're not here because of the pull of the town but more a reluctance to continue. There's a Czech couple in their 50s who have walked the Appalachian Way and who look subtly tough, but even they feel defeated by today's conditions. The rain may have now eased to the point of a consistent drizzle but standing in it and waiting for hostel opening time seems a better deal than carrying on.

It's another *donativo* – a big one that houses ninety people in the same room. There's a tumble dryer in the washing room which I get to first, and I selfishly chuck my wet clothes in. I return a few minutes later and discover a full-scale row going on. A Spanish man wants to jump the queue and is waving what was quite possibly a pair of training shoes earlier this morning. They're unrecognisable now beneath several layers of La Rioja clay. Nobody wants to yield their position in the washing and drying queue and he's furious. If he were a bit friendlier about it, he might have got somewhere, but his face is going purple and he's getting unpleasant and aggressive. He's not too happy with me either as I don't know when the machine will finish drying my clothes. The next people in the queue are the Spanish couple who helped with the cooking in Estella and I am able to break the machine's cycle and chuck their clothes in with mine. This infuriates the shoe man even more and his temper is not helped by a sign being pointed out to him which says that you can't put shoes in either the washing or drying machines. The angrier he gets the more the rest of us find him amusing. This isn't the right pilgrimage attitude to have but he is winding me and several other people up severely. I want to think that we are holding up the Camino spirit and he's the one attacking it.

When I return to the main room, it looks like one of those buildings which has been converted to house the survivors of a natural disaster. It has filled up quickly and there are clothes hanging on the ends of beds, backpacks everywhere, and dampness in the air. The bunks are pushed together in twos which means that I'm sleeping alongside a beautiful Canadian woman called Carrie. She's in her twenties with dark red hair and dazzling blue eyes. She is really good fun and laughs a lot, particularly about our sleeping arrangements. There are few things less romantic than sharing a space with eighty-eight other people, especially since two of them, namely her mother and her aunt, are occupying the bunks directly below. It could have been worse, just. The incredible snoring man from Los Arcos is here so I fear for the night. He's at the other end of the dorm but the distance doesn't look big enough.

It's still pouring in the afternoon though not with the same intensity as before so I make a move to venture back into town. Carrie looks up with interest.

"Are you going to have a look around? Can I join you?" A big grin forms on her face. "I mean, if we're going to sleep together we should get to know each other first."

I can't help but smile back, "Does your mother know you say things like that?"

"Yes, she does", comes a friendly voice from the bunk below, "And my daughter has been warned about it!"

I'm more attracted to just having a wander and finding out a bit more about the fiesta but Carrie's interested in buying supplies. I manage to steer her away from the scene of my earlier embarrassment where I'm probably already an anecdote, but Nájera is big enough with a full range of shops to choose from. There's a funfair set up and one of the squares is dominated by a temporary stage. The town is getting ready to party and the celebrations will be getting underway just as pilgrim bedtime approaches.

Over a beer, Carrie tells me she's from New Brunswick and has a Master's degree in Spanish Language and Literature. She has always loved the country and is taking up a teaching post in the Extremadura region after the Camino.

"Will the family be staying with you too?"

Carrie's effortless smile widens. "No. they're only here for the Camino. Anyway, as we're getting on so well. I think you should meet them." I've dreamed of meeting women like Carrie and when I do, I'm old enough to be her father and more worryingly, Caitlin's old enough to be her mother.

Later that evening I have a non-descript dinner in a small restaurant with Carrie and her mum and aunt – we're bunk friends and this means we're practically related - and are joined by an Australian couple who are trying to do the Camino by only using hotels. It's an interesting idea but the semi-detached approach doesn't really appeal to me. I want the full pilgrimage experience and I don't like the idea of cutting myself off from everyone else. The snoring, the over-crowding, the moaning about washing space – it all comes with the deal. It's only when we head back and become aware that the dormitory has turned into the Spanish version of the Black Hole of Calcutta that I think the Australians may have a point after all. It's incredibly hot and humid in the dorm with a strong smell of wet clothes. I can also hear the unmistakable sound of the Los Arcos snorer getting into his stride. Carrie and I sigh over what might have been and wish each other a good night. It's never like this in Barbara Cartland novels.

There was a band doing the tour of the town last night. They serenaded us at about midnight, which was not exactly welcome as most of us had been asleep for two hours by then. There was also live music from the stage about a quarter of a mile away and I vaguely remember being awoken in a daze by the strains of *Unchained Melody* at stupid o'clock. It is in situations like this that you realise how much the Camino really puts you at odds with normal life. We're all settling down to bed when the rest of the nation is heading out to party. There's a cultural barrier in place. The pilgrimage is a foreign country: we do things differently here.

It is another early start and mercifully, it isn't raining. The first part of the walk is along a road which shrinks to path size to go through a narrow valley. It is shrouded in total darkness and the only things that can be distinguished are the stars above. Slight fear turns to absolute elation when I stop, turn my eyes to the heavens and realise that I'm experiencing the closest I had ever come to total silence in my entire life. No bird song, no distant traffic; if I hold my breath there is nothing to hear at all. It's truly beautiful and I stand there for a few minutes taking in huge lungfuls of air and holding it in for as long as I can. There is an incredible sense of peace in just looking upwards. I know I may never experience something like this again and it's milked for all it's worth. These are infectious moments, before increasing light wakes up the birds and I hear the familiar sound of stones being kicked on the path behind me.

I have breakfast in Azofra which is busy with pilgrims when I arrive. The conversations are lively with most of the talk being about the rain yesterday. According to the television in the bar, there's a big sun over all of northern Spain and there's a cheer when we all see it. There's still the aftermath of yesterday to deal with first.

Soon afterwards, the Camino leaves the stone paths and roads and moves back on to the familiar red clay soil of La Rioja. It is still heavily muddy from yesterday's rain and it's a case of negotiating the way through it rather than walking on its surface. The more sensible walkers tend to ignore the paths and walk on the edge of fields when they can and there's a fair amount of opportunity. Whatever is grown there has been harvested and the stubble provides a more solid base underfoot.

It's a gentle but lengthy climb up towards the next village and I stop at a picnic area along the way to make a few adjustments to my rucksack. There are several people here and a couple is bravely lying down on the stone benches and taking in the feeble sunshine. Rather peculiarly, we're on the fringe of a golf course which seems strangely incongruous given that there can't be any major centres of population for miles. It looks and sounds deserted which makes it even more of an anomaly.

I pair up with an Australian woman called Olivia who is another easy-going pilgrim. She did the Camino the previous year and expresses an intention of doing it for a third time if she can. I've noticed her before as she's formed an improbable double act with another Australian called Nita. They're an odd couple with Olivia being a good six inches taller. They were in the same place as me last night and Nita has become famous in pilgrimage circles for going through the cupboards of hostels when she arrives to look for leftover food, which she then utilises herself. They both tend to seek out the municipal *refugios* and *donativos* because they are cheaper. At first, I was appalled at this cheapskate attitude but the more I think about it the more I think they are following in the spirit of the original pilgrims. They too had very little and Nita cooks her meals for anyone who is interested. They were very popular yesterday evening as only a few of us decided to venture outside.

There is no sign of Nita at the moment and, from what I can make out, Olivia and she only met on the Camino and they don't plan anything together. It's just that until this morning I have never seen one without the other. Olivia finished her Camino last year at the end of November and her first thought when she got back to Australia was to do it again in better weather.

"I also left something behind here," she says rather cryptically. She also talks about how difficult she found it to talk about the walk to her friends back home. "It's all about feeling and it's very difficult to convey that."

For a minute, I think I'm going to be subjected to bucketloads of unwanted mysticism but Olivia proves to be excellent company and barely mentions her previous Camino again. In fact, she doesn't talk about this one either, unless prompted. A lot of the conversation is about changing careers, which is a staple Camino topic. She's contemplating moving from secretarial work to physiotherapy and wants a bit of thinking time to see what her options are and what direction she goes in.

Together we march through Ciriñuéla, which appears to be a planned village situated on top of a very windy hill. The houses are all newly built but very few of them appear to be occupied. Many aren't even finished and I imagine they were designed to house the people who aspire to play at the golf club. There's a strange aspect to the place - an odd mix of housing estate and open prison. The rattling wind just adds to the atmosphere of desolation. According to Olivia, it looks like things haven't changed at all from the year before. Given the economic downturn in the country at the moment, the place may not have a future at all, unless they tear it all down and build a wind farm. Despite the modernity and the fact that the sun is shining it still manages to look drab and unwelcoming.

From here, it's a blustery descent from the new to the old and a first view of the town of Santo Domingo de la Calzada. It lies in the middle of a huge plain and there is nothing else to see in any direction for miles. It's a very sparse scene which gives this view a particularly strong visual presence. The scene is tarnished a little by the ubiquitous out-of-town warehousing but it promises much more than Ciriñuéla and is named after one of the people who helped create the pilgrimage route that we walking on.

Santo Domingo was born nearby in the village of Villamayor del Río sometime during the eleventh century. He was originally destined for the monastery but was turned away because of his illiteracy. Instead, he dedicated his life to the Camino by building roads and bridges. He was also responsible for the pilgrimage hospital in Santo Domingo, which is now an elegant looking Parador, and he was behind the church which is now upgraded to a cathedral. He's now entombed there and it bears his name. An impressive legacy after an unpromising start.

Apart from being an odd mix of styles and dedicated to its builder, the cathedral is also remarkable because it has a chicken coop inside which is constantly populated by two birds. The reason behind this is a legend which involves a pilgrim couple and their son

65

who stop in the town en route to Santiago. They stay in an inn where the innkeeper's daughter takes a shine to the son but he thwarts her advances. In revenge, she hides a silver cup in his bag and reports him for stealing it. He's condemned and hanged. For reasons lost in the midst of time, the parents continue on their way, oblivious to his fate until they find him still hanging and breathing when they're on their way back. They rush to the sheriff's house where, on hearing their story, he replies that their son is no more alive than the cock and hen he's about to eat. At that moment, the birds leap off his plate and crow loudly. Although prone to foolish statements, the sheriff knows a miracle when he sees one and shoots out to chop the boy down from the gallows. All of a sudden, a dead saint arriving on the shores of Galicia in a stone boat from the Holy Land doesn't seem that mad in comparison, does it? Santo Domingo appears to have been quite active on the miracle front and the town is sometimes referred to as the "Compostela of Rioja".

The town itself doesn't disappoint and there is obviously something big going on. People are in their glad rags hanging around outside the church and I assume, this being a Saturday, that there is a wedding underway. Eventually, some men emerge from the church carrying a statue – presumably of Santo Domingo – on a wooden frame. Music is played and the men dip their shoulders to allow the statue to sway. The statue and the watchers may enjoy it but agony is chiselled onto the faces of the carriers as they contort their bodies under the carpentry. This is then followed by eight people dancing in a style that is part Morris dance and part Madness video, before the procession moves on down the road.

Olivia and I view this sitting on a wall with a couple of German pilgrims while eating improvised sandwiches. Most of the town is with us as well and there's a lot of noise and cheering. It could be a lively day in Santo Domingo and it looks an interesting place to stay. It's not every day you see poultry in a church and a dancing statue, and the celebrations seem likely to continue. I don't really feel tired. It has been a straightforward 21km to get here and I feel healthy enough to carry on a bit longer. I'm also not sure I can handle any more late night singing.

It's another ninety minutes to Grañon, which has the geographical significance of being the last stopping point in La Rioja. Olivia comes as well and our reserves are gently sapped by a walk that's largely uphill on rough ground which snakes its way through grassy fields of emptiness. It's worth it for a glorious moment when the village approaches and all you can see is the top of the church tower, which, due to the slope of the meadow, looks like it's sprouting up from the ground in a Terry Gilliam sort of way. It is only when we get to the village that we find out that we're actually going to be staying in that tower overnight.

It's the quirkiest resting place so far, situated on three floors with the middle one housing the kitchen, dining room and showers. Washing is hung up to dry on the top floor in a draughty, bare stone room, which has a cave-like appearance and a chaotically uneven floor. There is a dormitory outside it and another one on the first floor but there are no bunks or beds of any description. Tonight's sleeping will be done on very thin, and it has to be said uncomfortable-looking mattresses, though there are blankets provided as well. It's a pretty safe guess that the humidity of previous stays won't be a problem this evening.

After Nájera and Navarrete, it's nice to be staying in a village again. Grañon is a sleepy place on top of a hill and you get the feeling that unlike other villages the Camino passes through, it could probably exist without the passing trade. It's a largely agricultural area and there are several farms scattered on its edge. As far as the average pilgrim is concerned, it has a couple of shops and a bar, though my pilgrim colleagues strangely underuse the latter. I try my slightly improving Spanish out on the bar owner but, in a matter of seconds, I resort to Italian. He's another one who thinks I'm German and it's starting to annoy me. I feel like beginning every introductory sentence with the phrase, "I'm not German". It certainly makes for some linguistic confusion in the bar. I finally get my beer but it's a lot harder to explain that although I may look German, speak bad Italian and happen to be wearing an Irish rugby jersey, I am in fact, British. Trying to convince him I'm Anglo-Hispanic is going to be a step too far and it still feels totally fake. I'm more like the archetypal Englishman abroad. I haven't resorted to speaking slowly and loudly but I can feel that I'm not far off doing it.

The focus of tonight's entertainment is not going to be the bar but the church we are staying in. There is a seven o'clock mass which is followed by a fabulous communal meal of salad and pasta, paid for by pilgrim donations from the day before. Although the *menú* *del dia*s have been good, they are starting to get same-y and I'm getting a bit sick of *flan* – the Spanish version of crème caramel. There are about thirty of us staying here and we sit at three long tables that we earlier rearranged under the supervision of the *hospitalero*. Everybody is in good spirits and there is much chatter and the sound of laughter. It is one of those times where company, location, and food combine to make a special atmosphere and an unforgettable evening. The food is followed by night prayers in a small chapel nestling in the roof of the church. There's a doorway from my dormitory straight to it, though you would never know it's there. The chapel itself is lit by small tealights and looks down the nave of the main church to the altar at the far end. There is a simple, but highly atmospheric multi-lingual service of prayers and readings read by us pilgrims, which bring us back to the spirit of the Camino and partly takes our minds off what we'll be sleeping on when we head back to our respective dormitories.

Last night after prayers, we were all given some herbal tea to drink to aid sleeping. I can tell you now that it has an effectiveness rating of approximately bugger all. It is partly the mats, the snoring, and the fact that someone decides to get ready for the next stage of the walk at about 4.30am, but they all add up to an uncomfortable and chilly night of broken sleep. I'm plainly not alone in feeling this way, as there are several bleary-eyed people sitting down to a communal breakfast. Compared to last night we are monastically quiet and there is little discussion over the bread and jam.

I've never had breakfast in a hostel I've stayed in before, and this means, for the first time on the Camino that I head out into perky daylight. Of course, there is less chance of getting lost, and the yellow indicating arrows which are not so discernible to a half-asleep bloke waving a small torch about at random on a dark path which may or may not be there, are clearly evident. However, there is something magical about walking when the light emerges and gently brightens the world around. There's a certain purity to the early morning radiance which doesn't last too long, and the experience is glorious.

Shortly after leaving Grañon I edge out of La Rioja, which will probably put an end to my grape stealing for the foreseeable, and I'm now in the region of Castile y León. There are no rivers or bridges to mark this boundary, but instead there is a tall, thin and incongruous plastic billboard located in the middle of a field. It shows the designated route of the Camino through the province and, stuff me, it looks a scarily long way. Like most pilgrims, I tend to look at the walking on the basis of what I have to do the following day, and it's a daunting proposition to be confronted with what the next fortnight holds all at once. So daunting that I can't take it in and decide to ignore it.

If the truth be known, it isn't a great day's walking and I do all of it on my own. Most of the path runs alongside the main Logroño to Burgos road with the occasional detour to take in a village. The sky is a high grey, which threatens rain but fails to act on it. There is a stop in Vilamayor del Río, home of Santo Domingo, to have lunch with an Italian couple who also stayed in Grañon last night. They are interested in whether I think Tony Blair is a war criminal, and what my opinions of Silvio Berlusconi are. There's an agreeable unorthodoxy to be having a pub conversation in the middle of nowhere on a picnic table on a Sunday morning with a couple of people I haven't met before. They are a friendly enough pair but won't be drawn on talking about the Camino when I try to bring it up.

There's a temptation to stay in Belorado. It's a substantial place of a couple of thousand inhabitants (In comparison to Grañon, which has about fifty) but a lot of it really does look as if needs a coat of paint, or the attentions of a bulldozer. Some of the buildings go beyond simple inattention, and actually look war-torn. Walls are falling down and crumbling away, and there's a sense of civic neglect as you walk through parts of it. For all that, it would still make for an interesting stop, especially if the hostels have beds instead of sleeping mats.

Tosantos is the ultimate destination for today and, unlike Belorado, there's only one place to stay. It's another *donativo* and another stab at communal living. Sadly, no belfry this time but rather a 300-year-old timber-framed house which you enter via a sturdy, oak door. The key for it is the size of a small rifle. Due to the age of the building, the wooden floors, beams, and doorways warp and slope at alarming angles. God knows what it must look like when you're drunk - it's confusing on the eyes even if you're not. It's another night on a floor and there's a reasonable chance that an unguarded roll in a sleeping bag could send me hurtling towards the stairs at a rapid rate, knocking down anything that gets in the way.

The village, while pleasant enough, isn't going to find itself on many postcards. There's a sense of mild rural chaos to it, with farm animals roaming freely in the streets, providing a steady soundtrack of braying, bleating, and mooing. There is a busy road which divides the village amenities - the church and the bar - from the rest of Tosantos. On the other side, rows and rows of tables and chairs have been lined up. Not for the first time this week, my arrival coincides with some sort of local booze-up. Four immense paella dishes, each one carried by four people and resembling a slightly smaller version of the Jodrell Bank telescope, are manhandled across the street and put in place. It looks like the village is about to settle down to an afternoon of food and drink on a heroic scale.

The hostel is looking ahead to eating too, as pilgrims continue to come through the door. Olivia arrives in the company of a couple of goats, quickly followed by the German, Michael, whom I'd met on the road to Nájera. There is also another athletic looking Hungarian man who comes in. Gradually the kitchen fills up, and we are given various tasks to do to prepare for the evening meal. Soon it echoes to chopping vegetables and international conversation, while the sounds of an entire village getting pissed about 30m away can be heard through the open windows. This evening's hostel offering is salad, followed by tomatoes with garlic. The main course is chorizo and potato stew, which floors Michael as he's vegetarian. The meal is convivial but somehow not as casual and freewheeling as yesterday's effort; something I personally put down to the lack of wine. From the good humoured and increasingly loud background noise coming from outside, I'm guessing this isn't a problem in the vicinity of the church. Our eating is much more subdued, and is accompanied by the sounds of a CD playing orchestral versions of 1980s hits; tomatoes are consumed to a strings-dominated version of Nik Kershaw's *Wouldn't It Be Good*.

There is another night prayer and this takes place behind a well-hidden and not quite full-size door on the house's first floor. Once you negotiate your way through that, you are confronted with a room which slopes steeply uphill like a tiny lecture theatre, to a series of seats against a wall. There is a small altar in one corner of the deep end, and prayer sheets are arranged by language in a cross shape next to it. The ceremony follows a similar procedure to the one last night. There are a few minutes of silence followed by readings and prayers in alternating languages. Afterwards, a box is opened containing prayers written by pilgrims who stayed here exactly twenty days ago. These are distributed to us to be read aloud. The rationale behind this is that the people who wrote them would now be in Santiago, and so their prayers have relevance again. Eventually, the pieces of paper with the prayers on will be burnt in the church on the village's saint's day in August.

I feel really uneasy about this. I don't like the idea of reading someone's private intentions, even if they are anonymous, and the person who wrote them is 500km away. It feels intrusive, and it turns

71

out that the pilgrims haven't held back in what they have written. In some cases the prayers are moving and talk graphically about personal loss and sadness; a French pilgrim breaks down in tears as she reads out the story of the death of a child, but I can't help thinking it's a bit ghoulish. It also makes me think that I'm not doing the walk for the right motives. A lot of the people around me are heading to Santiago for highly personal and tragic reasons, which very rarely come to the surface in normal conversation. Here the barrier is broken and it's uncomfortable.

Personal losses were a factor in me coming on the Camino, but they were those that affected my friends. Earlier in the year over the course of about a fortnight, three of them suffered a death in the family. One of them, Sally, actually worked on the same floor as me at BBC TV Centre. We would meet up a couple of times a week for a tea, and she would talk about her father and the circumstances of his death. I would not so much try to say something positive, as avoid uttering something trite. It made me think of my own dad and how much I loved him, and how Sally's feelings mirrored my own. What finally pushed me into action was an email about a week later from another friend, Margriet. I'd sent her a message to apologise for missing her birthday, only for her to reply that sister had died as a result of complications giving birth a few days before. Margriet's sister was six years younger than me. Life's vulnerability was highlighted, the dream of walking the Camino grew in importance, and it couldn't really be put off any longer. Suddenly the job didn't really seem that vital anymore, and I decided then to give it up. This was going to be the year.

We are offered the chance to write down our own prayers and intentions under the same proviso that they'll be read out in twenty days' time. Despite the serious misgivings, I decide it is what my friends would want, and I write down their names and circumstances as dryly and unemotionally as possible, before placing them into the box provided. I think the priest back in Los Arcos was wrong; I don't think you can have enough prayers.

There is another communal breakfast this morning but it seems that most of the effort went into last night's meal. There is some bread but not nearly enough and it's just about better than nothing. As this is a *donativo* hostel, it could be down to the lack of collected money from the day before, making it a pilgrim-induced situation. I then have a sense of guilt for mentally complaining, as most places I've stayed in so far don't bother with breakfast in any way, shape or form. It's a pilgrimage after all and nobody gets to Santiago without a lot of help along the way; people like Doña Felisa's daughter and those who operate the pop-up Camino picnic tables. We would be helpless without them. It's time to think more like a pilgrim, less like a grumpy sod and accept every bit of help as it comes. It also means not winding up shopkeepers about where they obtain their banknotes nor annoying my fellow walkers when they want to wash and dry their shoes. With these thoughts in mind, breakfast now becomes a gift. It also helps by delaying my departure time and allowing the rain, which has been constant all night, to stop.

It's back through more cornfields and familiar looking villages, as the way edges gently uphill. At about 10am I come to the snappily titled Villafranca Montes De Oca, which is big enough to have a choice of eating opportunities. It also has a large lorry park that caters for drivers along the N-120 road that heads into Burgos. My dad was a fan of lorry drivers because he always stressed that the best way to find good food in Spain was to follow them. There is quite definitely a truckers preference here, and with the ringing endorsement of a long-dead father in my ears, I cling on to their shirttails and follow a couple to a clean and friendly bar which has hot chocolate and sells welcoming *boccadillo*s of belt-straining proportions. There is a clientele of extremes - drivers and walkers - but there is no demarcation between the two and we mingle at the bar and at shared tables. The Spanish-speaking pilgrims exchange conversations with the drivers and the major subject to affect both groups is the thought of on-coming rain.

I join Jan and Andrew whom I have been greeting for several days and who were on the same dining table as me in Grañon. They are easy to spot on the road as Andrew wears a garish blue puffed up jacket which is unlikely to have been bought in a camping shop. He is a lot tougher than the rest of us, as he's been wearing shorts for most of the walk. I've never really spoken to them before and put them down as a couple. It turns out that geographically they couldn't get much further apart. Jan lives on Skye while Andrew is from Brisbane. They got together on their second day and have walked together ever since. They are now at the stage when they are finishing each other's sentences. I couldn't endure walking with the same person for ten straight days but they are undoubtedly enjoying each other's company. They are both retired and Jan has taken on the walk for spiritual reasons. She talks about having been on retreats and sees the Camino as a logical extension of that journey. Andrew used to be a teacher and a rugby league coach and is clearly a man of few words.

"To quote Sir Edmund Hillary", he drawls, "I'm doing it because it's there."

There doesn't sound like a huge amount of conviction behind his words and I rather get the feeling there may be a lot more to it than that. There is a tough exterior there and it isn't going to crack, at least not yet.

It takes longer to say Villafranca Montes De Oca than it does to walk through it. Soon the yellow arrows point sadistically uphill to the Montes de Oca themselves. There have been several climbs over the past few days, and indeed this morning, but they have been gradual and after a while, you stop really noticing them. This is an ascent up a path that takes the incline head on, and will take the Camino beyond 1000m in height for the first time since the Pyrenees. It is also going to take me through woodland for the first time since heading towards Los Arcos.

What starts off as a slender path soon spreads out into something dual carriageway-sized that has been slashed through the trees to provide access for logging activities. It's an ugly and muddy scar but the occasional lorry and the distant sounds of chainsaws do something to alleviate the feeling of isolation. Because of the rolling nature of the path, it's difficult to see other walkers and it's unsettling. There are three peaks of 1,100m, but each climb is swiftly followed by an abrupt descent of 100m or so, to accommodate a river valley. There are many cyclists around today who are experiencing the exhilaration, and enduring the torture of the cruelly hilly terrain but walking pilgrims are as rare as a good breakfast.

Meanwhile rain starts to fall in a sporadic but darkly alarming fashion. The Montes De Oca were a favourite spot for bandits to prey on early pilgrims and you can see why under this sky. There's also a reminder of more recent atrocities as the route passes a rather stark non-descript obelisk which is a memorial for those who died in the Spanish Civil War. Because of the logging, it's difficult to see how such an area could have such a treacherous reputation. It feels benignly dull. Before this morning, I'd actually missed walking through trees but now after three hours of ambling along this straight, unattractive path I am heartily sick of the bastards.

Lunch is had in San Juan de Ortega – St John of the Nettle. St Juan was a follower of Santo Domingo and followed his leader's aims in creating suitable roads and bridges for pilgrims. Evidently, civil engineering and sainthood go hand-in-hand in this part of the world. More importantly, he founded a monastery here in the twelfth century which provided shelter in one of the most dangerous areas of the journey to Santiago. The chapel is designed in such a way that at each equinox, the rays of the setting sun illuminate the Virgin Mary in the scene of the Annunciation. As I am fast discovering, the Camino is as much about the places you don't stay in as the ones where you do. I'm tempted to take shelter here if only to have a sense of the past, to share the feeling that my medieval counterparts must have had when they'd survived one of their more perilous days. Now it becomes another stopping point but there's relief in that; there is an open bar and an open bar means food.

I break what seems like a Camino taboo by sitting outside and talking to a French cycling pilgrim. He is fully aware that walkers and cyclists don't really mix but understands why the divisions occur.

"You see the same people day after day," he explains slightly wistfully, "We cycle greater distances, there is greater variation. We know we won't see the same people again."

He goes on to admit that he is jealous of the bonding that exists among the walking pilgrims and expresses a desire to do the Camino on foot one day. The cyclists have an added problem that many *refugios* don't take them and even the ones that do often wait until very late in the day to allow admittance.

Like a couple of places I've walked through in the past few days, Agés suffers visibly from the difference between having money and not having it. Many of the timber-framed houses have been renovated with impressive results. It should look gorgeous but an equal number are in a state of serious neglect and several have fallen down completely. It gives the village a very disjointed look; it reminds me of yesterday's walk through Belorado, and the similar mixture of extreme effort and inattention, often in buildings found right next to each other.

The place I'm staying in is spacious and clean and is perfectly located i.e. it's above a bar. There is one modern dormitory and it's pristine, as too is the bathroom. Of course, the major advantage is that there's not a lot of legwork involved in getting to your evening meal. To my great delight, my fellow lodgers include Carrie, her mother, and her aunt. There are more Canadians in the shape of Herb and Brian and I'm introduced to them by Linda (Carrie's mother) as "the man who slept with my daughter in Nájera". If they're slightly disappointed by the subsequent story they can rest assured that they couldn't be as gutted as I was. After the mildly embarrassing beginning, the company and conversation is convivial, to say the least. We are later joined by Michael and Olivia who were planning to walk onto the next village, but had been tipped off that there were no beds left. It's the first time I've heard of people being sent away from a hostel.

We are all doing well and are in good spirits and it is an evening of optimism and pilgrim tales. On the lengthy subject of mad pilgrims we have come across, Herb and Brian have met Steve, the French rucksack bore. Apparently, he was having an ankle strapped up in Estella a few days ago – so much for his carefully chosen boots. I'm told to watch out for a British bloke who calls himself "Luck" – he's apparently easy to spot because of his blond dreadlocks. Herb memorably describes him as "having overdosed on spirituality" and being "deeply shallow". A warning is also issued regarding Dave from Vancouver who apparently looks a bit like Lee Marvin and is noticably incapable of silence. His name provokes groans from the rest of the party but I haven't had the pleasure. For some reason, Brian refers to him as "BC". I hope I get the chance to introduce him to Caitlin and they can cancel each other out. Herb and Brian have yet to meet her but Linda has some advice for them.

"Say she's 39 and looks old enough to have a 21-year-old daughter. Seize the moment of surprise on her face and walk away as quickly as you can before she compares you to a Latin American country."

Generally, though, our impressions of our fellow pilgrims are positive and as Olivia rightly points out, "God knows what they think of us".

Rather strangely, one question that barely gets asked on the Camino is why you are doing it. Herb brings this subject up and suggests that the question is asked but it's unusual for somebody to give a straight answer to it. It is almost too personal, like "how much do you earn?" Fortified by a lot of wine I put Herb's theory to the test.

His eyes twinkle and he smiles and says "A multitude of reasons, Rudy."

I know he's not going to say what they are. Having read some of the prayers at Tosantos last night I don't think I really want to know. If there are personal tragedies involved no-one's admitting to them here. The Canadian family hints at the physical challenge while Michael has spiritual leanings. He's been seen clutching a spiritual self-help book, but to his credit, he doesn't mention it, and I can guarantee that I'm not going to ask him about it. Brian suggests that people who do tell you why they are going to Santiago should be avoided at all costs.

The joyous evening ends far too quickly and as we're heading back upstairs, Linda taps me on the shoulder. "No sleeping with my daughter tonight!"

I'm tempted to reply, "No, not a wink," but I'm not sure how it'll be received.

Carrie just offers a resigned "Oh Mom!"

One of the great things about staying above this particular bar is that it's open at 6am for breakfast. I'm first down and am served with great cheerfulness by the woman who signed me in yesterday afternoon, and then served the food in the evening. All the places I've stayed in have provided a friendly welcome - bar one of course - but this has been the best so far. Over a hot chocolate and a muffin, I am encouraged by the sight of a large yellow sun shining over Burgos in a newspaper weather forecast. The city is today's planned destination, and it's an encouraging sign, as there are hills to be conquered between now and then, and I really don't fancy the rigmarole attached to donning the poncho again. This buoyancy and optimism lasts about as long as it takes to get through the front door. It's the coldest morning of the walk so far and there's a whistling wind that pierces, needle-like, through exposed skin. I can barely make out the stars in the sky and the outlines of the hills are scarcely visible. I'm walking into autumn.

If there was one fault about the hostel in Agés, it is that there wasn't an awful lot of drying room and my previous day's clothes are still damp. I've pinned yesterday's socks to my rucksack and was hoping to get them dry along the way, but by the time I reach the next village of Atapuerca it feels like they have frozen solid. I'm feeling fairly similar despite wearing my full complement of layers for the first time. There's a real cold edge to the morning which walking only goes some way to alleviating.

Atapuerca has a history way beyond the lifespan of the Camino. The earliest human remains ever found in Europe were discovered here and it's now a UNESCO heritage site. There's evidence of human activity going back a million years, though on today's evidence, you can't help thinking why they chose somewhere so gloomy to set up a community.

The road to Atapuerca has the double whammy of being both badly lit and surprisingly busy, given the hour of the day. There's a real feeling of defencelessness every time a car shoots past. The best I can do is pull as far from the road as possible and shine my torch down to increase my visibility. There's also a sense of relief when the Camino moves onto a path, though this is tempered by the fact that it points upwards as far as the eye can see. On this particular morning, the eye can't see that far at all. The sun may have appeared but everything at ground level disappears into thick mist after about 10m. If you want the full experience of the medieval pilgrim this is as close as you can get. Indeed, it seems there's no path to speak of anyway, and it's a case of following the smoother parts of the exposed rock outcrop where the yellow arrows have been carefully sprayed.

With each step upwards, it gets colder, visibility decreases, and it feels more desolate. So much for the bloody weather forecast. By the time I get to the top of the hill, we're into full-blown *Wuthering Heights* territory. A simple wooden cross marks the summit while nearby, people have made their own crosses on the ground using loose stones. Basic messages have also been written, like "have faith" and "follow your heart". I'm seriously tempted to add my own - something along the lines of "be true" or possibly "fuck me, it's bleak" - but these aren't the kind of conditions you really want to hang around in. More oddly, a little further on is a large standing stone which is surrounded by a spiral path of rocks – as many as thirty loops in total. This is a meditation walk where you concentrate on following the path to the centre. There are no takers on this particular morning but it is an ethereal image in the fog. Apparently, on a good day, you can see Burgos from here. At the moment, I can barely see my feet.

There's still some mist on the descent side of the mountain but there's enough visibility to make out the washed-out colours of the fields below. There are no signs of human activity at all but somewhere down there is Cardeñuela, which will provide a chance to warm up and wrap my mouth, and possibly my pinned socks, around a mug of hot chocolate. It takes about half an hour to get there, by which time the sun is making good on the promise of the weather forecast and finally boring its way through the greyness. Thawing out has become less of an issue but a rest is needed before the final march into Burgos. The bar has conveniently left basic street maps of the city centre for pilgrims to study and take away, so it can't be too far off. The reality is, it is, and it isn't.

I'm no stranger to tedious walks; just mention the name "Southport Pier" to me and I break out in hives, but even that stroll pales into insignificance compared to the march into Burgos. It starts off by going across a bridge over a motorway and then goes around a disused airport. That's the exciting bit out of the way. It's then a walk down a perfectly straight road flanked by warehouses, miscellaneous business premises, and car showrooms. The road continues without variation in direction or decoration for what feels like an eternity. Somehow, the word "dull" doesn't even begin to cover it. There is no café or bar to stop in and the main worry is being complacent - missing an arrow and having to walk back along the bloody road to find out where I should have turned off. I've gone from rural to urban drabness in the space of a morning. I can only assume this isn't part of the original pilgrimage route, but it fulfils the idea of penance beautifully.

Of course, need increases with desperation. After about fifteen minutes of trekking down Tedium Street, I quite fancy a sit-down and another hot chocolate. About twenty minutes later, I feel like a small beer, which after more walking soon expands to becoming a large beer. By the time a bar actually comes into view - and believe me it takes about an hour - I am almost on my knees with a mixture of tiredness and boredom. I order two pints at the same time and drink them with very little gap, one after the other. It's a beer that tastes of survival. Well, the first one does. The second tastes of stupidity. The walk isn't even over, but Burgos cathedral is in sight and there is an accompanying relief that I no longer have to stay on the same road. If I ever move here to live, at least I'll know where to buy a car.

The *refugio* is close to the cathedral and has only been open for a few years. I don't believe I'll ever spend a better few euros on the Camino. You could be forgiven for thinking that you're staying in a modern museum. It's been well thought out. The bunks are on several floors and there are partition walls carefully separating you into your own alcove. There are sinks at the end of each row of beds and a generous number of bathrooms. On the ground floor, there's a kitchen space with tables and drinks machines. It's clean and spacious with lots of natural light, and is big enough to house over a hundred pilgrims without any hint of cramping or anyone arguing the toss about who's next in line for the washing facilities. Historic it certainly isn't, but I know that I'm going to stay in places a lot more basic than this, so I see it as an unexpected treat.

I have decided to have a rest day tomorrow and stay in Burgos. I've been on the go now for just under a fortnight and I think I've earned a day off. I'm slightly worried about the big city experience after Pamplona, but Burgos is a gorgeous place with beautiful squares and narrow streets. I can even just about forgive it for the road that had to be walked down to get here. It's turning into a really hot day and I sit down to a sunny lunch outside a riverside bar. The idyllic setting is ruined, though, as I'm attacked by wasps. I could hardly call it a swarm but there are enough of the stripey bastards to take my mind off my food and devote my energy to taking action. I find myself waving my arms about like a possessed Keith Moon while my chicken lies largely undisturbed on the plate below.

There's not much luck with the food in the evening either. A few of us who could be labelled "The Friends of Olivia" have got together in search of an evening meal. We must look like an odd bunch, even by Camino standards. There's another British man who must be in his mid-forties and looks like the only person ever designated too scruffy to attend a Levellers gig. There are a couple of high-spirited Germans, Horst and Torsten, whom I met in Santo Domingo and who are walking the Camino at the rate of one week every year, a Belgian bloke, a Swiss man who doesn't talk a lot, an elegant Dutch woman in her thirties called Corinna, me and Olivia herself. Everyone is in a manifestly good mood, even Corinna, who has been looking like she's been drinking vinegar instead of water over the past couple of days. I say everyone, but I am fulfilling the role of the Ancient Mariner and being the miserable sod. The evening will not linger long in the memory. We end up in a fast food pizza place which is a lot more ghastly than it sounds. The food is appalling, made worse for me by the fact that we are in a city that is famous for its gastronomy. It's also so grubby that I'm tempted to wipe my feet on the way out. I look to be the only one who is bothered, but at least I'm having another day here, which I can use to sample the grub. All around me there are smiles and laughter and I've clearly inherited the misery baton from Corinna. The only plus of the evening is seeing Burgos lit up at night. It is astonishingly beautiful, particularly the gate of the Arco Santa María, which shimmers like gold as we walk past.

We demolish a couple of bottles of wine back at the hostel and take advantage of the late licence to stay up until a decadent 10.15pm. Somehow, it feels like a wasted evening. After the walk in the town and then the lunch and dinner experiences, Burgos has a lot to make up for tomorrow, but I'm hopeful. As it said in the stones this morning, "Have faith".

The hostel in Burgos has very strict rules on leaving - it has to be done between 7 and 8am. There are even airport style announcements telling you how long you have to go. The *hospitaleros* were quite adamant that you can only have one night here and yesterday, when I was signing in, they refused to admit a couple of people who had spent the previous night elsewhere in the city. Not that I want to stay there again, lovely as it was. I'm after a night off from the Camino experience and my first task is to find somewhere else to stay, something that is greatly aided by the map I had picked up in Cardeñuela yesterday which thoughtfully lists hotels.

There's something quite beautiful about having a roam around a city before most of the inhabitants get on the move. It's worth it this morning to see the impressive spires of Burgos cathedral disappearing into the mist of early light. My fellow pilgrims start heading out of the city on a course I can only assume (and hope to God) is less tedious than the one coming in, leaving me to have a wander around the deserted city squares and watch them come to life.

I bump into Carrie and the in-laws, as I've started calling them, outside the city's other hostel. They have never voiced it before but although Carrie's walking timetable is flexible, the mother and aunt have a limited time to finish the Camino in order to catch a flight home and they already think they're a long way behind schedule. There's a certain panic associated with them this morning as if they've just become conscious of it. There's a bit of hurried conversation but we linger over some photographs before I guide them on their first few steps out of the city.

Finding a guesthouse is reassuringly straightforward and I get a room at the first place I turn up at. It's on the unfashionable side of the Río Arlanzón, away from the cathedral in a place which has unrestricted views on the rather dull shopping street below. I think I'm on to a loser when I am taken up to the hotel by an elderly man who then struggles to open the front door. When he does manage to do it, after a few frantic minutes of fumbling with the key, several people stare out of their rooms to gawp at who has just come in. It's what you imagine the previous inhabitants of the hotel in *The Shining* to have looked like. I am at least thirty years younger than the faces that stare back at me, and possibly fifty years younger than the decor. I am guided along a purple carpet down a green walled corridor and finally shown into a room that has gaudy orange and yellow walls. If Edvard Munch ever designed a hotel room, it would look like this. It's a box to induce nightmares, and with a swirling carpet design of blues and yellows, everything seems designed to make sure that your night will be a restless and unpleasant one. I can imagine emerging tomorrow looking exactly like the other guests, aged and slightly frightened. And all because I wanted a room with a bath, or in this case, something twice the size of a washbasin that I can just about get my feet into. As hotels go, it's cheap and it's clean, but somehow a bunk bed in a room full of people who can imitate animal noises in their sleep seems like a rather more attractive alternative. There are other hotels but I don't really want to spend more time looking for one when there's a city to explore. I hand over €25, which is roughly my daily budget on the Camino, to the receptionist, with the aim of not coming back there until I absolutely have to.

The first port of call is the cathedral of Santa María. I have to admit that I normally get bored senseless looking at churches. I have been dragged around a few and have spent a large amount of time in them for various reasons. The novelty wore off several decades ago. Having said that, Burgos Cathedral is worth a couple of hours of anybody's time. It was built over four centuries and finally completed in 1567 and is very much in the gothic tradition. Inside it's divided into over twenty chapels; each one is distinctly decorated with remarkable carvings and paintings, more often than not beyond the point of ostentation. Right in the middle is the resting place of local hero, El Cid. He was born here in 1040, roughly the same time that the Camino was starting to emerge, under the name of Count Rodrigo Díaz de Vivar. He fought alongside King Ferdinand I's son Sancho against the Moors and Sancho's brother, Alfonso. He actually died in Valencia but after a couple of re-interments, his bones found their way here. For a man with such a profile, this is the least ornate part of the entire building, though in this place that's very relative indeed. Just about every part of the church is extravagant on the eye and it would take days to really do it justice. There are some truly breath-taking works of art on display and the choir stalls are perhaps the most beautiful examples of woodcarving ever displayed, but how prayerful you may find the building is a moot point. It may be a cathedral but it's considerably more museum than church.

The rest of the day is spent wandering aimlessly in the sunshine. After days of overcast skies and occasional rain, this is the first really hot day in a week. I check the route out of the city for the following morning and find somewhere suitable to eat. I am determined to rectify the culinary wrong of the evening before and decide to seek out a restaurant and sample the local speciality of blood sausage and lentils with the aim of washing them down with a pleasant bottle of Rioja. My relaxed state of mind lasts until 8pm, or roughly dessert when I hear my name being bellowed across the square. I turn around and Caitlin comes into view. This is a bit of a surprise because, by my calculations, I thought she was still a day behind me. There is a big hug and I am then subjected to a lengthy monologue about what she's been doing since we last met. She is with a beautiful German woman who is friendly enough but struggles to get a word in and, by the look of her, I imagine she's been in this situation for at least several hours. There is much more gushing followed by an invitation to meet up for breakfast the following morning;

"We can walk together, it'll be fun."

For one of us possibly. I know immediately that this is a seriously bad idea. I don't want any more group activities after the pizza nonsense of yesterday evening and I really enjoy the solitary walking. Racking up more than 20km in the heat is going to be hard on the feet and I don't really want it to be hard on the lugholes as well. There's a non-committal response backed by the almost certain knowledge that I'm not going to show up at the breakfast rendezvous time she's suggested. The final nails in the coffin of the "say yes" policy were hammered in last night and it finally gets buried now.

Tomorrow we will be entering the Meseta, a largely shelterless plain of wheat fields, which will make up the next week's walking. It's the area of the Camino that most polarises walkers. Some see it as an endurance test of total monotony while others regard it as a place of beauty with wide-open spaces allowing for peaceful contemplation. It's also claimed that the sparseness of the backdrop can lead to madness. Given the state of some of my fellow pilgrims, I wonder how I'll be able to tell. One book, *El Camino Iniciático de Santiago* divides the Camino into several religious sections with the Meseta cheerfully representing "spiritual death".

I saw Francine and her husband earlier in the day and their group isn't going to risk a potential descent into insanity. They going to take the bus to León and carry on from there, which means that I won't see them again. There's a certain sadness to that but at least I had a chance to say goodbye. There are several people I've already met whom I won't see again but I don't know who they are. I think back to the meeting with Carrie this morning which did have an air of finality about it. Friendships are fleeting and brittle on the Camino, just like in life. Here I am philosophising and I haven't even entered the bloody Meseta yet. Maybe Francine's group knows something I don't. The intention at the beginning was to walk the whole Camino and that still holds. If that means psychosis starts tomorrow followed by spiritual death, so be it.

Walking in and out of cities is never going to be enjoyable, but at least leaving Burgos is a lot more pleasant than walking in. True, it involves walking close to a railway line, crossing over a motorway and passing a factory, but by the time shadows start to form, I am on the edge of the Meseta, with just the birds and the butterflies for company. The cereal crops have been harvested and the fields are various shades of brown. In the early morning light, the fields have a lunar quality, with occasional thin wisps of waist-high mist stretching across them, but by the time the afternoon comes, you are half-expecting Clint Eastwood and Lee Van Cleef to ride past on horses. The soil looks as if it's been raked repeatedly until sand appears. From an unpromising beginning, it turns into a truly beautiful walk. The only people I see are those cycling the Camino, and I thrive on the solitude. There's a lot more of these landscapes to come so I'll see if the novelty wears off, but today's isolation and silence have been truly hypnotic. Today's a short stage of about 20.5km, and for well over half of it, it is largely flat. There's a bit of a climb to get on the Alto Mesta and then there's a steep descent into Hornillos del Camino, which is where I'm going to stay tonight.

I doubt if there's a bigger contrast between two consecutive stopping places on the entire route than between here and Burgos. Its pale sandstone buildings look suitably weathered in the intense sunlight, and I doubt if it's changed for several centuries. It's a world away from the past couple of days, and once again there's a feeling of how a big city distorts the Camino experience. It's back to the simple life. Hornillos has the four things a true pilgrim needs; a bar, a *refugio*, a pilgrim-friendly shop and a church, and they are all within metres of each other. To be honest, we could probably get by on just the first two, and the shop is over 50m away which, by this place's standards, is a bit of a slog. The hostel here is clean and simple and, of course, comes with the warmest of welcomes.

One of the downsides of the Camino is that it can be a bit of a mad rush to secure a bed somewhere. This is particularly true today where Hornillos is the obvious destination to stay after overnighting in Burgos. The city has around one hundred and fifty *refugio* beds but Hornillos has only thirty-two. There are no clear stopping places before, and the next two options are 5km and 10km further on. This hostel is full most nights. I haven't really been affected by the bed scramble so far. As I tend to start earlier than most, I tend to stop earlier too and with the exception of the first day, my walking has been done and dusted by 2pm at the latest.

Whether it's a big city or a hamlet, the routine barely changes. You sign in, pay and get your *credencial* stamped. Then you find your bed (sometimes allocated, sometimes not), have a shower, and wash the clothes you've just walked in and then try to get to the clothes line before anyone else. The washing sinks are outside today, and there's enough drying space for everyone so the major source of pilgrimage tension is gone. One of the things I was advised to take before I went on the walk was this amazing soap that works for skin and fabrics. Over the past couple of weeks I've discovered that what makes it truly special is that it's equally useless for both. I've got to the stage now where I use it out of habit. It certainly doesn't seem to affect my personal hygiene in any significant way. I can recommend the ultra-light camping towel, though. It does feel like you are rubbing yourself down with Velcro but it works. I take an opportunity to wash it, which results in it becoming several hundred times heavier than normal, and it puts the washing line under considerable strain. Even after it's been wrung out several times it's still outstandingly weighty. I hope that given today's heat, it'll dry quickly.

One of the good things about staying in Hornillos del Camino is that there is absolutely nothing to do, and the hot afternoon sun adds to a really lazy atmosphere. After two days in a city and its accompanying distractions, life has slowed down to a agreeably sluggish speed and this is the quietest place so far. It's hard to believe that I started out this morning in Burgos. Being here is a more intense Camino experience – the only people around are pilgrims: their prominence restored after being rendered invisible in the chaos of the big city. In Hornillos del Camino there is nothing to visit or explore, and it's a good time to reflect and just be.

My reflection is aided by the seductive heat, a couple of cans of beer, and the shade of a parasol in the small square across from the bar. I have walked about 300km so far and it's been largely trouble free. I certainly don't feel any more Spanish but this is because of my own ignorance. It's almost as if I believe that I'm not actually in Spain at all. My father came from the region of Cantabria which is green, mountainous, and as far removed from the geography of the Meseta as you can possibly get. It might as well be another planet when compared to the Costas. Thinking about it leisurely, it dawns on me that I'm due south of Cantabria and probably as close as I'm going to get on the Camino to where he grew up.

My thoughts are disturbed by a voice that pierces the warm stillness in a loud and irritating fashion. Its source is a grey-haired, red-faced Canadian who matches the description given by Brian at Agés the other night. He does bear a striking resemblance to Lee Marvin, albeit a more benign version. This must be the famous BC. I had initially (excuse the pun) thought that this was because of how he introduces himself; "Hi I'm David from Vancouver BC", but by the time this afternoon is over, I'm convinced that it stands for "Boring Canadian". On a sweltering, languid afternoon where time passes leisurely, and when people are barely talking above a whisper, he totally fails to capture the spirit of the moment. This being Hornillos, there is nowhere to run to. He's giving a summary of his Camino, and indeed his life so far, to a couple of middle-aged German women who listen with a grace and politeness that is well beyond the call of duty. His voice carries easily though, and within half an hour and with barely a pause, the entire pilgrimage population of the village knows that he deals in real estate back home, has three children, was divorced recently, started his Camino in Roncesvalles and thought he'd lost his wallet in Pamplona when in reality it was in his rucksack all along.

I seek sanctuary on the steps of the church which is not really far enough away, but it reduces a bit of the noise, and the afternoon drifts sleepily by with no great urgency. I'm joined by an Australian couple, Jim and Sue. They both look as though they spend a lot of time out of doors and it turns out their main hobby back home is sailing. They trained for the Camino quite seriously back in Perth with practice walks up to 40km long, which possibly explains why they appear to be glowing with health and look like they have just been photographed for a camping magazine. Meanwhile, I'm feeling decidedly lumpy in their presence, and sweating like a pregnant nun.

We decide to carry on our conversation over dinner; we're not exactly spoiled for choice when it comes to venues - it's the bar or nothing. There are only five dining tables in the *comedor* at the back, and they are full when we finally summon up the legwork to travel the 20m from outside the church. Mercifully, BC is already eating and his voice is largely drowned out by the hubbub of bar conversations and general pilgrimage chatter. We have to wait for about half an hour, which gives us a chance to consume a bottle of Rioja in the front part of the bar. We are joined by a frail-looking Colombian journalist with a wizard-like beard and friendly eyes. He's a welcome addition to our company, and comes with positive pilgrimage anecdotes which he delivers in excellent English. He can't be that fragile either, as he started his walk in Le Puy in France, so has been going three weeks longer than I have. More bottles of Rioja are jovially emptied in no time at all, as the world's hardest working waitress effortlessly clears and re-lays tables, and then keeps everyone fed and watered without anyone being neglected. It's another excellent meal and what my first night in Burgos should have been like; somewhere cosy where laughter can be heard and pilgrimage tales can be exchanged. I don't know whether it's that time of the Camino or the wine is getting to me, but the walk seems to be full of people who look like someone else at the moment. There's a dead ringer for Alexei Sayle in my dormitory tonight and he's sharing a bunk with the Canadian Lee Marvin. The madness may have started already.

25th September: Stage 15 - Hornillos del Camino to Castrojeriz

It is another day of walking in blazing heat. I start at about 7.30am and feel the sun rise over my shoulder and gradually spread its light over the vast emptiness of the Meseta. I love the sparseness and silence of it all. It's MAMBA (Miles and Miles of Bugger All) country. There's a bit of uphill at the beginning but then the world becomes flat, arid and uncomplicated, with the only signs of activity belonging to those who are heading west on foot. There's a pattern to today, which involves walking pretty much in a straight line to a ridge on the distant horizon, and then on arrival the view opens up again and another ridge appears ahead. There is absolutely no shelter at all and it's the kind of day when seeing a tree becomes a real talking point. The fields are all bare and the land is unforgivingly sunburnt. With wide landscapes and a fair amount of flatness, the views are expansive and compelling.

There's a magical moment this morning, which must have been felt thousands of times over the previous centuries. Just when I'm heading towards a low ridge and starting to think that the Meseta is totally devoid of buildings and permanent inhabitants, the path dips sharply into a fold in the landscape and the domed roof of a church slowly reveals itself. As the descent continues, more buildings emerge and eventually Hontanas comes into view. This is perhaps the definitive pilgrim village because there is no other way that you are likely to come across it. It looks like a truly memorable place to stay. Just the nature of how you walk into it makes you think it's special, and there's that perfect untouched feeling to its streets and buildings. This is the overnight stay that got away.

I time my breakfast brilliantly. BC is already in situ but he's reattaching his rucksack as I settle down to some bread and jam. I've barely spoken to him but I'm wary of Brian's words back in Agés. I'm sure he's innocuous enough but I don't think he does silence particularly well and, as I'm fast discovering, silence is a huge part of the Meseta's charm. I manage to avoid him for the next few hours but it has to be said that he's a gregarious pilgrim and over the course of the day he pairs up easily with other walkers. Every time it looks as if I'm going to catch him up, I decide to have a stationary water break and let him get away. I decide on the general rule that if I can hear him I am too close. In the general silence of the Meseta, half a kilometre usually does it.

Apart from Hontanas, the other interesting stopping point is the ruins of the monastery of San Antón. You actually walk under an arch that connects the monastery to a church in what is a case of ecclesiastical overkill for such a small place. The monastery dates from the twelfth century and sheltered pilgrims even then. It was infamous in the past as a scene of miracles, particularly the curing of "St Anthony's Fire", or ergotism. The order of St Anthony claimed that the cure was using the power of love, or "Tau", in its healing regime. The T-shaped Tau is still one of the symbols of the Camino. The miracle had more to do with the fact that Santiago-bound pilgrims ate wheat bread rather than rye bread which attracted the offending fungus. Modern pilgrims are a cosseted bunch; the only food danger now is overdosing on the *menú del dia* staples of pork and *flan* and getting a dodgy bottle of wine.

You can still stay in what is left of the monastery. It's probably a raw experience but almost certainly a very memorable one. From my quick look in, the only habitable part of the building still has a wall missing. Even so, it's a warm day and there's a certain appeal in staying here, but I'm not battle-hardened enough to try.

It's approaching midday and, despite the relatively level route and the short distance of today's stage, it's a struggle in the heat. Thankfully, I can see my destination from San Antón: the town of Castrojeriz. It's a striking place, situated diagonally on a hill, below a ruined castle, and there is a reasonable chance of making it there before I pass out. It's a bloody near thing, though. It's one of those places that doesn't appear to get any nearer no matter how much you walk towards it. It is another hour before arrival and then there's the bonus slog of walking through the town to get to the hostel. It takes a good twenty-five minutes from one end to the other and the route is all uphill. As a cruel coda, my chosen digs are then at the top of some steps. I make it to the front door almost on my knees. Even then, it isn't open and isn't going to be for another hour.

Not a lot seems to happen in Castrojeriz; it's not so much sleepy as catatonic. Apparently a thousand people live here but you wouldn't think so today – it's quiet to the point of sinister. There are no sounds apart from pilgrim footsteps and the gentle breeze blowing against the buildings. It looks and feels totally uninhabited. According to my handbook, the town comes to life at the end of July for the garlic festival. Apparently, there are competitions to make garlic plaits followed by garlic soup and garlic chicken tastings. It must be a riveting few days. It's a good job is doesn't clash with Glastonbury. Today you could be forgiven for thinking that the place has been abandoned, or is in a permanent state of siesta.

Then again. it could be making up for a very active past. The Romans came and so did the Visigoths. The Christians and Arabs fought here in the tenth century, but I doubt if anything significant has happened here since. It is a suitable destination, very much in keeping with the enduring quality of today's walk. Right from leaving Hornillos this morning, there's been a feeling that things haven't changed on this part of the Camino for hundreds of years. There have been very few modern intrusions, with only a rare car or two on the road between San Antón and here to break up the natural peace. In Castrojeriz, the only thing that spoils this eternal setting is several kilometres away, and comes in the form of more wind turbines. They occupy the surrounding hills in huge numbers, and on an ageless day like today they look completely out of place and just wrong.

I manage to summon up some energy to have a bit of a walk around and manage to find an open shop and a local inhabitant. Like most Camino stores I've come across, it stocks pretty much anything you ask for, from fruit to walking boots, despite not being particularly big. I rather get the feeling that you could ask for an outboard motor and the shopkeeper would have a rummage around the back and come up with the goods a couple of minutes later. I compare ponchos with the overpriced affair I bought in Logroño and stock up on chocolate. The *refugio* is open when I get back and I sign in to the sound of New Age music being played in the background. There is nothing particularly New Age about the *hospitalero*s or the accommodation. The dormitory looks like a school gym and there are bunks around the perimeter and thin mattresses in the middle for latecomers.

At one stage there were seven pilgrim hospitals in Castrojeriz. There are four now and guess who's staying in mine? BC has appeared, but happily he's staying in the basement because he says somebody has complained that he snores too much. Apparently, boring for Canada doesn't come into the equation. He's adamant he doesn't snore and has been voicing this to whoever happens to be near. Alas, I'm in the wrong place at the right time. He does present me with a verbal open goal, though.

"Well, you know what they say, you either snore or toss."

I defy any of you who find yourselves in this position not to volley the ball home with enthusiasm and aplomb. Getting him to admit that he is a tosser made me feel better for a few seconds at least, though the brief satisfaction was more than matched by the guilt. Castrojeriz should easily be big enough for the both of us and I should be able to avoid him for the rest of the day.

Even on this particular Friday night, nobody appears to venture out much. It's a bit windy, which takes the sting out of the heat and makes it a pleasant evening to have a walk around. I sit on a bench overlooking the valley and surrounding hills, and feel that the town has got under my skin a little. After an afternoon of snooping around and exploring the narrow roads and paths, I've really grown to love it, though I would be hard pushed to tell you exactly why. There's something quite beautiful about its remoteness and serenity. I don't think I've been anywhere where life has slowed down so much. It very much fits the pattern of the walk since leaving Burgos. Apart from the castle above and the distant ruins of St Antón, there are no other buildings in sight. Even the wind turbines can't spoil the moment. I don't think I've ever felt as calm and relaxed as I do now, with the sun setting, my eyes fixed on the surrounding hills and a breeze blowing through the town. I doubt I will ever again. I think I could happily live here. Bring on the garlic.

For a sleepy place, there are a number of venues to eat and some of them have enough customers to be classified as busy. I could count the number of non-pilgrims in the town on the fingers of one hand before, but evidently, they gather in cafés. I eat particularly well in an ornate back room which looks like it should belong in a castle but in fact lies behind the curtain of a nondescript bar. A couple of other pilgrims have discovered it too, and we nod our hellos to each other and work our way through the *menú del dia* - garlic soup regrettably not available - while the waiters are spectacularly liberal with the wine. So much so, in fact, that when I leave and feel the cold night air on my face, I realise I don't know exactly where my hostel is. All I can remember is that it's near the highest point of the town, so I keep heading upwards while my watch counts down to the 10pm curfew. I make it with a couple of minutes to spare and endear myself to my fellow pilgrims by kicking over some walking poles on my way in, their metallic rattling giving rise to some semi-conscious murmurings of disgruntlement from the surrounding bunks.

It is another rough night, despite my taking out the insurance policy of downing more wine than usual, purely as an aid to sleeping you understand. Part of the problem is that my top bunk is about the width of a lolly stick, and you try turning over in a semi-comatose state when there's a very real prospect of ending up a couple of metres below in a crumpled heap, impaled on your neighbour's walking poles. It's stop-start sleeping until 6am, when I am woken by everyone else stirring, and the now familiar rush to get to the bathroom. For once on the Camino, the idea of a lie-in really does appeal.

The most difficult part of today's walk comes right at the beginning, with a 150m climb away from Castrojeriz which is undertaken in the semi-darkness, and with the accompanying soundtrack of heavy breathing. It's worth it though. An extravagant sunrise is taking place behind me, illuminating the castle above the town and the surrounding plains. All around, the vastness of the land is opening out and changing colour in a grand display of natural morning pyrotechnics.

Apart from that early scramble, it's a simple walk that copies yesterday in that it involves following a natural path to as far as the eye can see, and then keeping going as the horizon pulls away in front of you. It's a topography of fields, more wind turbines, and precious few people. The first village on today's route is Itero de la Vega, and that is 10km away, which means well over two hours walking. With the sun rising unopposed in the sky it's going to be another hot day, and just getting there could be a bit of an ordeal.

As it transpires, the first refreshment break comes considerably earlier in a very unexpected and welcome way. Another pop-up feeding-stop has been set up at a picnic site about an hour into the walk. There is coffee, sandwiches, and fruit, thoughtfully laid out on picnic tables, all provided by volunteers with welcoming smiles. It's all the more delightful for being a surprise, and it's located in just about the perfect place for today's stage. There's an opportunity for a rest and a chance to catch up with other walkers. I've no idea what motivates these friends of the Camino to set up a mobile café – they shrug their shoulders awkwardly when I ask, but admittedly that could just be my Spanish - or how profitable the operation is, but I'm extremely glad they appear today. The plan is to walk about 25km, which is considerably longer than the past couple of days so fuel stops are going to be vital. This halt represents more than the food and drink though, it's the feeling of being helped along the way, and that's a huge morale boost. It means that pilgrims cluster together again and feel part of a group. There are conversations and laughter, while struggle turns to smiles when a new walker arrives. It's an extremely well timed stopping point, and without it in this heat, I could see myself entering Itero de la Vega on my knees.

After a short descent over another ridge, there's a marked change in the scenery. The russet cornfields are broken up about a third of the way to the horizon by a significant band of trees that cross the path. Trees have been something of a rarity over the past few days so seeing them here in such numbers borders on the freakish. It turns out that somewhere in the middle of this woodland is the Río Pisuerga, which marks the boundary between the provinces of Burgos and Palencia. Just before you get there, there is a solid, square building which is one of the more famous *refugios* on the Camino. It's around eight hundred years old and is run by the Italian Confraternity of Saint James. There's no electricity, so the communal meal that is provided could be interesting; evening illumination is provided by candlelight. Despite being at the more basic end of the lodging experience, it looks like an intriguing and beautiful place to stay but I've thought that about pretty much everywhere I've passed since Burgos.

A glorious centuries old bridge takes you across the river into Palencia, where it's not just the trees that grab the attention; there is the novelty of some green fields as well, though normal service is resumed shortly afterwards as the countryside edges back into brown. Eventually Boadilla del Camino comes into view, where I know several of my fellow walkers are planning to stay. It is now a small farming village, though it was an unlikely hotbed of pilgrimage activity in the past. There are two hostels here including the one where I have lunch. It's an impressive place too, with a big garden and a small swimming pool. After a 35 minute re-charge, I head out to see the Czech couple I first met in Nájera, and who have been walking in a similar pattern to me over the past few days. Rather more disturbingly, BC is on the next table and wants to know where I'm heading. Rather stupidly, I give him the right answer of Frómista.

"Me too," he says, "save me a bed".

Terrific. Can't wait. It's around now that the Czechs look at me with what look like knowing smiles and say that they're staying in Boadilla for the night. It could be a coincidence but I doubt it.

I have developed a plan for dealing with BC which would involve me telling him that I'm from "T.W." (What do you mean; you have never heard of "The Wirral"?) and then bore him with made-up stories about the place: how Birkenhead was the centre of European commerce until it was bankrupted by the "Great New Brighton Earthquake"; how Hoylake was originally going to bid for the 2012 Olympics until it was undone by a dirty tricks campaign by London - that sort of thing - just to see how much he believes. As I'm the only British person around at the moment, there might be some mileage in it. Whether I can convince him that satellites are launched from Parkgate and that Churchill co-ordinated World War II from Tranmere Rovers' home ground remains to be seen. I'll work on it though. Bloody hell, the Meseta allows your mind to wander very easily.

On leaving Boadilla, the route follows a towpath alongside the largely idle Canal de Castilla. It was originally built to transport grain but the only people who use it now are anglers and canoeists though neither group appear to be active today. For the last fifty odd years, its only practical function has been for irrigation. The trees alongside it provide some much needed shade, though it's so breezy that I have to keep hold of my hat. Eventually Frómista appears on the horizon, but it's not a church that first catches the eye; it's a couple of huge grain silos. The fields of the Meseta have been harvested, and it's easy to forget that this is a major farming area of the country. Entry into the town comes via a lock-gate on the canal, which is the first of several in a rather underused lock staircase.

Frómista is a bit of a shock to the system after the past couple of days. It has tarmac roads, zebra crossings, and people travelling in other directions apart from west. It's an odd mix of the old and the new, with the main focus being the deconsecrated church of St Martin. It was sanctified around the same time that King Harold was discovering catching arrows would never make it as a future Olympic Sport, and is regarded as one of the best examples of Spanish Romanesque architecture in the country. There's been a bit of twentieth century restoration but it has remained largely the same for the best part of a thousand years and it has a timeless quality to it. It's a compact building devoid of large towers and domes but under the main roof there are hundreds of sculptures of animals and people, intricate in their design. It's commanding without necessarily being showy and is all the better for it.

It's a great day to see it too. The sun is searing through the clear windows giving it a cheery appearance. I don't know whether it's the brightness, or the fact that it's been deconsecrated, but it's not the kind of place you feel the need to whisper in. It seems to welcome noise and there's a good echo to it. There is still a specialness about St. Martin but without the oppression of religious interference.

The church is in the centre of a square and is surrounded by buildings which are more 1986 than 1066, including my *refugio* for the evening. I am back in a small dormitory again, and in the bunk above me is the Alexei Sayle lookalike from Hornillos. He got here before me and I don't remember seeing him along the way. It turns out there's a reason for this. His feet have swollen to the point where his boots no longer fit and he's using a taxi to cover a couple of stages, before continuing to walk on Monday. There's something about this that doesn't sit right with me, but also I can't help thinking "there but for the grace of God go I." My back hurts a bit but my feet are in remarkably good nick. It's hard to believe that a week ago, I was in Grañón, and it's been two weeks since I was in Pamplona. Sometime in the next few days the halfway point of the journey will be reached.

Apart from the unfamiliar sound of traffic, there have been a fair few explosions this afternoon. These have been fireworks going off to celebrate a wedding, and a strong smell of cordite lingers over the town in the evening. I manage to avoid the overtures made by BC to join him for dinner and instead head off to a busy café on Frómista's main drag. On the wall is a large television showing a Latin American music channel, but the rhythms are drowned out by the sounds of people enjoying their Saturday night. Playing cards are being thumped on tables with unnecessary violence while spectators

99

huddle in groups, giving their vocal support. There is barely any standing room and I am pointed upstairs to a narrow deserted mezzanine floor - the location of the *comedor*.

I've been surviving very easily so far on the *menú del dia*. The choices may be limited, particularly if you have seen similar menus for the best part of three weeks, but generally the food has been very good. Tonight's is the best of the walk so far, and I take my time eating my meatballs and lentils so I can cast my eye on the people of Frómista revelling in their Saturday night. Unfortunately, although the food is good, there's a shortage of red wine and I'm given a bottle of something that resembles nail varnish instead. I do finish it though, just to make sure it's as bad as I think it is.

On the way back to my bed I bump into Caitlin's sidekick from Burgos. Despite being German, her name is Manuela and she could easily pass for being Spanish with her olive skin and raven black hair. She is still walking with Caitlin which makes me think that she must have the patience of a saint; either that or she's deaf. It means that Caitlin is in Frómista too, but since I haven't heard her all afternoon, I can only assume she's staying elsewhere. Sure enough, as I'm walking past St Martin, I hear her voice and find her holding court at a table in a nearby bar.

Manuela suggests a drink and I accept, hoping I can speak to her rather than have my ears pummelled by Caitlin. The quality of the wine here far outstrips the stuff I have just been drinking and Manuela is a lively drinking companion. She's a lawyer in Hannover and speaks excellent English and Spanish. Just as we start swapping Camino experiences so far, Caitlin realizes that her captive audience isn't big enough.

"We stayed in Castrojeriz last night. What a boring place! I expect you hated it, Rudy. It isn't really you, is it? Oh by the way, what happened to you in Burgos? Did you oversleep? We had a great time that morning, didn't we, Manuela? It reminded me of when I was in Nicaragua."

I'm so pleased I didn't bump into her yesterday. I doubt if I would associate Castrojeriz with a truly special moment of serenity and calm in my life if I had. I'm struggling to understand why Manuela walks with her. Maybe after a few hours Caitlin yields a bit and lets somebody get a word in, or becomes entertaining. The man sitting next to me is another walking companion she has picked

100

up - her Camino is starting to look like a walk down the yellow brick road. He's a very pleasant guy from Florence who, judging by this evening's body language, is more interested in Manuela than listening to Caitlin. There was a huge temptation to ask him what Latin American country he resembled, but I barely get the chance to speak to him. Caitlin is in a loud mood and is reluctant to close her mouth and give her brain a chance. Dinner with BC may not have been a bad option after all.

Today's stage is the first time since day one where there is a choice of routes to follow. The destination is always going to be Carrión de los Condes, and the alternatives are either walking along a new footpath, or *senda*, by the side of a main road, or take a longer option along an old Roman path that avoids the traffic, and ushers you past fields and farmland. I take the bucolic alternative, knowing that it will put about 3km on the journey, but it's likely to be a more pleasant experience. It will also be following in the footsteps of the Roman Emperor Trajan who was born in Spain and did his bit by building this particular part of the way.

It all starts off in thick fog and it is a good 40 minutes before a village comes into view. I was rather hoping to have breakfast, but nothing is stirring and there are no signs of any life at all, let alone an open bar. After a few minutes of contemplating alternatives, I see a torch beam struggling through the misty half-light. Attached to the torch is another pilgrim who also looks as if he's searching for somewhere to rest. His name is Valerio and he is a drama student from Pisa. He is more prepared than I am for the lack of bar facilities and rather generously gives me some of his chocolate as we head together through the grey world. Surely, no man can offer more. I am humbled by this gesture as the only way you'll get chocolate out of me is via a mugging. Valerio is quickly promoted to friend for life and, with his English being as bad as my Italian is, we get on brilliantly. He doesn't look particularly Italian with short red hair and intense blue eyes. He worked as a waiter in London and I've lived in Italy so we swap cultural differences, while heading into the rural mist in search of somewhere to eat.

Today's experience of the Meseta is a major contrast to what has gone on before. Even when the light does penetrate, visibility is minimal and, after the wide expanses of yesterday's walking, this is a much more claustrophobic experience. The diversion along Trajan's road takes us on the edge of cultivated fields and irrigation channels but with no sense of the great beyond at all. It's a largely noiseless monochrome world that we amble through, punctuated by the occasional sighting of a farmhouse and the sporadic barking of unseen dogs. Valerio is the only other person I've seen since I left my *refugio*. The extra 3km has bought us some silence but nothing in terms of visual stimulation. Above all, it hasn't brought us breakfast.

The fog doesn't lift until about 10am by which time we have, as Elvis Presley might have put it, returned to *senda*. The stone path runs alongside the main road into Carrión de los Condes and it's a tedious bit of walking. It's been cut into the terrain and only occasionally are you able to poke your head above the arable dunes to the vastness of the plain beyond. However, if the choice is walking along a soulless path or facing the oncoming traffic on a major road, there is a clear winner. It is a long couple of hours before Valerio and I find somewhere to stop, and it isn't the most salubrious of surroundings. It's an unlovely pilgrimage café by the side of the road, but it's open and we're hungry. It does have a garden though and we sit outside, despite the fact that the sun hasn't had a chance to warm up the countryside, while an orchestral version of Meat Loaf's *Bat out of Hell* plays out in the background. We are joined by some of the regulars. The Scottish-Australian coupling of Jan and Andrew are already here and have clearly not tired of each other's company. I haven't seen them for a few days, but they are injury free and in good spirits. The Czech couple arrives just as Valerio and I prepare to get moving again, and we exchange Buen Caminos and say we'll meet up in Carrión.

There is another stop about an hour later when we reach Villalcázar De Sirga. The Knights Templar had an influence on the Camino, and this is the first place where you can actually see it. It comes in the shape of Santa María la Blanca, one of the most impressive churches on the route. Modernity is kept to a minimum here and it's difficult to separate church and surroundings in terms of architectural style. Santa María is regarded as a national monument but it's not an easy building to take to. On this particular morning, it's cold, stark, and doesn't feel particularly welcoming, but we walk around in a suitably reverent and mesmerised silence. There's a statue of Santa María La Blanca herself, which was famous during the middle ages for its miracle cures. Santiago is not neglected here either and I chuck in a euro to illuminate a rather extravagant panel which depicts the life of St James from his first meeting with Jesus, up to his arrival in Galicia. When the light on the panel fades, the somewhat gloomy atmosphere returns and lingers in every alcove and aisle; the air feeling arctic and stale. The melancholy feeling continues when we leave the church. Low clouds have grouped together and the lustrous sandstone of Villalcázar De Sirga is slowly fading in front of us, adding to its somewhat woeful demeanour.

I part company with Valerio who decides to press on to Carrión while I decide to prolong the break in a café. I am joined by an elderly looking Frenchman who looks faintly ridiculous with his thin legs hanging down from very wide shorts. I quickly reverse my opinion of him when he tells me he started his walk in Paris, which means he is covering double the distance I am. I think my legs would be in the same state if I were doing the same thing. He retired several years ago and did a week's worth of the Camino the previous year. It plainly wasn't enough, and so back in July, he took his first steps from Notre Dame Cathedral. I ask if he's had any problems and he shakes his head.

"I get a bit tired sometimes," is all he will add.

I am in temporary danger of inadvertently picking up new walking partners as I bump into Caitlin, who has Manuela and the Italian man from last night still in tow. Thankfully, she has only just arrived in Villalcázar and I am on my way out.

"Let's meet up in Carrión," she grins after some enthusiastic hugging.

No. Let's have bamboo inserted under our fingernails instead.

Carrión at one time supported thirteen *refugios* and even now, there are still a generous four to choose from. I decide that after the modernity of yesterday evening, and inspired by my experience at Santa María La Blanca, it's time to have a night somewhere more traditional in the shape of the thirteenth-century convent of Santa Clara. Allegedly, it once provided a resting place for St. Francis of Assisi when he made the journey to Santiago and it has the bonus of being just about the first building you come across when you enter the town.

I am greeted in English in the cloisters by the *hospitalero,* which is a bit of a surprise.

"Come with me" he smiles, "and wash your head."

Of course, this is a religious building, steeped in Camino history and centuries of tradition have to be respected. I am obviously about to take part in a ceremony of humility and benediction that St Francis and thousands of pilgrims since have undertaken. I am just contemplating my spiritual preparation for this ritual when my head connects forcefully with the doorframe of the office. This is followed by a few ungodly and universally translatable expletives. By the time I raise my head again I see the *hospitalero* looking at me severely.

"I told you to wash your head," he sighs. And if the bugger had told me in Spanish, I would have understood him perfectly.

Santa Clara is a bit unusual as resting places go, because I am actually sleeping on a bed. Not a bunk or a mattress, but a proper bed. There are just four people to a dorm too. I'm followed in by Richard, the Frenchman from the café at Villalcázar. Already in situ is another Frenchman, a jovial man in his fifties called Bernard while the final bed is occupied by a smiley Italian called Giovanni. It is a cheery dorm, to say the least, and I'm determined to add to the bonhomie. I've gone through a whole morning without seeing BC and anyone thinking I'm German.

Carrión is a lively place for a Sunday, with the squares and the bars all being particularly busy. It's not just pilgrims either. The residents are taking advantage of the heat and have come out to enjoy it. There's no mistaking the Camino links though. The local cafés and bakeries all appear to be trying to outdo each other with large signs in their windows advertising how early they open in the morning, and much they welcome pilgrims. They may all be open at stupid o'clock tomorrow but it is tricky to find anywhere open right now. I manage to locate a sweet shop which bizarrely also does a nice line in bread and cold meats. I stock up because tomorrow's stage looks like the most remote to date, and villages are few and far between.

I also have a good look at another famous pilgrimage bridge; this one spans the Río Carrión, and I'm going to cross it in early morning darkness tomorrow. The gentle heat of the afternoon gets to me and I have a brief doze on a bench overlooking the river. I am rudely awoken, not by children throwing stones for a change, but by the sound of engines revving nearby. I look up to see a collection of familiar looking small cars. There are about ten of them, small in size and each a different colour, making them look like Smarties on wheels. I've openly stumbled across a gathering of the Seat 625 appreciation society, or possibly a themed dogging afternoon. I quickly rule out the latter. No-one could have sex in a Seat 625 unless they were a gymnast. My family had the same type of car when we stayed in Cantabria when I was younger. It feels like a sign, another piece of my past life, a time when I felt a lot more Spanish than I do now.

If there's one thing that marks Carrión as being different to most stopping points on the Camino, it's the fact that it's big enough to accommodate a lot of pilgrims, but small enough not to swallow us up. There are familiar faces everywhere this afternoon on the streets and in the cafés. Being here is a happy full-on pilgrimage experience. A pleasantly lazy day is followed by an evening service at the church which bucks the pilgrimage trend by not being dedicated to Santa María in her various forms. There's a pilgrimage blessing included and as I haven't had one for about ten days, I thought I'd better go in case the last one has worn out. Blessings so far have normally lasted about ten minutes, bolted on at the end of a mass, but this one stretches to a separate service of about half an hour. We have the readings in six languages, and also have to deal with a googly that none of us is expecting – the Camino hymn. I didn't know there was one and I'm clearly not alone. It is played from a CD and is a ghastly sub-Eurovision ditty whose chorus scans with the words to the rugby song "My Husband's a Bricklayer" – Oh the benefits of a Christian Brothers education.

Sixty pilgrims stare at each other and wonder if they are the only ones who hate the song and then notice a similar recognition in everyone else's eyes. That will be a *nul points* from the jury then. None of us appears to have heard it before and I don't think I'm alone in hoping I never hear it again.

The blessing makes me late for the dinner appointment I'd earlier arranged with Jim and Sue. I see Michael again for the first time since Burgos and he joins us for an excellent meal of good food and laughter. There's a huge amount of jealousy from my fellow diners who are staying in different *refugios* when I tell them I'm sleeping in a bed tonight. You know you are on a pilgrimage when Jim asks mournfully to tell him what the experience is like when we meet tomorrow.

28th September: Stage 18 - Carrión de los Condes to Terradillos de los Templarios

Despite being in a room where the door refuses to close and where the bed sheets are made of paper, I manage to get my best night's sleep in a week. I definitely have something to boast to Jim about. Giovanni and Richard leave very early and, just to make sure you have no chance of a lie-in, the warden bangs on the door at 6.30am even though kicking out time is officially ninety minutes later.

I have breakfast in the same restaurant where dinner was eaten yesterday evening. They appear to be playing a CD of every song you've ever forgotten from the 1980s – Matt Bianco's *Sneaking Out The Back Door With a Grin*, or *I'm Not Scared* by Eighth Wonder. Music has played a strange role on the walk so far. I had every intention of writing down the songs that go through my head every day but gave this up early on as they all had negative titles like *Surrender* and *Don't Come Close*. A few of the hostels have music playing when you walk in. There was the New Age stuff in Castrojeriz while Tosantos had managed to acquire orchestral versions of songs like OMD's *Enola Gay*. Yesterday it was Meat Loaf at the roadside café, while a hot chocolate in Logroño was accompanied by the career highlights of Tears for Fears. The Camino tradition goes back hundreds of years but the music legacy only appears to cover a couple of decades. Still, at least the Camino hymn is pushed out of my head.

The main feature of today's walk is that the first 18km doesn't include a village or any other obvious stopping point. After leaving Carrión, the route consists of a country lane which then diverts onto an original Roman path, the Via Aquitania. Daybreak reveals a broken chain of walkers in front and behind on the straightest, flattest path I've ever seen. For two hours, there is absolutely no deviation whatsoever. Over the previous few days, the countryside had at least been a bit bumpy but now it is level to the point of monotony. There is also the strange abundance of trees that line the path but are neither close nor tall enough to provide any useful shade. There aren't thickly planted either so there's little to obscure the capacious views of nothingness that lie in all directions. It's easy to forget that we're walking half a mile above sea level.

It's tricky to find a suitable place to have a comfortable stop and enjoy the food I bought yesterday. At about 8.30am I stumble across a picnic area with four tables. There is only one other inhabitant and it is BC. He looks like he is getting ready to leave but I decide it isn't worth the risk so I press on with the aim of giving it another half an hour or so. Just as the trees thin out and the scenery opens up a bit more, another picnic table comes into view. It's concrete, outstandingly unattractive and surrounded by litter but I don't care as I am starving. I improvise an inelegant chorizo *bocadillo* while BC crunches his way along the path shortly after I've settled down, and he is long gone by the time I've finished.

It is back onto the straight red-earthed path and a further plod. On days like today when all is flat and largely featureless for as far as the eye can see, you can understand why pilgrims use the Meseta to construct life metaphors. I'm not immune to it and come to the conclusion that every day the Camino throws up some sort of challenge. It may last a few minutes or take up the whole day's walking but there's something to be overcome every day, and life is just the same. Sometimes life is a flat walk of boredom and sometimes it's climbs and descents. Not profound I know, and maybe I'm no different from those walkers who spend their afternoons reading through their well-worn self-help books. It's easy to understand why people feel a little bit unnerved by the Meseta's expansive terrain. There are a lot of walkers about today, but I imagine doing this stage when the path is deserted must be very unsettling indeed. It's not hard to comprehend why this part of the walk has been seen to represent spiritual death. I'd still take it over the walk into Burgos though, which I've now decided must represent eternal damnation.

There is a bit of excitement at around 10.15am when the path actually deviates slightly to the left, and there are moments afterwards when it goes up a bit of a slope. On a day like today, this passes as a major event. All in all, the way is pretty much constant and dull, and it's over four hours until I get to the first village, Caldadilla de la Cueza. I've nearly caught up with BC but he stops off in a bar and I continue around the corner to eat the rest of my food and have a brief conversation with one of the locals who wants to know if I support Manchester United. I think I'd prefer to be called German.

The yellow arrows now point away from the ancient Via Aquitania and onto to a modern *senda* which twists its way alongside a main road. There are now some up-hills and it becomes difficult to open your mouth without swallowing flies. In the distance is Terradillos de los Templarios; an unassuming sort of place which is just short of being halfway along the Camino. In the midday heat, it might as well be Santiago, as it looks a bloody long way off to me.

While I was walking in a straight line this morning, my mind was meandering elsewhere, and I came up with a way of classifying walking distances. Anything under 22km constitutes a sprint while 22-26 km equates to middle distance. Anything above that and we're into marathon territory and today's stage just about does that. I really feel the pain of the last few kilometres. The heat takes away any advantage provided by the flatness of the terrain and it is with some relief that I take advantage of the first stopping point I come across. It's just outside the village and looks like a small-scale Lego version of Southfork Ranch. It's back to the modern again and this time it comes with a restaurant attached. I've never been in one of these hostels before so I think it is about time to give one a go. As it works out, there's no real option in Terradillos as the two *refugios* are the only places to eat. Michael is here and, to my horror, so is BC. I had a night off last night but this still means that four out of the last five nights have been spent with him. Having said that, this is the first time in the same dorm. I may be doing the man an injustice and judging him too much on the words of others - I've barely spoken to him after all. Mind you, I have listened to him quite a bit.

After staying in three towns in a row, it is time to adjust to doing nothing again. It's a strange environment being stuck in an incongruous-looking building in the middle of nowhere. There's a wire fence around the comfortable grounds and it's difficult to know whether to feel liberated or imprisoned. There are worse places to be staying; it does have a bar. It's a different feeling to doing nothing in Hornillos; there you are tied to the village, whereas here all the facilities are inside or within the grounds. I would happily fall asleep in the garden but, although it's sunny, there's a cold wind blowing.

Only one of the narrow sides of the building provides any protection and it's the least aesthetically pleasing part of the complex.

I'm using the weather conditions as an excuse to wash my towel again. My fellow pilgrims aren't helping and many seem to think that washing that has been blown onto the floor is there to be stood on. I get angry with an unapologetic Swiss pilgrim whose feet are firmly anchored on my towel, though he claims ignorance when this is pointed out. Clearly he's mistaken it for some novelty blue coloured grass. With a sense of relief, I bump into the ever resourceful Valerio who lends me a couple of clothes pegs. There is a real danger of my clothes being blown away and discovered with footprints all over them. There could also be a chance that a pilgrim gets found in a shallow unmarked grave after being strangled with a wet cloth. It really is curious that the only time there's been any tangible ill-feeling between pilgrims is when it comes to the area of drying clothes.

Time is idled away until 7pm when dinner is served in the restaurant. Once again, I am in the company of Richard who flies the flag admirably for la belle France and refuses to accept that any of the country's current problems are its own fault. He blames Germany in particular and chooses to do so just as Michael joins us, along with another German woman, Cristina. In fairness, both take it on the chin and land a few good-natured blows in return. In spite of the subject matter, we are laughing a lot more than the other tables, which is always a good sign. I've escaped direct contact with BC but he's in earshot on the next table, peddling tedium about several ex-wives.

A few years ago, I went to watch a battle re-enactment in the incinerating heat of high summer in the Czech countryside. Over the course of about an hour, there was constant gunfire, substantial use of cannon and the whole thing was explained by an enthusiastic narrator with a microphone, and a PA system that was worthy of an Iron Maiden gig. The performance ended with the crowd cheering and more firearms being discharged. The reason I mention this is because I managed to sleep through absolutely all of it. I only know what happened from what my friends told me, and what was in the newspaper the following day. I thought this meant that I could close my eyes and ignore all the intrusive sounds the world could provide. I was wrong.

After going to bed just after 9pm yesterday I'm wide-awake four hours later as that is when the World Snoring Championships starts. There are ten of us in the dorm and half sound like they are taking part. BC is demonstrating his versatility by proving that he can be a pain in the arse at night as well as during the hours of daylight. He sounds like he is machine-gunning seals. Even worse is the guy in the bunk above him who imitates starting a tractor while playing a kazoo. It is relentless and they are not alone. The man above me is making strange submarine sonar noises. The decibel count is truly astonishing. Snoring has been an issue before on the Camino but this is a completely new level of earache.

At about 2.30am I reach under my bunk to feel if my walking poles are sharp enough to cut out someone's heart. I'm tempted to say something but, judging by the sounds of the bedroom farmyard, none of the perpetrators is likely to hear it. Eventually, thoughts of mass slaughter get overtaken by avoidance strategies. I stagger into the adjoining bathroom, sit on the floor and speculate if I could spread myself out and rest here. It is far from ideal but it could be a goer. Rather surprisingly I'm joined a couple of minutes later by my former roommate from Carrión, Bernard. He has also been struggling to sleep and he's been wearing earplugs. In fairness, he's a lot closer to the epicentre than I am. Just as we are trading noise-related metaphors, the bathroom door opens again and we are joined by a Danish woman who has a tired but murderous glint in her eye. Luckily, it's not directed at us and she joins our escape committee. We use the time not to moan but to swap Camino stories so far, while the bunk beds continue to rattle next door. Bernard then announces he has some wine in his rucksack explaining that he always carried two bottles of water plus an extra one for wine "in case of emergencies."

The Danish woman thinks this is incredibly funny and asks Bernard if he has a baguette as well.

"Of course," he replies, "and some camembert too!"

Seeing the look of tired surprise on our faces, he quickly backpedals and laughs. "I don't really. I ate them with my onions earlier."

The Danish woman mentions she has some cards with her and I remember that I still have some chocolate left. I hesitate briefly about surrendering this but I remember the kindness of Valerio a couple of days before and recognise that the Camino is forged in the spirit of brother and sisterhood, not to mention occasional adversity. As improvised parties go, I don't think I'll ever have as strange experience as sipping wine and eating chocolate on a communal bathroom floor while playing poker, using toilet paper as chips.

We edge back into the dorm at around 4-ish though nothing appears to have changed. It is a good forty-five minutes before I manage to close my eyes successfully. I'm up again at 6am and if BC even looks at me today, he's going to be found face down in a drainage ditch. Just as the Inuit have two hundred words for snow, I'm developing a similar vocabulary for snoring. Some of the words even stretch to more than four letters. After yesterday's experience with the clothes drying and the overnight racket, the grumpy pilgrim is back.

I can't wait to get out and put some distance between me and everyone else, but there is a worrying start. When I put on my backpack there's a slight twinge in my right shoulder. It doesn't appear to be anything major but it's perceptible. I suppose it's about time there is some evident wear and tear on the body as the feet are bearing up remarkably well.

I'm led into the first village of the morning by a skinny tabby cat who is rather intent that I should follow it. It keeps looking over its shoulder to make sure I'm right behind. Right at the entrance are houses that are cut into the hillside with chimneys sticking out of the grass. Middle Earth exists in the middle of the Camino. The cat is the only moving thing I see for about half an hour. When I do stumble across some pilgrims, they come in the welcome shapes of Jim and Sue. It is impossible to stay grumpy in their company, and over hot chocolate and coffee, they both laugh heartily at my overnight experiences. They were in the other hostel and had an evening of total tranquillity, joy and undisturbed sleep. They still haven't stayed in a bed though so I'm clinging on to that boast.

Sahagún is given a good write-up in my guidebook but it doesn't look particularly promising from a distance. To be honest, it doesn't look good close up either, but it was once a powerful and flourishing town. For nine hundred years, it was the site of the most important Benedictine monastery in the country but only remnants of it still exist. It was also the site of a university and this image of a thriving seat of learning is particularly hard to understand when the place gives the impression of being near the end of a slow and painful decline.

The way into town is alongside a new and barely used road. Despite Sahagún's ecclesiastical history the most dominant building is a grain silo which looks like an over-large cinema. The yellow arrows allow a detour to take in an old church and bridge before the route heads past a couple of barns. I keep expecting to turn a corner and find myself in a nice part of town but it just doesn't happen. It's not unpleasant by any stretch of the imagination but it's a place that has considerably more of a past than a future. I go off-Camino to look at some ecclesiastical ruins but the whole town looks in a bad way, scruffy and dirty. Even the main squares look shabby. Unlike other places I've been to, there doesn't seem to be any cause for optimism here at all. Despite its obvious neglect, history alone dictates that it must be an interesting place to stay. It's not just its pilgrimage heritage. It was a Roman town long before the Camino came into being, and it also has links with Charlemagne. I do spend some time having a walk around and have a lengthy lunch break at a café in the town's main square. I can't write-off Sahagún completely, and there are enough signs that my feelings would change if I stayed here overnight. The isolation would appeal in the same way it did at Castrojeriz and there may be beauty in the evening light. It will certainly be more distinctive than last night's hostel but the town is rather awkwardly placed in terms of the next part of the journey, for me at least.

Outside one of the hostels here is a statue of St. James dressed as a pilgrim. This is a common image along the route and it portrays the saint dressed in a hat and carrying a staff and a gourd. You can see similar representations of him in shops and signs. It hasn't sunk in before but there's obviously a whiff of vanity about the bloke if he has dressed up to travel to his own shrine. Maybe he wants to know whose bones are buried in his cathedral.

I leave via the impressive, if unstable-looking, Arco de San Benito and across a Roman bridge and find myself back in the blazing sunshine and following a main road. There are alternative routes for the next few hours that will affect the next day's walking. I can spend tomorrow either following a *senda* or take in Spain's finest example of surviving Roman road. No contest really but there is the problem of a starting point. To walk on the Roman road, I'll have to head to Calzadilla de los Hermanillos today which is slightly further than the alternative route destination which is Bercianos del Real Camino.

I have to make the decision just after midday when the sun is belting down unopposed and another two hours of walking is starting to look like a tough call. I decide to go Roman and straight away, it feels like a bad idea. To get on the appropriate route I have to negotiate the crossing of the busy N120 road. Pedestrian aids are conspicuous by their absence and it's a quick run across several lanes of traffic. I don't think I've had to run on the Camino before and it's a bit awkward when you're carrying a backpack and a truck is bearing down on you.

I have certainly not chosen the more popular route of the day and there is only one walker ahead of me, too far away to be identified. As I follow at a distance through the village of Calzado, the quiet is shattered as a huge dog leaps out at him, barking with impressive ferocity before being yanked back to a safe distance by its tethered chain. It's enough to make the walker jump significantly and to move away at great speed. It terrifies the life out of me and I'm a couple of hundred metres back. I read a lot about dangerous dogs being a factor on the Camino but I haven't really come across any. This one doesn't look particularly friendly - the fact that it appears to have an iron bolt around its neck instead of a collar, and is tethered by what looks like a battleship chain doesn't help - but I walk past it on the opposite side of the road, while it lies motionless and growls softly to suggest that it could make a spring if it could be bothered. There are no sudden movements and my blood pressure remains constant. A useful lesson is learned. I decide that where possible in the future, I'll lag behind my fellow pilgrims as we walk through villages so I can use them as dog bait and be forewarned.

After Calzado the road turns to stony path which leads through fields parched orange by the heat. I'm feeling orange too as the afternoon shapes up to be the warmest part of the Camino so far. It must be well over thirty degrees and this is turning into a footslog of ambitious and draining proportions. There is absolutely no shade to be had and my water bottles are dangerously empty. The track heads towards some woodland but even when I enter the trees there is no respite. The path is wide and the trees are not close enough to provide much-needed cover. There is a water fountain indicated on my map but I certainly don't see it. To be honest, seeing anything is difficult as the sweat is pouring into my eyes. This is one of those moments when you just count down the minutes until the walk is over. The walker ahead of me is clearly suffering more, as I am reeling him in quite rapidly. To my delight, when I get close enough to make identification easier, I discover that it's Bernard, the wine carrying Frenchman. Together we make it into Calzadilla de los Hermanillos, advertised - as all places on the Camino are in Castile y León - with a large plastic sign showing the amenities and the route through the village. Just as we are entering, we pass a group of pilgrims who are planning to kick on to the next village, even though several don't look capable of getting to the other side of the road. At best, they have another couple of hours walking to go and have to deviate from the route to get to the *refugio* at El Burgo Ranero. I don't think I've got more than thirty minutes left in me and Calzadilla is going to suit me fine. It's been a truly energy-sapping few hours but one thing I notice is that my earlier shoulder twinge seems to have disappeared.

The hostel is open but deserted when we arrive there. We stand around for several minutes and have a bit of a look around. It's a

115

small place with sixteen beds in cubicles of four. Soon a woman appears from outside and we go through the usual formalities of signing in and getting our *credencials* stamped. The rules of the curfew are explained too, but by now, we're used to the fact that you have to be in by 10pm. To be honest, most of us will be tucked up well before then anyway. Whether we sleep or not is, of course, another matter. As Bernard and I are going through the pilgrimage washing rituals, Michael arrives followed by Richard. Yesterday evening's political discussion on Germany versus France has not affected their Camino spirit. After introducing Michael and Bernard to each other, we decide to split up and explore Calzadilla.

It has to be said that it's a weird looking place. It's greener than pretty much everywhere I've walked through in the past couple of days, but what makes it truly odd is the housing. There is no crumbling adobe here. Many of the streets are made up of double-fronted square terraced houses made of red brick, which gives it a sort of *Coronation Street* feel to it. They are immaculate to look at and a lot of them have been recently renovated. The thing that sticks out is that they have steel shutters on the windows and many have steel doors, giving them a "just been boarded up" look. It doesn't resemble anywhere I've been too before in my life, let alone on the Meseta. The use of steel makes it look like a planned slum but many of the houses are beautifully maintained, as if they were built the day before. The wide streets are largely car-free and deserted. I don't know what my idea of a typical Spanish town should be but it certainly isn't this. I've got used to sandy stone places in various states of disrepair but this really is decidedly odd and if anything, slightly British. It's a long way from anywhere and the sense of abandonment gives it a unique and slightly baleful character.

True to form, I find the bar which is on the way out of town. It does have something that the rest of the village is lacking and that is people. Granted, there are only three of them and one of them is serving but it takes the known inhabitants of the place to four. After a quick beer, it's time to regroup and determine what everybody else has discovered. Michael has found the village shop which is near the rather large pelota court. It's a good job he stumbled across it because I certainly wouldn't have done. There is nothing to advertise its existence at all and its opening hours aren't exactly pilgrim-friendly. Luckily, we get there just before closing time.

Tomorrow's walk involves 18km before getting to another stopping point so having supplies to dip into is vital. It's another of those places that looks incredibly small but appears to stock everything. Of course, my demands aren't particularly great and consist of sandwich making materials and large slabs of chocolate. Apart from the shop, there's a travelling van doing the rounds this afternoon selling fruit and fish. How much wisdom there is in selling both types of foodstuff together is debatable, as the apples I buy have a distinct aquatic smell to them. The van does bring the inhabitants out of doors though and there are smiles, waves and warm "Buen Caminos" thrown in our direction.

The evening is a relaxed an extremely pleasant one. There are only eight of us staying in the village and we all meet outside Calzadilla de los Hermanillos' only restaurant *La Trajana* for a meal. Bernard is insistent that we should rock up for an aperitif and we met up with a Quebecois couple in their mid-fifties I would guess, and a French pairing of a similar age who are sitting outside. The French couple are from Lourdes - I would have thought they would have been sick of the idea of pilgrimage - but they distance themselves from their town's shrine, which they seem to regard as a major inconvenience. We are soon joined by Richard and Michael and conversation flows freely and happily. While the others celebrate St Michael's Day with San Miguel beer, Bernard sees no reason to break with tradition and I hate to see a man drinking wine on his own.

We are the restaurant's only clients and we head indoors where good pilgrimage food is eaten, more wine is drunk and much multilingual bollocks is talked. We are attended to brilliantly by the efficient and entertaining owner and it's been the most enjoyable evening of the Camino so far. Despite the fact that half the group are new to me, and I only came across Richard and Bernard two days ago, we talk together like old friends. There's a lot of laughter as stories are swapped with Bernard talking very entertainingly about our struggle to sleep the night before. I mention using Bernard as dog bait, which he takes very well. The Quebecois talk about the semi-mythical British bloke called Luck whom I still haven't met, though from the sound of it this is no bad thing. Once again, nobody mentions exactly why they are doing the Camino and there is no talk of getting to Santiago. We all are focusing on now with an occasional nod to tomorrow's walking. We may not meet again as a group and we all are experienced enough now to be aware of it. We're living this moment as a one-off and enjoying every second of it. I just hope all this bonhomie can be converted into relaxing sleep.

30th September: Stage 20 - Calzadilla de los Hermanillos to Mansilla de las Mulas

This morning is in marked contrast to 24 hours ago. I slept straight through to 6.30am and woke up with no thoughts to murder any of my fellow pilgrims. The weather doesn't look too promising when Michael and I head back to *La Trajana* for breakfast. The road looks damp and, rather worryingly, there are no stars visible. This is not the stage to catch some bad weather, as there is going to be nowhere to shelter for the next four hours. It turns out we have nothing to worry about as daylight brings a lot more optimism; a blue sky emerges, streaked with high clouds, and it looks like we're going to get away with it.

It's a stretch of modern road before Roman rocky path takes over. All around, the earth is recognisably arid and if there was rain last night, it certainly didn't fall here. The route fulfils the cliché of being largely straight and can be quite difficult in places, but it certainly has more romance and a sense of history than following a *senda*. It's also a lot quieter, and that's not just because BC must be on the other route. It was the right decision to take the ancient path, though I know I wasn't thinking like that in the early part of yesterday afternoon. Whatever the walk today throws up, it will have been worth it just for last night at *La Trajana*.

Having walked on my own for a lot of the time, I pair up with Michael today. He's a tall, balding bloke in his early thirties and, for the purposes of this trip, he's growing a black beard. He is an interesting person to talk to. I do fear the worst early on when it becomes clear that he seems to have read every self-help book known to man, and religiously carries a copy of the book *The Power of Now* with him. However, if he does have mystic tendencies he keeps them to himself. He tells me about his experiences in Ireland, and about his journey to Macchu Picchu, which he describes in tourist terms rather than anything spiritual. He doesn't appear to be doing the Camino for therapy reasons, at least no more than the rest of us are.

It's another day of wide flat topography, interrupted only by a railway line, which we gradually approach on our left. No trains pass us for the entire walk and, as there are only eight of us on this part of the Camino, there is a real sense of isolation. I'm actually pleased I'm walking with someone, as this is another backdrop to induce madness. There is virtually no movement anywhere and there's not a breath of wind in the air. A lot of the day feels like walking into a painting. We overtake and are overtaken by the Francophone couples as breaks are taken and food consumed.

There's nowhere obvious to stop on the route at all and lunch is only taken out of necessity, when we come across an unattractive grassy hillock which just about has enough space for both of us to sit down and spread out a bit. It is also close enough to have an unrestricted view of the world's most underused railway line. We put together our roughly improvised *bocadillo*s but soon get distracted by some activity back on the path. A colony of ants are marching across it in an endless line of determined organisation. We watch them in silence, on their purposeful mission and it becomes almost hypnotic in its effect; it is the only non-Camino movement we've seen all day.

Michael and I eventually part company when Reliegos comes into view; he's heading there while I decide to press on to Mansilla de las Mulas. Mansilla is another place that pre-dates the arrival of the Camino. It was a vital intersection of trade routes and the Romans saw it as important enough to put a wall around it - I actually enter it by a Roman gate. By the 13th century, it was the largest and richest town in the area. It gets its name "de las Mulas" - of the mules - because of the cattle markets that existed there. Over time, it also became a pilgrim-friendly halt, boasting several churches and other places for pilgrims to rest their weary heads.

There's only one hostel now and I'm not exactly impressed with it. I don't know if it's something to do with the greying skies when I get there, or that I arrive just as the *hospitalero*s are leaving for a break. While certainly not hostile, the greeting is efficient rather than friendly. It's quite a big place and has evidently been here for a long time, as the wooden floors and stairs have warped considerably. There are several dormitories, and space is very much at a premium. Bunks have been shoe-horned into rooms and, given the topography of the flooring, may have been packed in to make sure that they don't shift during the night. It's noisy too and every sound can be heard through the walls and floors. Outside there's a central courtyard which doubles as a dining room and drying area for clothes. The washing facilities and showers are hidden away in the corners. It's the busiest *refugio* I've been to since Burgos, as pilgrims converge again after a day of differing routes and lay up before heading on to León tomorrow. There is hardly any table space to be had and there's a lot of eating and drinking going on. There's genuine delight in seeing Rod and Cassie again for the first time in eleven days, as well as the Colombian journalist I last saw in Hornillos. He warmly takes my hand in both of his and asks me how I am. It's particularly pleasing as the vast majority of the other people here are strangers.

I have a bit of a wander around the town, which looks pleasant enough, even under melancholic cloud. Of course, several hundred years of decline has faded it a bit, but it seems to be holding its own more successfully than Sahagún. Then again, it's a lot closer to León. As evening starts to descend, the courtyard and the kitchen fill up once again, and there is the sound of communal meals being prepared and general activity. There is also an annoying Norwegian sod with a guitar. When I go down there to check on my washing, he's trying to lead a sing-song. Are we going to be treated to something by The Beatles or a chorus of *Daydream Believer*? No, we get Radiohead's *Street Spirit*, a right cheerful karaoke favourite, that one. It is enough to send me straight out and back into town, where I sit in the square for a few minutes. I'm soon joined by the local town drunk who tries to engage me in conversation and manages to hold out for several minutes before asking me for money.

Mercifully, when I come back to the base, there's nobody dangling by their neck from a rope, despite the Norwegian's best efforts. Just as I'm arriving, I see Bernard heading out. I haven't seen him since breakfast and I assume he's going in search of his aperitif. Rather regretfully, I turn down his dinner invitation as BC suddenly hoves into view, and it's clear that they're going off to eat together. I'm openly lacking the pilgrimage spirit here and Bernard is visibly more open. It's going to take more than an aperitif to get me through a meal in the company of BC. I'm sure he's inoffensive but there's something about his desire to talk all the time that really winds me up. Or maybe he's just better at making friends than I am. The "say yes" policy comes back to mind and I have a rethink by balancing Bernard's jollity against BC's ability to irritate. It's too late though, as they've headed off and I don't know where to.

There's a major drawback of staying in places of any size on the Camino, and I've never really thought about it until now. There are more places to dine, and of course, pilgrims spread out into different cafés and bars. Yesterday in Cazadilla, we were all thrown together in the evening. as there was only one place to eat, and we enjoyed a concentrated dose of Camino spirit. Here it's considerably more diluted, with pilgrims scattered across various watering holes. The most memorable evenings so far have been those when random pilgrims join up because of where we're staying – the nights in Estella, Grañon, and Agés - as well as last night. Tonight I pay for my lack of goodwill towards BC by dining alone.

I don't remember a huge amount about the Spanish food of my childhood. During the walk, I've become reacquainted with crème caramel under its Spanish name of *flan,* as it's a constant on a *menú del dia.* This evening I rediscover noodle soup. It looks a little bit like orange-coloured frogspawn and it's certainly not something that I remember eating at home. I don't know when I last consumed the stuff, but it must have been with my father and that would make it more than a couple of decades ago. I must have stopped eating for a few moments as I trawled my memory in vain for a definite recollection. It's a similar feeling to seeing the Seat 625 cars at Carrión. It's another piece of my childhood coming back to remind me why I'm here. I'm recalled from my trance-like state by the reappearance of the waiter who asks me if everything is fine. I reply in the positive, but find myself holding back tears. I haven't cried about my father for years and I can't believe that my emotions had been activated by a bowl of soup. I feel a bit self-conscious: the restaurant is a lively place – there's much alcohol-induced frivolity behind me as a German and an Italian are celebrating the fact that they've cycled 160km in one day – but rather abruptly, I feel very lonely indeed. I hope to God that Norwegian bloke has put a stop to "sing-along-a Radiohead" for the night.

I may have done the *refugio* an injustice. It's another restful night and it's a good place to have secured a bottom bunk, which I've now decided is the better deal. It is more than just the fear of falling off the top one. Trying to fumble a descent on a dark morning in a confined space in near silence is no easy task. There's a significant risk of trampling on the lower pilgrim and then kicking over their rucksack for good measure. Waking up a dormitory is not a good idea, and experience so far would suggest that you will be earmarked, treated with caution and talked about at pilgrimage meals all the way to Santiago.

The bottom bunk provides safety and gives you a chance to use the space underneath to lay out things for the following day. It's also a convenient place to sit while you're getting dressed, though in this particular case there is a significant risk of smacking my head on the bed above. As there isn't a huge amount of space in any dimension in this dorm, getting dressed is always going to be awkward, but at least it's happening without getting in anyone's way.

One of the reasons I like heading out so early each morning is to look at the last vestiges of the night sky. I don't really pay much attention to the heavenly bodies in normal life, but I'm measuring my time on the Camino by the phases of the moon. The position of the stars has also become familiar and it's got to the stage where I can make a sensible attempt at using them for simple navigation. There is a full complement this morning, their brightness fighting against a lightening sky and they are slightly skewed from their normal position. The path is twisting away in a more northerly direction as we head towards León. This slight change is even more pronounced when the darkness fades away and the sun rises, casting shadows in an unfamiliar direction.

I enjoy it while I can, as there's not a lot of nature about today. After a week of wide panoramas where there has been little in the way of non-pilgrimage related movement, and where motorised vehicles have been pointed at in wonder, we're heading towards the next big city. Inevitably, the walking isn't particularly pleasant. It starts on a path below the main N601 road which is busy with commuter traffic. It is the noise that's the hardest to deal with after 36 hours of almost total stillness; it's abrupt and intimidating. Then there is the visual threat. Matters have to be taken into your own hands on a couple of occasions when the path disappears and the only thing separating you from oncoming traffic is a painted white line at the side of the road. Rather swiftly, you become aware of just how exposed you can be. Today's stage is only 18.5km but there is going to be a huge amount of concentration needed over the next few hours. The contrast between yesterday's walking and today's is staggering and very unnerving. There will be no insect watching today. Those who took the *senda* alternative might have less of a culture clash to deal with but I'm finding traffic more intimidating than I've ever found it before. The Meseta has definitely softened me up.

If the normal road is bad, the terror is cranked up several notches by crossing the bridge at Puente Villarente. It's a long time since I've seen a lorry, let alone shared a crossing with one. Again, there is no pavement and there's only enough space to shuffle sideways next to the railing while facing down the oncoming traffic. There is space but the margin of error is negligible and there's a real worry that a connection with a truck wing mirror could send you sprawling over the parapet and falling helplessly into the river below. It's not a particularly long bridge but crossing it seems to take forever. It you are feeling a bit sleepy when you get to the bridge I can guarantee that you'll be wide-awake at the other end of it, as all the senses heighten and dangers become life-threateningly obvious.

There's a brief respite as a pavement materialises after the bridge but a kilometre further on, a road has to be crossed which gives absolutely no help to the pedestrian whatsoever. It's a couple of lanes of constant movement with cars travelling at speed. If the Meseta represents spiritual death, the walk into León represents a chance to look mortality directly in the eye. If you make it across the road, things get considerably easier. After a couple of hours of brazening it out against the road users, it's back onto a path. Not an attractive path I grant you, it rolls through scrubland and around the back of warehouses as the city comes nearer, but it's much better than the nerve-shredding alternative. If the road into Burgos is incredibly dull, the way into León is a bit too exciting for its own good.

After negotiating oncoming HGVs, feeling your way across the bridge of death, and traversing the road of extinction, there used to be one other chance for fate, or more specifically, motorised transport, to finish you off. This was an unassisted crossing of a dual carriageway with a minimal central reservation. Today appears to be death-wish day. The good news is that this particular dice with death has been eliminated by the building of a footbridge. The bad news is that it isn't open yet. In the meantime, a diversion has been set up which takes in the back of some more warehouses and up a residential street to a hill which overlooks the city. It's a serious detour in terms of time and distance and it's a portentous warning of the walking days to come. As well as the city spread below, the mountains which have been barely in view over the last eight days are now sharply in focus. The days of the flat Meseta are nearly over. The descent into León is down a sandy path that emerges through some trees and it's now that I get my first proper view of the city and its cathedral.

The sizeable diversion, which takes in the first distinct ascent in a couple of days, enables us to cross the dual carriageway about half a kilometre down the road from the unopened footbridge. Once you get into the city, it is a quickish and safe walk through the residential suburbs to get to the central hostel which is situated in a convent.

It is an austere place with a welcome to match. The curfew is half an hour earlier than normal at 9.30pm and I half-expected to be told that this will be followed by fifteen minutes of self-flagellation in the bell tower. It's that kind of place. I suppose the feeling is that if you survive the walk into León, you'll be happy with anything. It certainly hasn't worked with Michael who got here before me, took one look at it and decided to walk straight back out. Given that we pilgrims aren't exactly a fussy bunch when it comes to resting our heads it doesn't bode well. I decide that I am made of sterner stuff and, apart from anything else, I'm knackered. There are some positives; there's a lot of space between the bunks and the floor looks level so it's a visual improvement on last night's experience.

León is the last of the big cities on the Camino before you reach Santiago. It has an Irish pub named *Molly Malone's*, a *Dickens Tavern* and a restaurant called *Captain Haddock*, but I can forgive all of this. It's clean and there is a lot going on. Unlike Burgos, the cars come close to the city centre giving it an occupied and noisy feel. The buildings are a summery ochre colour, with the focal point being the cathedral. It is more understated than the one in Burgos, though I seriously doubt if any building could say the opposite. It is a riot of stained glass which gives the inside a dark, but not sombre, appearance. There's a high vaulted nave and a beautiful rose window. It certainly looks the part and it feels like a church, and I spend the best part of an hour in there just sitting alone with my thoughts and enjoying the reverential silence.

Another famous city building is the former Monasterio Hostal de San Marcos. It was designed for pilgrims but is now geared up for the wealthier traveller as the Parador Nacional. It is audaciously grand with a palace-like facade over 100m long. The arched front door alone is about the size of a living room. I'd like to play the Camino inverse snobbery card here and say that I'm glad I'm staying in my convent because it provides a more authentic experience. Pilgrimages are supposed to be austere, I'm mixing with people going through their own personal trials, and we're sharing the experience of hardship and struggle together. I would be lying, though. I quite fancy a kip in a posh hotel, particularly after seeing tonight's venue, and this certainly looks like the place to do it. With its forced elegance on display, there's a desire to know what the pilgrim of a few hundred years ago would have found inside it and how many people could stay there. I'd also like to know if Spain has other desserts, apart from *flan* and rice pudding. I've decided to stay another day in León but I think a night in the Parador might cost more than my expenses for the entire journey to Santiago. I've decided to book a room in a cheap guesthouse for tomorrow night. It's tiny, and in financial terms, it lies somewhat closer towards the hostel end of the market, though it does have the luxury of a carpet.

León provides that guilty feeling again of being in a big place with enough distractions to take you away from the spirit of the Camino. There is little time for reflection or just being, as you are caught up in a world of shops, museums and people. The ability to slow down is taken out of your hands, and you are surrounded by people who are in constant movement. There is a stark reminder today of the conflict between Camino and urban life, as a German pilgrim has had her passport stolen from her backpack as she was having a drink. It's the first time I've heard of any crime affecting someone on the walk.

As I'm sitting at a café table scribbling postcards, a beer arrives for me that I quite definitely haven't ordered. As I'm about to remonstrate with the waiter I get a tap on my shoulder from a Spanish man who is on his way out of the bar. He points to the beer and says, "For you."

I'm surprised by the random act and if it's his way of buying friends, it certainly works for me.

He then points to my Irish rugby jersey. "You Irish were so friendly to me when I was on holiday there. I love you people."

I just manage to say "gracias" and am about to go to explain that I'm considerably more Spanish than Irish but he moves at greater speed than my brain works in a foreign language, and he's heading down the road with his friends before the right words form in the wrong order. Feelings of guilt well up in me, but I take it as a sign that I have to do something equally kind and random to somebody else on the Camino.

This isn't the first time today that the jersey has led to a misunderstanding. Earlier when I was booking my hotel for tomorrow, I was asked to sign a docket that stated that my nationality was Irish. This was despite the fact that the receptionist took every other detail from my unmistakably U.K. passport. I haven't worn the jersey that often because the weather has been very warm. I'm beginning to wish I had now. My blue England cricket hat, which I wear every day, has barely garnered a comment.

The city is gearing up for a medieval festival. Stalls are being set up and there are strolling minstrels from Oviedo and dancers from Valencia practising their routines. As I am walking around the site of the accompanying market and admiring the tat on display, I'm hailed by Bernard who, needless to say, is sitting in a café with a glass of wine in his hand. With him are most of the diners from the night in Calzadilla. Bernard signals to a waiter to bring another glass but his request either is ignored, or goes unheard. I'm still a short distance away but I shout "jefe" in the direction of the waiter. He turns round with great speed and looks slightly embarrassed. I smile and ask him for a glass and he goes off straight away with some urgency. After the humiliation of trying to pay for a drink in Pamplona, I can't begin to tell you how good this feels. I can't keep the smile off my face, like a baby who has just learned to walk. In the past three weeks, I've inherited some Spanish spirit at last. It

127

feels incredibly significant and I find myself doing a fist pump and shouting "Get in" – something I've never done before in my life. I can feel – really feel - my dad being proud of me. It completely baffles the Francophones, who look on utterly bewildered until I try to explain. The Quebecois woman looks at me curiously and I know what's coming next.

"I thought you were German. You have a German first name."

This is beginning to worry me a bit but I thought the explanation was an easy one. "If I was German and Michael is German. Why were we talking in English to each other the other night?"

The Quebecois woman acknowledges that this was a problem she had thought of before, "I thought you were doing it for us."

"But we spoke French for most of the evening. At least you did and I tried. For everyone's benefit."

Bernard laughs having heard me explain my German problem before to him, but never seen it acted out. "You have a German first name, a Spanish surname and you're wearing an Irish rugby shirt and you tell me your hat is English. I've heard you speak French – well it's nearly French. People will be confused. It's natural."

I can't really argue with that. I was rather hoping for a bit more dissent from the others though, when it came to Bernard's assessment of my linguistic ability.

A couple of wines later we are on a search for something to eat. This takes us to Plaza San Martin, and a restaurant which appears to specialise in Desperate Dan-like meals. For once, we ignore the *menú del dia* and decide to splash out on the local delicacy which is lamb's feet. Delicious though it is, I can't really enjoy it and it is nothing to do with the food or company. All the Francophones are staying in León's other hostel which is further away from the city centre, but has a positively decadent curfew of 11pm. I have to keep looking at my watch, as I have to return to the Middle Ages for 9.30pm. It is hard to relax and eat when you know you've got to run back in a short time to make sure you're not locked out. This causes great amusement among the other diners who enjoy the teasing. It doesn't help matters knowing that I got lost on my way to the convent earlier in the day. I'm not at my best running drunkenly down cobbled streets in sandals in a geographically complicated part of town.

I make it back with seconds to spare and find myself gate-crashing a sing-song in the back yard. I get in just as a Russian girl is explaining that she is going to sing an old Russian song about "a soldier who is going to die in the morning and he writes a letter to his wife". So, a couple of notches up on the cheerfulness scale from Radiohead then. After the dirge, a nun arrives and announces that she plays the guitar too. By the way she grabs it I think for one majestic second that she is going to play it with her teeth. Who knows - we might have had a chorus of *The Wind Cries Mary*. Sadly, the instrument is then passed to the previous evening's Norwegian and the opening chords of *Street Spirit* ring out again. Mercifully, the nun gives us the option of being led quite literally to sanctuary, for night prayers in the convent chapel. Never has a bit of Latin seemed so attractive.

There were about twenty nuns in evidence for evening prayers, matched by a similar number of pilgrims. The service was a little disjointed as we didn't know when to join in, or even if we were supposed to. It was pleasant and it almost took my mind off the fact that a quarter of a mile away, some of my friends were getting slowly and meaningfully drunk. The solemnity worked for me because against all odds, I have a great sleep.

Yesterday I met the Canadians, Brian and Herb, whom I hadn't seen since AM (ante Meseta). They were having a rest day in the city and had stayed in the convent the night before. I think it is fair to say they were less than impressed. They tipped me off about what happens in the morning and they were absolutely spot on; I was prepared for battle. At around 6am there was a mad scramble to the bathroom, hardly surprising given that there are only two sinks, two showers, and two toilets in a very confined space. I was up fifteen minutes earlier, and breezed through my ablutions as chaos started to build around me.

The hostel promises breakfast but there is only table space for about twenty people – enough for about a fifth of those staying. It looks cramped, and I decide to give it a miss fearing that restricted elbow movement may prevent me from eating anything anyway. I'm followed out into the waking city by some Brazilians who think I'm following the Camino out of town. What I'm actually doing is wandering around trying to find a place to mail my postcards. I suppose I could have told them…

It is a lovely solitary day, which involves revisiting the cathedral and checking the way out of the city for tomorrow morning. It's not easy to navigate your way out of any sizeable place on the Camino, and things have been made worse here by the overnight growth of the medieval market. The new tents and stalls have blocked out many of the way markings. Considering I'm taking part in the ultimate medieval activity, I feel very disconnected to what's going on. There's a demonstration of folk dancing in the street, along with falconry displays, plus the fully occupied stalls selling New Age tat, sweets and various sword and chivalry themed rubbish. There's also the highest concentration of busking statues that I've ever seen in my life.

The city is full of familiar faces. Bernard is staying in León for an extra day as well, and I also bump into Jim and Sue and have a drink with them. Rather sensibly, they've decided to avoid the convent and are staying in a hotel for a couple of days. Sue went to a convent school in Australia and clearly wants to keep as much of a distance from nuns as she possibly can. Jim's delighted as his dream of sleeping in a real bed is going to come true. I also see Caitlin a couple of times. She still has the Italian man and Manuela in tow, and we only have a brief conversation in which she describes all the places she has stayed in since Burgos, forgetting that we have seen each other since then, and throws in the occasional tedious anecdote to illustrate her point. In one pilgrimage guide, it suggests that pilgrims should be open-minded and shouldn't judge others. That's me totally buggered then, and I'm not alone.

In the evening, the city's bars are packed and the market is also heaving. It is all rather loud and slightly overwhelming, and the coping strategy is to sit, observe, and not get involved. A Mendelssohn concert is taking place in the cathedral - I can see Michael in the queue for it - but I have an odd urge to be alone; always a bit tricky on a Friday night in a big city. I sit on a bench opposite and look at the facade as the evening sunlight fades and the blue sky goes through the gears towards darkness. The moon is almost full and I think back to the morning when I left Viana when it was little more than a wispy crescent. There are a lot of families out, and small children are bouncing footballs, while others are being pushed on small tricycles by their parents. I watch them with an odd mix of envy and nostalgia. My dad must have done the same things with me, but of course, I can't remember them, and right now it hurts. This will be an unmemorable evening for all of them, and it really shouldn't be. It is the very ordinariness of it all that makes me feel sad.

When I head back to my guesthouse I become conscious of the fact even though I'm staying in a place without a curfew, and have greater freedom to come and go, it has resulted in me going to bed at exactly the same time as yesterday. My room overlooks the Plaza

Major, where a temporary stage has been built and there is a band warming up by playing some Celtic music. Oh God....

Sure enough, my sleep is disturbed by the sound of accordions, mandolins, and general drunken revelry. Anyone would think it was a Friday night in a major city. The concert eventually winds down at about 2.30am, but what I didn't know is that Plaza Major has a fruit market on Saturdays, and once the music stops, the vans start moving in to set up. It's better than the snoring, but only just. It certainly explains why the hotel owner was grinning like a concussed nun when she took my money.

The walk out of León is not an easy one, even when you've recced it. There are no major physical challenges but the route is not direct, particularly when there's a medieval market in the way. You do get a farewell tour past the best buildings the city has to offer, guided by brass scallop shells embedded in the pavement. It takes in the cathedral before going in a roundabout way to the front of the Gaudi-designed Casa de Botines, before passing the Parador. Due to its convoluted and illogical nature, the way out possibly owes more to the León Tourist Office than to Camino tradition. Then again, there is little danger of being knocked over a bridge by a truck.

I have enjoyed the city but having a rest day now somehow doesn't feel right. León, like all the cities I've walked through, has always been an integral part of the pilgrimage route but even so, urban life seems like an anomaly on the Camino. The problem is one of perspective. Because of their size, it's easy to consider a city to be more important than places like Hornillos del Camino or Puente de Reina, when in reality each place has the same value. They are different but they are equally part of the same experience. By giving myself an extra day in León and Burgos, their importance becomes exaggerated. Approaching a city on the Camino is a bit like promising yourself a post-pub kebab: you look forward to it and guiltily enjoy it when you start, but just afterwards, you really wish you hadn't bothered. I like both Burgos and León and would happily visit both of them again but I am finding out that they don't really fit in with what I want the Camino experience to be.

There is nothing wrong with rest days, but maybe they should be more arbitrary. A lot of hostels don't take kindly to you having an extra night so it's understandable why it's attractive to stay in the cities where there are other places to stay. In addition, it has to be said that, time-wise, Burgos and León are well positioned for days off. A more Camino-intense option to a complete pilgrimage-free day is to choose to walk shorter distances and have more overnight stays. It would mean stopping over in places like Sahagún, which, having heard the opinions of other pilgrims, I really wish I'd spent more time in.

The excitement of coming to a big city is negated somewhat by the walks in and out of them. The walk out resembles the way in, through dreary suburbs and an industrial estate, though without the potentially lethal encounters with traffic. It's easily a good couple of hours of urban hiking along wide pavements, which eventually take you to the unattractive district of La Virgen del Camino. Its romantic name comes from 1505 when the Virgin Mary appeared to a shepherd and asked him to throw a stone, promising that a chapel will be built where it landed. If you want sheep now, you will have to seek out a kebab shop but there is still a church here - a basilica no less. It dates from the 1950s and is a good example of why you should never give an architect a pencil and a bottle of vodka at the same time. You can certainly describe it as striking, but I am hard pushed to find positive adjectives for it. It is grey, angular, and looks like a fan heater propped up on stone legs. Thirteen tall, thin, bronze statues, representing the Virgin herself and the twelve disciples of Jesus, decorate the façade. The whole complex is overlooked by a towering concrete crucifix, which looks like an electricity pylon and doubles up as a bell tower. I am sure its design is lauded in some circles but I can't take to it at all. It does fit in with its surroundings, in that there is nothing even slightly attractive about La Virgen del Camino; its purpose seems to be to prolong the city boundaries along a major artery. Thankfully, it is León's last fling.

I could continue to walk along this route but there is a more rural option, though initially this is merely relative. I head left at a fork and follow the yellow arrows which lead away from the main road, and along bridges which cross motorways and a railway. The countryside eventually takes over again but it is not the unfiltered, rustic topography of the days before León. There are still grain fields, but they are mixed with scrubland and trees. I am easing out of the Meseta and in a couple of days' time, it will be back to the mountains. I'll miss the plain. I have loved its sparseness and placidity, from the lumpy lunar fields of the first few days to now. I have enjoyed the endless horizons and its silence and simplicity. I have never experienced anything like it before, and it is as far removed as possible from any vision of Spain that I had previously. I have walked through spiritual death and really enjoyed it. There has been luck involved, as the rain in Spain stayed mainly off the plain. One day of torrential downpour falling on the shelterless upland could have made it a completely different experience.

After about 25km of uneventful walking, I get to Villar de Mazarife. It is a place of colourful buildings and total serenity. Well, I thought so until I noticed the crosses nailed to outside walls; I may just be entering vampire country. My fears are not particularly assuaged by a man coming out of his house, pointing a broom skywards and ranting unintelligibly for a few minutes. Some of the houses are truly elegant but, like Calzadilla de los Hermanillos a few days ago, there are a few buildings with the forbidding steel shutters and doors - a strange sight in an otherwise tidy-looking village.

Despite its air of remoteness, it quite definitely looks inhabited. There are people washing cars, walking dogs and tidying gardens. Around five hundred people live here and it looks like the perfect antidote to those who want an easy commute to León but don't want to live there. There are a couple of shops, with one of them filling the traditional role of stocking everything that the under-resourced pilgrim needs. There are three *refugios* here and, judging by the lack of pilgrimage traffic on this alternative route, I stand an outside chance of getting a dorm to myself.

There is a logic to my choice of shelter. I decided to invoke the spirit of Agés, which now seems a very long time ago, and select the one that is situated above a bar. After doing my washing and having a walk around the village, I have a quick look around the church of St James and then reacquaint myself with the joys of thoughtful idleness – something that was virtually impossible to achieve in the noise of León. Sitting down and watching what little of the world that is on show comes very easily indeed.

Food is served at 7pm. I'm definitely staying in the right place, as a few minutes later, pilgrims start coming in from other *refugios*.

Sadly, one of them is Caitlin - no wonder the locals have crosses nailed to their walls. She walks in on her own but I'm convinced that she doesn't do "by herself" and I'm proved right. She spots me straightaway and totally fails to get her brain in gear before her mouth starts to motor. Seconds later Jim and Sue walk in and they are followed by a rather lovely German woman who witnessed "the ranting man with the broomstick" incident with me. They settle at a different table and I lose my chance of interesting dinner conversation and a possible clumsy attempt to talk to another pilgrim in a language I can barely speak.

Caitlin has a favourite mantra this evening, which is "Everybody has a story", but all I hear is hers. She refers to meeting interesting pilgrims but doesn't go on to elaborate. Over the main course, she tries to link the beauty of the Meseta with the music of Elton John. Apparently, I haven't lived until I've walked across that lonely landscape with the sound of *Can You Feel the Love Tonight?* blasting out of an iPod. Off-hand, I can't think of anything worse. I don't know of any other pilgrim who's brought an iPod with them, or even thought about it. It seems to defeat the purpose of getting back to nature and the essence of pilgrimage. It probably explains why she's not particularly good with quiet and didn't enjoy the Meseta too much in its natural state. She briefly tells me that her improvised walking group of Alessandro the Italian man and Manuela has splintered, due to Alessandro's romantic interest in Manuela and Manuela's lack of romantic interest in him. I know they were certainly together yesterday afternoon in León because I saw them. She offers no further information on where they might be and continues on her theme of matching a day on the Camino with a song. I've made the decision that if she mentions Celine Dion she's getting murdered and I'm reasonably certain that no jury in the world will convict me. In the subsequent monologue, it's clear that Depeche Mode's *Enjoy the Silence* won't get a mention.

At the end of the meal, we are given a complimentary glass of orujo, a drink distilled from grape skins and seemingly diluted with paraffin. It is questionable whether its gift is a gesture of hospitality or a veiled threat. I remember it from previous trips to Spain because one of my relatives used to make it, even though no one in the family would go near it. I am not the most discerning of drinkers. In moments of stupidity, I've knocked back Swedish whisky, Czech pastis and the soapy water that passes for beer in Luxembourg but, after a quick sip from the glass in front of me, I decide to follow in the Noriega tradition by drawing the line at orujo. Caitlin knocks it back effortlessly and finishes my glass off as well.

I keep an eye on Jim and Sue's table and at the first possible moment after they've finished eating and space becomes free I join them, albeit with Caitlin in tow. They're staying around the corner and are not too impressed with the accommodation.

It did offer a meal but Jim scowls and says in a disapproving Australian drawl, "It was vegetarian and we weren't having that."

It turns out that they have planned the rest of the route to Santiago and know where they're going to stop every night for the next two weeks. Normal pilgrimage conversations don't go much beyond the next day's destination and I'm reasonably certain that's how Jim and Sue have planned their walk so far. Santiago still is as far away to me as it was on day one. I'm not even sure where I'm heading tomorrow and I'm torn between a short day's walking of about 16km to Hospital de Órbigo, which is where Jim and Sue are heading, or pushing myself to a 30km plus blockbuster that will take me to Astorga. Caitlin is undecided but is edging towards the shorter day, which might inspire me to put a bit of distance between her and me. The hike to Astorga isn't flat. It is also 7km more than I walked today, and 2.5km more than I've walked on any stage before. Is it worth putting myself through that just because I find Caitlin a bit annoying? Then I think of Elton John singing *Can You Feel the Love Tonight?* and decide that the answer is an emphatic "Yes".

It takes a certain skill to kick over a rucksack, which dislodges a chair, which in turn knocks over some walking poles, in a dormitory that has the highest space-to-bunk ratio on the entire Camino. I can't even blame alcohol, as I went to bed relatively sober last night. Just about the only thing I do right this morning is not switch on the lights. Luckily, the consequences aren't too great. There are two bunks in the room but only one other bed is filled. I know absolutely nothing about my roommate apart from the fact that he's male. We didn't speak to each other at all last night and I imagine that he won't be in a hurry to talk to me today. He remains motionless in his sleeping bag as almost everything else in the room clatters to the floor, though he is possibly harbouring murderous thoughts.

There is a breakfast advertised but nobody seems to be occupying the bar. After a bit of hanging around, I head out and meet an advance party of Germans who were staying in one of the other *refugios*. For the first time in a fortnight, rain spots start to darken the road, which fits in with the forecast I saw on the television yesterday evening. It means a bit of readjusting, which is just as well as the dull pain in my right shoulder has reoccurred. I put on my rucksack cover, which dislodges both my water bottles which now sink inaccessibly to its bottom. I also take out the dreaded poncho and am quickly reminded me why I really hate it. It takes a couple of unnatural spasm movements to get it over my body and rucksack. The rucksack cover is probably fine on its own but I don't want to take the risk. The uncomfortable action is accompanied by swearing and cursing and consists of the first coherent and grammatically correct words of Spanish I've uttered since I entered the country. After taking a few minutes to get into shape for wet weather trekking, the rain stops almost immediately though the swearing definitely continues.

I stay on this road for well over an hour - thankfully it stays largely traffic free - and enjoy the last part of relative flatness I'm going to encounter on the Camino. The mountains are worryingly close now and tomorrow I'll be a good couple of hundred metres higher than I am now. For the best part of the last fortnight, the daily variation in height has barely exceeded 60m, and significant climbs have been rare.

I arrive in Hospital de Órbigo after about three hours. I may regret my decision not to rest here overnight, as it is in contention for the nicest place I haven't stayed in. The centrepiece is a thirteenth-century bridge supported by twenty arches of varying sizes that crosses the Río Órbigo. At about 300m, it's the longest one on the entire Camino. Back in 1434 a knight, Suero de Quinones, decided that he would fight every *caballero* who came across the bridge on the thirty days around St James' Day. This belligerent declaration had nothing to do with drunken bravado and everything to do with an affair of the heart. He did this to free himself from the fetters around his neck that he wore every Thursday as a symbol of his unrequited love for a noble woman. When it came to the fighting he hedged his bets a bit by roping in nine of his friends to help him, and together they dispatched one hundred and sixty-six knights, allowing de Quinones to free himself from the shackles of love. Ah, the things they did before agony columns, therapy, and Jeremy Kyle. What the slain cavaliers thought about being attacked unprovoked by a lovesick madman is alas not recorded.

The Camino goes right over the bridge and there is a bar at either end, a superior bit of town planning. It then goes along the main street until the town ends rather abruptly. It is only 10.30am and the earliest that a hostel is likely to open is not for another couple of hours. There's a really strong desire to stay here. It's an impressive and beautiful place but it feels like an act of laziness to stop and hang around after what feels like a short walk, so I decide to push on. This means committing myself to Astorga and passing the 30km in a day mark for the first time.

It's another day of alternative routes and I decide to go for the slightly longer path option, rather than walking along the main road. The way into León is still fresh in the memory, and I'm not sure I can deal with the noise. There are also more villages attached to this option, which means comfortable places to stop, and more water filling opportunities. It will, however, put another 3km on the journey, so whether this will make sense at the end of the day remains to be seen. Either way, it's still a long way to Astorga and it's all uphill.

As the morning progresses, this decision climbs the charts rapidly to become the worst I've made so far. The next few hours sap the energy cruelly, not helped by the path below my feet. I walk on a surface of red sand and loose pebbles, which falls and mainly rises across the rough countryside. The early spots of rain this morning were replaced by an optimistic blue sky but, since Hospital de Órbigo, the horizon has been mottled and grey. The sky has mirrored my mood. It's stayed dry, but the humidity is significant. I traipse up and down through lumpy fields, my straining ankles acknowledging every shift in gradient. There's also a sense of loneliness; since Hospital, I've barely seen anyone else. This is not the place to break down or get injured. Water may be easy to find but help certainly isn't. After the hill climb to Sanitibáñez de Valdeiglesias, there's 16km of nothing until my destination. This now has all the hallmarks of a really badly thought-out day and one that's been undertaken for completely the wrong reasons. Hospital de Órbigo is looking more and more attractive the further I walk away from it.

Somehow, the Camino is looking after me. Just as things are getting difficult and more and more negative thoughts spiral inside my head, a short attritional climb up the side of a field reveals an almost mirage-like view of wonderment and relief. Another group of people has set up an improvised stall next to a barn. It is well over two hours since I passed through a village and, indeed, last saw anybody at all. The vision lifts the despondency, and several hours of accumulated negativity disappear in seconds as fruit juice and other assorted calories are taken in. I also have the novelty of talking to some fellow walkers. There are about half a dozen of them - all Spanish - who look as relieved as I feel. I haven't seen any of them before, and the reason for this is that they only started their Camino in León. Part of me wants to indulge in pilgrimage one-upmanship and boast about crossing the Pyrenees and experiencing spiritual death, but I don't. The fact is I'm absolutely delighted to see them, and their presence banishes the negative aspects of walking in total isolation.

Just as welcome as the drinks stop is my first sight of the towers of Astorga Cathedral. Every now and then, you get a sense of what it must have been like to undertake the Camino hundreds of years ago, and this view is one of them. There's a sense of achievement and history in getting here. A few minutes later, I come to the cross of San Toribio. It's a famous pilgrimage landmark where, according to legend, the former bishop of Astorga cleaned his sandals after being expelled from the town after being falsely accused of a misdemeanour. So incensed was he that he didn't even want to take the dust of the town with him. I look down on my shoes and can still notice specks of the red clay of La Rioja on them from a couple of weeks ago.

One of the skills I've picked up on the Camino is to measure distance in terms of walking time, and the guess is that my destination is just over an hour away. Although you look down on Astorga from San Toribio, the town is built on a hilltop and has a fort-like quality to it. This means that it's a down and up walk to get to it, and the body is suffering a bit. It's back on a road to get there, and the final hill into Astorga nearly finishes me off. It isn't particularly steep but it comes at the end of a lengthy day which hasn't really been comfortable since I left Hospital de Órbigo about four hours before.

Happily, my shelter for the evening is situated right at the entrance to the town. From the back, it looks a bit like Colditz, but it turns out to be a warm and welcoming place. Inside it is decorated with blue highlights and waves, which make it look like a sports centre swimming pool, while feeling a bit like a school. It's the largest hostel I've stayed in so far with one hundred and fifty beds, but it has been divided up in a complicated way into several small dormitories. As it turns out, I'm in one with five women and in keeping with the pilgrimage theme of the day, I haven't seen any of them before. Like all other places you stay in, you have to sign in. I'm right at the bottom of today's page and am the only one staying here so far who started in France. There are only three people who didn't begin in León

Astorga is really rather lovely. It's big enough to be interesting but doesn't feel like a town. It is Roman in origin but became an important pilgrimage stopping point in the eleventh century, as it's where the Camino Francés and another route, the Via de la Plata which starts in Seville, intersect. As the land isn't particularly suited to agriculture, the local commerce depended on the carrying trade. One result of this is that Astorga developed a chocolate industry, as cocoa was transported through the town from the ports on the

Galician coast. There are shops devoted to the stuff and there's even a chocolate museum. There's also a museum dedicated to ham, and if I can find one that has a similar reverence for alcohol I'm moving here permanently and bugger the Camino. Regrettably, in keeping with the dismal planning which has dominated my day, I have arrived in food heaven on a Sunday and absolutely sweet football association is open.

Perhaps the most famous building here is the Palacio Episcopal or Bishop's Palace, which houses the Camino Museum. It was designed by Gaudi and, like his Casa de Botines in León, it's the usual striking display of turrets and fairy tale touches. I can't vouch for the interior because, not surprisingly, it's closed. Rather strangely, so too is the Catedral de Santa María. I assume this is because of renovation work rather than taking religious observance in directions that were surely never intended.

It is a lively place, even on a greying evening. The terrace bars are busy with families, and there are children running around in the squares, presumably looking around to find something other than a bar that's open. It may be regarded as a bit of a heresy but for once, I'm pleased to be somewhere that is not exclusively occupied by walkers. It's also a happy town; everybody seems to be smiling and this can't help but rub off on me, on a day when smiling, has been something of an effort. Despite the tiredness of a lengthy walk, there is a feeling of rejuvenation taking place. I manage to find a mass to go to in a church near my *refugio,* and then stumble across a rare shop with an open door, which specialises in local produce. There are rows and rows of butter biscuits, along with chocolate in slabs you could tile a roof with. You can buy chocolate flavoured with practically anything, and it comes in a variety of colours. Purely for research purposes, I buy a couple of hefty bars, one pink and the other orange. I'm not sure how attractive it is to eat something that looks as if it glows in the dark but hey, it's chocolate. The extra weight may be a problem tomorrow, but I can always use them to fend off potential bandits and muggers.

Astorga isn't short of places to eat, and I settle down in a large *comedor* which has an even split of pilgrims and natives. Just as I'm about to attack my pork and chips, my roommate from the previous evening comes in. The first instinct is that I have been hunted down for the crimes against sleep committed this morning, but it turns out that his appearance is a total coincidence. We share a chatty meal, which is a bit strange considering that we didn't speak to each other at all yesterday. I put this down to another change in the Camino spirit, and it's not a positive one. After several weeks on the trail, we have become used to seeing people and then not seeing them, so we have stopped being overtly friendly as a matter of course. Why invest the effort if this is the only time we meet? However, when we do see someone again familiarity becomes a lot more important and reassuring. Having spoken to a few people in the hostel and in cafés this evening, it's clear that there's a change happening in all of us as the Camino enters its next stage, but I can't put my finger on what it is. Conversations sound different, attitudes have altered, and those of us who started in France are not the same people now. We are also mixing with the newcomers who have begun with the finishing line already in sight. We can all be classified as pilgrims, but that is where the uniformity ends.

I enjoy a deep sleep that can only come with contented exhaustion. It's an interesting walk today. The Meseta is finally over and today's stage heads consistently uphill for around 25km. The early rays of morning light up a green valley and give some scary definition to the approaching mountains. The days of big skies and wide huge vistas are in the past, and we are heading into the region known as the Maragateria.

I have to admit that I didn't know a lot about the history of the area before my walk, but I soon discovered that nobody else really does either. Even the origins of the word are obscure, and theories range from it coming from the eighth century King Mauregato of Asturias, to being the name given to the offspring of Moorish-Gothic immigrants from Mauretania. There's also a much less romantic theory that it's simply a corruption of the word *Mercader,* which means merchant. The area has its own ethnicity and the people here are described as proud and strong in character. What can't be disputed is that they made their living from the carrying trade which, apart from cocoa, meant the transportation of fish and precious metals. With the arrival of the railway, the trade collapsed, and people started to migrate out of the region in search of employment. The result of this is that many of the settlements were abandoned. Nowadays the area consists of about five thousand people stretched over about fifty villages. The Camino goes right through the middle of it.

There is a threat of rain in the air and there is a constant battle in the sky with grey fighting blue, creating dramatic shading on the world below. It's about an hour before I get to the first village of the region. There's not a lot to Murias de Rechivaldo, but what there is shows no signs of any degeneration. It's little more than a road, but there is a bar which provides a useful stopping place for breakfast. Soon afterwards, road turns into path, and this is followed by the first significant shift uphill of the day.

Eventually, I stumble into El Ganso. While some of the villages of the Maragateria are undergoing something of a revival because of the Camino, this place is bucking the trend. Even the more prosperous places I've walked through today have abandoned housing but here it's difficult to find anywhere that looks occupied at all. It's eerily silent. Many of the grey stone buildings don't look as if they've been inhabited for years. Some have roofs missing and are overgrown with weeds. You can't help thinking about who once lived here and under what circumstances they left. There is also a question about what it would take to make it have a future. Under a dull sky, and with the wind blowing, it looks more desolate than anywhere else I have come across so far, possibly in my life.

People do live here though, and there are a couple of places to stay. Also in El Ganso is one of the Camino's best-known non-religious landmarks; the *Meson Cowboy*, an American western themed bar. It's not the most salubrious of places; it looks like a converted garage, but the owner has tried to make an effort. There are Stetsons attached to the walls and hanging from the ceiling. A couple of guitars are carefully arranged on shelves, and pictures of cowboys placed behind the bar. Even with a few western themed paintings on the walls, there is no way on the planet that you're going to imagine Calamity Jane or Jesse James propping up the bar. This would be an odd place anywhere in the world, but in somewhere as isolated as El Ganso it's positively freakish. There are no swinging saloon doors to walk through, and although I'm not greeted with a "howdy partner", the welcome is friendly, and it has to be said that the cheese *bocadillo* is superb. I'm joined by several other walkers whose bemused looks when they come into the bar are a sight to behold. Possibly all this walking is making us have a group hallucination.

The path out of El Ganso follows a largely deserted road which has been slashed carelessly through woodland. There is anxiety about the weather as the gaps in the sky have closed up and the threat of rain is now turning into a promise; it's just a case of when. I'm lucky; I'm heading out of Rabanal del Camino when the generous drops start to fall. The original plan was to walk a further 6km to Foncebadón, but with the heavens looking unyielding, it makes sense to call it a day here. I've achieved a respectable 23km and, as I would be walking uphill and visibility is fading, it feels a bit reckless to continue. I am also suffering a bit. Today has been a bit of a toil and this could easily be a knock-on from yesterday's 30km effort. I can feel the stones under my feet and I've been particularly good at stubbing my toes all day.

It's not a bad place to stop either. Rabanal is another favourite pilgrimage haunt. Again it's little more than one upwardly sloping main road but it's a place which has done well out of the revival of the Camino. Most of the houses look smart and the number of empty properties is small. It feels inhabited, if not necessarily lively. There are four *refugios* here, one of which is run by the British Confraternity of St James. Regrettably, it isn't opening for a couple of hours and this isn't the day for hanging around so I head off elsewhere. There's an open hostel situated away from the main drag, with a rectangular courtyard which I'm sure must be lively when the weather's a bit more favourable. A covered bar sensibly takes up one side while opposite is the main dormitory; a big, one-roomed place with about sixty beds in it. Basic food is provided - but amongst Rabanal's other attractions are several restaurants, one of which boasts an English menu advertising "friek eggs" followed by "custard sing" and I'm not going to miss out on trying those.

It is noticeably cold in Rabanal and there is close to nothing to do. The rain certainly doesn't help. I'm getting used to doing nothing, and indeed, I'm trying to embrace it. I positively enjoyed the lazy afternoons of contemplation in Hornillos del Camino and Mazarife but "being" is hard going today. I don't see any of the regular walkers either and although the hostel gradually fills up, all the faces are strange ones. Many are taking advantage of the covered courtyard bar and there is certainly a relaxed, chatty and cheerful atmosphere.

The palpable change in pilgrimage conversations since León is particularly evident here, and I now realise what the difference is. Sometime tomorrow morning we will be reaching the highest point of the Camino: the iron cross on the summit of Monte Irago, but nobody is talking about the next day at all. The emphasis now is all about reaching Santiago. It's now not just Jim and Sue who have planned the rest of their walking schedule. There are people at the courtyard bar comparing notes and future itineraries, even though there is still by my calculations the best part of a fortnight and a third of the journey to go. I don't know if this is because of the high number of new pilgrims who only started the walk a couple of days ago, but something now appears to have been lost. Before we only talked about our plans for the following 24 hours and never really looked beyond it, but now there are people predicting where they will be in a week's time. It feels like the rest of the Camino is being wished away rather than being appreciated in the moment. A big city like León has enough international familiarity in its shops, buses and way of life to remind a pilgrim of what they've left behind and for some, that's their ultimate destination – a return to normality. There really is a sense among the walkers propping up the bar that the difficult part of the pilgrimage is behind them, or indeed never existed in the first place. I don't want to lose the sense of being fully absorbed in the day I'm living in, nor do I feel like tempting fate. In the past, pilgrims were well aware of the mountain passes to come where they were vulnerable to bandits and wolves. Those dangers may be gone and feasibly the greatest worry to the modern pilgrim is overdosing on meatballs, but there are still a lot more steps before any of us make it to Santiago.

I need some way of reconnecting with the idea of pilgrimage and this could be provided by Rabanal's monastery. There are no ancient footsteps to be walked into here - it was founded in 2001 by a German group of Benedictine monks. Every evening they sing Vespers in a tiny church which is in the process of being restored. If the monks are relative newcomers to Rabanal, the church certainly isn't. It's rumoured to have been built by the Knights Templars in the twelfth century. There are only two monks present this evening, and if the singing is left to them it would be fine. As we all have hymn sheets, some of my fellow pilgrims decide to join in and the solo voices of those versed in Latin are drowned out by the untrained enthusiasm of the masses. This rather deadens what could have been a moment of significance and spirituality, and turns it into a form of ecclesiastical karaoke. It is still an energising experience but it could have been so much more.

It is enough to drive me to drink, but unfortunately, I manage to choose a restaurant for my evening meal that has instigated wine rationing. Like most pilgrims, I survive on one big meal a day and it usually comes with a full bottle of red. Tonight there is no bottle and they haven't exactly been friendly with the size of the glass either. After the singing I've just heard, I could keep them in business all night. It might also be useful to knock me out tonight as the dormitory is going to be full and I'm guessing it isn't going to be quiet. I decide to pass on "custard sing". I've had enough singing for one evening.

I try to delay my departure today as I have romantic visions of watching the sunrise as I head uphill through the Puerto de Foncebadón towards Monte Irago. There is no chance of that dream working out. Mountain mist has descended and visibility is minimal. It's a tough if relatively short slog to Foncebadón, and along the way, the mist condenses into rain. It's also the coldest day of the Camino so far and there are fragile ice crystals forming on my fleece. The village at one stage enjoyed royal protection under the condition that the inhabitants looked after pilgrims and the path they walked on. At some point, there was a monastery here but the place lay totally abandoned for most of the twentieth century. It is cited now as a place that is being revived because of the new interest in the Camino. Even so, its standing population can be measured in single figures.

I can't make any judgments about the village because when I get there visibility doesn't stretch beyond a couple of metres, which gives it an intense ghostly quality. This feeling is enhanced by hearing noises of activity without actually being able to see what is going on. I can tell you there's a cross in the middle of the street, which I don't see until I nearly kick its plinth, but that's about all. And I thought El Ganso was God-forsaken. The only definite sign of life I come across is right at the end of the village when I narrowly avoid a head-on collision with a very angry looking goat who possesses sharpened horns and a bad attitude that is easily discernible despite the poor visibility.

It's another hour before I reached the Cruz de Ferro – the iron cross – which stands 1500m above sea level and represents the highest point of the entire Camino. I'm expecting something massive and ostentatious but the cross is about a metre high and perched on top of what looks like a telegraph pole. Traditionally, pilgrims are supposed to bring a stone from their own country and lay it at the foot of the pole to symbolise the sin that they have carried with them. The only thing I've carried of similar weight is a bar of Astorga's chocolate and I've only had that in my backpack since yesterday. The only reason it's still there is because I completely forgot I had it until I saw its rather radioactive looking pink glow this morning as I was packing.

Rather than sensing anything symbolic, my first reaction to this significant monument is one of disappointment. From a misty distance, it looks like a rubbish tip, and as you get closer it actually looks even worse. There are bits of paper, randomly strewn shoes and postcards in among the stones. It looks like the washed up flotsam from a shipwreck. It is not easy on the eye at all and I come close to hastily dismissing the entire thing. It's only when you walk up the cairn that supports the pole, which is strewn with these objects that it starts to make some kind of sense. Each abandoned item represents a petition for prayers: nearly all of them have messages written on them, as do many of the stones themselves. It's not really a morning to linger anywhere but I look at a few of the messages and feel overcome by the sorrow I read about. There are multilingual petitions for every form of human tragedy that you can imagine. A story written on the sole of tiny shoe relates the story of a child's last day after a long battle against a heart condition, and reading it feels like an intrusion. Even the casual way I picked it up seems wrong. Many of my fellow pilgrims have been walking with similar burdens, I'm sure, but they're never revealed. I don't know what BC or Caitlin's motives are for walking to Santiago. Behind the friendly exteriors, Michael, Jim and Sue, Brian and Herb, and any of the dozens of people I've spoken to over the past few weeks, may harbour personal tragedies on a par with those here. This is where the private becomes public and regardless of my initial feelings for this geographically-based shrine, it's clearly important for others.

I always struggle with visible signs of human prayer. It makes me feel small because it shows a depth of faith I just don't have. What was an eyesore just a couple of minutes before has suddenly become very moving indeed. While I'm reading some of the prayers and feeling guilty for being a grumpy pilgrim, there is a magical moment when the cloud lifts completely and a blue sky is seen above. Intense sunlight shimmers on the mountaintop for about a minute before the clouds roll back over and the mist closes in again.

Monte Irago also has a chapel, an unattractive modern addition to the setting. If every step on the pilgrimage is a prayer and every stone and object a petition, it feels unnecessary. It's as if the church is trying to take control of the personal petitions of the individual.

On this particular morning, it's closed anyway which rather defeats the purpose of it being there. Even if it were open, it's the iron cross and the messages at the foot of it that are more likely to inspire and provoke prayer. Not too far away is a stone platform with complicated instructions on how to be part of a human sundial. There won't be many takers on a day like today.

As well as reaching the highest point of the Camino, I'm likely to be descending about a kilometre today, by far the biggest drop in altitude on any stage of the route. It's twice as long as the descent on day one and so the potential for things going wrong is significant and it's not too far away from my thoughts. After about 200m of walking, the mist line fades away and, not for the first time, the reintroduction to a world of colour serves to lighten the spirits. I'm also lifted by the familiar sight of a nearly full moon posing elegantly in a blue sky. It's somehow comforting to see it again. It's also a relief to come across the hamlet of Manjarín.

Manjarín has a resident population of exactly one, which makes it the only place I have ever visited that has more signs advertising its presence than inhabitants. The man who keeps it alive is called Tomas. His house is the only one of a total of seven that is habitable, and even that is pushing it a bit. It doubles up as a *refugio* with spaces for about twenty people, and is obviously the spot to head to for those who wish to enjoy a more primal Camino experience than I'm prepared to undertake. Heating is supplied by solar panelling and open fires, and a communal meal is provided for his guests, along with weather information and a bit of Gregorian chant. He also supplies tea and coffee on a *donativo* basis to passing pilgrims, which is why I'm here. It's a good job he exists because there is nothing else for miles. There is a look of an improvised protest camp as you approach, but rarely has a warm drink been so appreciated. Thousands of pilgrims every year must feel the same thing. I have spent a lot of time speculating about the people who serve the Camino: those who look after accommodation or restaurants for the benefit of those whom they see only fleetingly. I'm also fascinated by the people who appear at exactly the right moment, for me at least, to provide food and drink for pilgrims. Of course, they get some money for their efforts but it must be a strange existence. In Tomas's case, it has to be a tough one too, but he will see more

151

smiles and experience more goodwill in a day than most of us see in a year.

The path levels out a bit after Manjarín before the descent begins in earnest. It still feels treacherous underfoot with exposed rock looking like submerged tree-trunks, worn smooth by hundreds of years of pilgrimage traffic. The path clings to the side of a mountain while a road twists and turns below. While I prod ahead carefully with my sticks, the air fills with the yells of cycling pilgrims enjoying the adrenaline rush of a fast unhindered descent.

Soon I get my first sight of my destination for this evening, Ponferrada. From this height and distance is doesn't look even slightly attractive. The most noticeable things about it are the cooling towers belching out smoke and layering a haze of smog above it. I might as well be staring at Widnes. I look in vain for its famous castle, but it is too far off and a long way down to pick out any kind of significant detail. There's a huge amount of disenchantment in this first viewing but hopefully, like at the iron cross at the top of Monte Irago and not like Widnes, things will improve with proximity.

It's another two hours of continuous descent before I come to another resting place, Acebo. If Foncebadón and Manjarín look isolated and austere, here looks like they've only just taken the wrapping off it. It is clean and prosperous and has a good road going through the centre of it. A goat staring inquisitively out of a ground floor window of one house, as I pass. More importantly, it has a bar, which has a pub feel to it. It also contains a couple of familiar faces in the shape of Jan and Andrew whom I last saw in Mansilla de las Mulas. It's good to see them because for some reason walkers seem a bit thin on the ground this morning. They spent last night in a *refugio* in Foncebadón, which they describe in glowing terms as the most atmospheric and peaceful of the walk so far. They actually walked up to the Cruz de Ferro last night and Andrew talks with some passion about how incredible and peaceful it felt in the moonlight. I've never seen him so animated, nor so overcome. The tough exterior of a couple of weeks ago has melted away. I speak too soon as he then comes back down to earth,

"Good job we went too because we saw fuck all when we walked past it this morning."

152

Jan looks like the kind of woman who would normally wince at that kind of language but she must have grown immune to it by now. She seems very ladylike and has a knack of looking less scruffy than the rest of us. I get the feeling that she is an experienced walker though, and I haven't heard her complain once about the route, hostels or other pilgrims. She's constantly smiling and I really should hate her for all of the above, but I don't. She's in danger of giving us all a good name. I'd love to know what she and the more rough and ready Andrew talk about over the course of a day. I can't see it being rugby league somehow.

I might have been envying the cyclists earlier but Acebo has a memorial to one who was killed outside the village when he was on the Camino. There are a few memorials dedicated to those who died along the way and I've passed several crucifixes today, including one just outside Rabanal. Most seem to have died for health reasons (though this is not true of the cyclist here who was hit by a car) and of course, if they weren't on the Camino their deaths wouldn't have happened. So is the dream to blame?

None of us knows when our time is due; the story of my friend Margriet's sister told me that. I admire them for trying to achieve something and not sitting back and dreaming about it. I've been thinking about the Camino for years and if it wasn't for the agony of my friends, I might still be at my desk at work, watching dawn break over the Unigate dairy in West London, and reflecting that I might walk to Santiago *someday*. In the many lessons being picked up along the way, the fragility of life seems the most important.

There is still more careful descending to do on the most brutal path of the walk so far. Exposed rock makes it slippy underfoot and there are near vertical descents on loose stones which have to be picked through carefully. Most of the paths that I've walked on look like they've been created, or at least amended, this one is as raw as they come and it's tough going on the feet. It hugs the sides of a small valley and there is a strong scent of eucalyptus in the air. Today also sees the first hints of Autumnal colours, with brown and orange patches on the opposite hillside.

I'm glad to see Molinaseca but because of the descent, it comes into view a long time before you actually get anywhere near it. Just as I'm approaching, it starts to rain and with this comes the temptation to hurry. A gentle slip, which leaves me off balance and in a hedge, cures me of that idea and I settle for a safe speed through the persistent drizzle. The angle of descent into the town ensures that the church is the last building you see, but the first one you actually walk past. It is then a walk across a Roman bridge and down a beautiful main street then out the other side. With the weather closing in and my legs feeling every metre of the ups and downs of 26km, I abandon any hope of making it to Ponferrada and stop at a *refugio* that seems to miraculously appear seconds after the decision is made.

I couldn't have chosen better. There are beds rather than bunks and they are well-spaced, making this look like luxury of the highest order. After a couple of nights staying in places where I barely recognise anyone, the first people I see here are Jan and Andrew again. Just after I emerge from doing my washing, I hear another familiar voice; it's a slow North American drawl and is unmistakable; I was convinced BC was a day ahead of me but here he is and he actually seems pleased to see me. We haven't crossed for six days and we exchange a few words as he places his things on the bed opposite. I've decided that I'm going to rehabilitate him in my own mind but I'm starting gently.

This is one of those *refugios* which provide an evening meal, and I don't think I'm up to sharing a table with him just yet. Just before coming into the town, I passed the French and the Quebecois couples that had been eating and drinking companions back in Hermanillos. If they're staying in Molinaseca they are certainly not here. There is no sign of Bernard the Frenchman either, with neither couple having seen him since León. I really hope he appears tonight - I might need some of his wine.

The rain eases off enough to sneak out and have a bit of a look around Molinaseca. Like many places, there is not a huge amount to it. Any traffic skirts around the edge of the village, leaving the main street almost silent. There are a few houses and bars along it but the principal activity of the locals is people-watching in the nicest and friendliest way. According to the Camino sign at the town's entrance, there's a shop marked but it takes some finding and looks nothing like a shop at all when you walk past it. I love these places now. They feel like the height of luxury and entering one is a bit like having a special treat. I stumbled through the transaction of buying fruit, bread, and cheese with my faltering Spanish which still involves chucking out words with no sense of grammar or syntax. I'm getting better, though. The shopkeeper hands me my change before asking me if I am German. Oddly enough, I haven't heard the question for a few days so I let him off and try to explain that I'm British. Well, sort of.

I get back as the clouds close up, and just in time for the evening meal. I position myself on one of three long tables next to Jan and Andrew, while BC chatters his way onto another one. He really does talk a lot and language appears to be no barrier – he just assumes everyone speaks English and carries on. We talk and exchange stories on our table but in between gaps in our conversation I appreciate that I'm a bit jealous of BC When all said and done, he's pretty inoffensive, more outgoing than I am, and he is making friends all the time, so who's laughing at whom?

It lashed it down with rain all night; you could hear it hammering uncompromisingly on the roof - well you could when the indoor racket subsided. Any kind and forgiveness-based thoughts I may have had for BC disappeared overnight in another evening of snoring-based disruption. I lived in hope that the rain would pass over or that lightning would disobey the laws of physics and strike inside a building. Neither dream is realised, and it is still soggy outside when I wake up, or to be more precise, get up. The hostel provides the usual half-hearted breakfast for the sum of €3. More bread than usual but still unimpressive, and I use some of the food I bought yesterday to make up the hunger deficit. There's going to be an early food stop in Ponferrada anyway. I delay my exit for as long as possible in the hope that it will dry up but it is no bloody use. The rain is outstandingly persistent and it's not going to be a day for wish fulfilment.

I am forced into action when I notice BC is almost ready to leave. I'm probably a bit faster than he is in terms of normal walking speed, and leaving now would give me a bit of a lead which will hopefully last all day. The actual result is that it does me no chuffing good at all. I follow the yellow arrows around the back of some houses and walk down a muddy path while the sensible walkers including BC keep to the main road. We meet up again about twenty minutes later and the only things I have gained are a ten metre lead and an awful lot of mud on my trousers. I let him go on ahead and fiddle about with my poncho as an excuse to slow down. It is a grim walk with frequent looks skywards in search of some cause for optimism but none comes. On the way into Ponferrada, I look behind me to see a line of what looks like waterproof hunchbacks in pursuit. We all have our heads down against the elements as we push determinedly towards the town

As the name suggests, you enter the town via a bridge and walk past a large yellow building that stands on the site of an old pilgrimage hospital. Then there is the town's most famous building. After constructing a small church in Rabanal, the Knights Templar got ambitious and built a castle here when the town came under their protection in the twelfth century. It's now a national monument but sadly, it doesn't open for a couple of hours. There's also a radio museum here but that's closed as well. I stop for the usual hot chocolate, hoping that my resting time will see the rain to ease off a bit and allows BC to pull a couple of kilometres clear. Two German women join me; they are doing the Camino as part of a gap year before studying medicine at university. I've seen them several times before and much to my embarrassment, I can't remember if they were staying in the same place as I was last night. It's another case of the Camino fatigue that has taken hold since León. I'm taking less interest in what's around me as Santiago comes closer.

The interesting parts of Ponferrada are on the way into it, though it has to be said that it looks better at ground level than it did from half a kilometre up yesterday. I ease into the newer part of town and look to find something distinctive about it, but it just looks like everywhere and nowhere. It's busy, noisy and looks complicated. It's not just the traffic this time, it's the fact that there's a choice of roads and that people are walking in all directions. I'm not used to people walking towards me in such large numbers. I'm not used to people walking towards me at all, and it feels more alien here than anywhere else.

Like most places of a similar size, Ponferrada is ringed by major roads and it's a zig-zag exit out of the town which is so indirect and distorting, that it feels at one stage that I've taken a wrong turning and am heading back into it. The fact that the arrows point in unexpected directions doesn't help, and when the walk goes through a courtyard belonging to a residential apartment block, there is a suspicion that the local youth might have got busy with some yellow paint after the bars had shut. It's a dull walk through some rather unmemorable suburbs which makes it hard to believe it's part of the same route that took us into Molinaseca yesterday.

After yesterday and the Cruz de Ferro, this is really bland hiking, not helped by the slowly easing rain. The only distinguishing features of the route out of town are a couple of churches with mosaic patterns on their outside walls. It may get worse in the future as Ponferrada is continuing to expand. One road I walk down has been sold for housing and what looks like allotments; elegant walls surround both types of plot but they make it all look very forbidding

157

and unfriendly. The powers that be in the town are obviously quite prepared to sacrifice the route of the Camino for a fist full of Euros. Why anyone would want their new house to be built on a road travelled by thousands of pilgrims anyway takes some thinking about.

The housing plots soon stop and I enter the fully built community of Fuentes Nueva. A bar is advertised and it's time to celebrate the improving weather and seeing the back of Ponferrada with the traditional pilgrimage lunch of a *bocadillo* and the added luxury of a small beer. I barely have my rucksack off when the bar door opens again and a familiar figure with a familiar voice stands there. BC has caught up with me yet again. I don't quite know how he's achieved this as I was convinced he was well ahead. I can't escape this one and it's time to grin and bear it. I do need a rest, or at least my feet do. My ears are just about to get another working over.

I'm spared from undiluted BC by the arrival of Jan and Andrew, and we all sit huddled over a small table. BC is in fine form as he talks about the universal spirit of the Camino, its friendliness and how he's met people from all over the world and been treated with kindness. Don't stay at this table too long then. Jan and Andrew agree and talk about various moments when they've been helped by people along the way. Their combined fervour outweighs mine significantly and I'm the only one on the table who has appeared to have lapsed into occasional moments of grumpiness over the past few weeks.

BC then goes on to mention his life back home. "I've just got divorced so I decided to come here. I really didn't want to go through another divorce but that's how these things work out."

I think to back to Monica and the train to Saint-Jean-Pied-de-Port and decide this time not to pursue the obvious line of questioning in case he decides to tell me. Jan and Andrew decide to ignore the carrot too, and Jan gets him back on the subject of the Camino spirit straight away.

I find myself eating my cheese sandwich and listening to the others talking happily about their experiences. I didn't realise Andrew did enthusiasm until yesterday and he is overdosing today, talking at great length about the scenery and the food. He is another one who enjoyed the Meseta. BC's stories too, are told with gusto, though whether they are interesting enough to repeat in the first place is doubtful. He's impressed with the whole experience and once again, I have slight pangs of jealousy. I can't deny that it's been a surprisingly enjoyable lunch and I get the feeling that it will be a "Camino moment" to be discussed at a later date.

It's dry outside when I head back out but the clouds continue to look ominous. It's been a day of attaching and detaching the waterproofs and it looks like it's going to continue that way. The walk out of Ponferrada is never going to be described as picturesque, but the morning's rain has made it an ordeal. Soon a significant moment arrives. The bridge over the A6 motorway is crossed, which means that all traces of urbanity are behind me. Even better than that, we are back in wine country.

I haven't really set myself a target of where to stop tonight. I am defying the growing pilgrimage trend of astute planning and playing it by ear instead. One potential place to rest is Villafranca del Bierzo, which doubled up in previous years as a mini version of Santiago itself. Pilgrims who were unable to make it the whole way could seek forgiveness at the local church. To get there would mean another tally of more than 30km of walking, and after this morning's attrition, I'm not convinced it's the occasion for it. Instead, my body suggests I call it a day in Cacabelos. I get here at about 2.30pm and, despite the clearing skies, I come to the conclusion that 24km is enough and where better to stay than in the centre of the local wine trade?

It is the biggest place I've stayed in since Astorga but only just about qualifies as a town. There are notable differences from Rabanal and Molinaseca, and it not just the smell of the wine, which lingers heavily in the air. The main street here is wide enough for two-way traffic and flanked with buildings with beautiful overhanging balconies. In addition, there are a lot of bars. It does have an air of a British market town about it.

One thing it does have in common with yesterday is that the hostel is on the way out. It's easily the most idiosyncratic *refugio* of my Camino so far and it's to be found in the confines of the parish church. The courtyard wall has a wooden frame attached to it, which extends inwards towards the church itself. This supports a roof and walls, which have been divided into units. Each unit has two beds separated by the width of a bedside table. There's also a shower and toilet block and, to liven the place up, all the exterior walls and doors are painted yellow. It's a bit like staying in an ecclesiastical Butlin's. Wherever you are, you step out and see the church. Jan and Andrew are already here, as are the two German women I spoke to earlier in Ponferrada, and we're all taken in by the quirkiness of the surroundings. It does have a flimsy look to it as if a stiff breeze or someone leaning in the wrong place could topple it all like dominoes.

Of course, the problem with such an eccentric place is that a lot is going to depend on whom you are going to share a unit with. The beds are allocated in order and I have the first bed in one room, which means the next person who comes in, be they male or female, will be with me. I am washing my clothes in a stone sink opposite the showers when I see the familiar Columbo-like shuffle of BC coming into the churchyard and counting down the cubicles. I haven't seen anyone else come in since I arrived and I stare with a growing sense of inevitability as he stops outside my door and then goes inside. I'd seen him a few minutes earlier having a rest at the entrance of the town which I assumed meant that he was going to head on somewhere else. After lunch today, I'm less hostile but I do know for a fact that he can snore for Canada. Happily, I'm in a place famous for its wine, and bloody hell, I think I'm going to need some. Tonight is going to be murder, maybe literally. The sleeping arrangements on the pilgrimage have led to some interesting nights. A couple of weeks ago, it was just me and Carrie and eighty-eight other people. Now I'm sleeping with another Canadian in the most intimate environment so far, and it happens to be BC. Bloody hell, Camino life can be cruel.

At the back of the church are a couple of stone benches under an awning where my fellow pilgrims including BC are congregating. A few others just sit on the steps outside their doors and exchanged pleasantries. BC sounds like he's about to embark on a stream of unconsciousness. Although he winds me up severely, I'm in the minority, possibly of one. People are listening intently to what he's saying and there is a fair amount of laughter. I drift back to my room just in time to hear the rain start to assault the roof. Somehow, it's reassuring to be lying on my bed just listening to it in splendid isolation. I only get up an hour later because of a need to eat. If there were any other scenario in my head, I would stay where I am. It is

160

horrendous outside. The sky is murderously black and the raindrops are falling with the weight of pebbles. It's raining so hard that it actually hurts.

Fortunately, it doesn't take too long to find a suitable bar with a suitable steak and chips on offer as its main course and a large vino accompaniment. The food is excellent and I meander back after overdoing it on the local produce, arriving back at the *refugio* at the same time as BC. He's been eating with the German women, and Jan and Andrew, and evidently has consumed less wine than I have. Then again, I don't snore.

It's not a shock that I don't sleep particularly well. I'm expecting the place to be cold, bearing in mind that my head is resting against a stone wall and it's pouring down outside, but the main problem is a more traditional one. What is unexpected is that the snoring isn't emanating from the other side of my unit. There is a space at the top of the partition walls so you can hear your neighbours and see their lights. In comparison, BC is positively tranquil and even he struggles with the noise. He gets angry with a couple of Germans who decide to have a conversation at 4am. Given the way that sound travels, it's difficult to know where they are, but BC takes no chances by standing up and shouting abuse in both directions.

It's a slightly delayed start under a broken sky. I am still out just before sunrise and, after several weeks of walking, it's apparent how much longer daylight is taking to arrive. It's another misty beginning, but within minutes, it becomes a beautiful and familiar tramp through vineyards. I meet a man who is studying his guidebook with a sense of bafflement, and asks for help. The problem is soon solved when we work out he's on the wrong page. He's another Canadian who must be easily in his sixties. He looks in far better physical condition than I am and this is backed up when we head to Villafranca together and I struggle to keep up with him. He's a pharmacist from Edmonton and is doing the Camino for the sense of the physical challenge. He looks like he could run up a mountain, assuming his map-reading skills put him in the right place.

We part in Villafranca. He's clearly a man in a hurry, while I'm quite definitely in search of hot chocolate. I can see why the place is a popular stop off point for pilgrims. It's bigger than Cacabelos and clearly has an identity that extends beyond the Camino. There are lots of cafés and shops, and it's big enough to have a good wander round and unwind. I can't unwind too much, but there is a strong temptation. I sit outside as the mist lifts and I can feel the first calming vestiges of direct sunlight on my face.

Uniquely, there are three routes out of Villafranca. One of them looks like torture on legs and is 40km long. There is no way I am touching that, so I decide to take the middle ranking route instead. It's a road that points threateningly uphill, and before you attempt it, there's a sign in several languages telling you that the route is extremely difficult. Even the Pyrenees didn't come with a health warning. I've never seen one of these signs on the Camino before but it is the suggested direction in my guidebook. The other possible path is alongside a major road, which has no appeal at all. I take some heart from the fact that the visible part of my chosen route is layered in concrete, but this soon runs out, the houses disappear and it narrows to the width of a path. Within seconds, it looks like a grappling iron would be useful to make the ascent a bit more straightforward. It's difficult, really difficult. I can feel the gradient attacking my knees, and progress is slow and painful. The path is a good, firm one but this is a stiff test, with frequent pauses to get my breath back.

It's now, in one of my increasingly lengthening stops for air and water, that I decide that ascents need to have their own grading system, and I come up with the "bastard scale" to measure walking enjoyment. The basic gist is that the more pleasurable the walk, the less likely you are to utter the word "bastard". It's a flexible system too, as it can measure both gradient and distance - at the moment it is mentioned every 15m or so. I didn't realise until today that you can shout and be short of breath at the same time.

I am still climbing after another twenty minutes but luckily the slope's severity decreases. Even so, every time I turn a corner my heart sinks as I see the path sticking to the mountain side and then disappearing from view at a higher level than the one I'm at currently. I'll need to devise a new scale for that too. I can't think of a suitable name at the moment but when I do, I guarantee that it'll have a few hard consonant sounds in it.

Mercifully, the climbing finishes before I do. My legs hurt and my lungs are bursting but I think it's worth it. At least that's what I keep telling myself. The alternative route, the soft option, is to follow a main road on the valley floor, which I can see now, and it's a bloody long way down. The vehicles look like ants and the noise of the traffic barely filters its way up here. It feels like I'm closer to the clouds. I stop for a few minutes to recover and take in the views

163

across the narrow green Valcarce valley. There's no sign of any other walkers on this route. There were a couple someway behind me earlier on but they must have turned back, put off by either the gradient or the loud persistent swearing from the pilgrim in front of them. I drink in the solitude and enjoy the satisfaction of making it this far. It's truly beautiful and peaceful, but then I think, not for the first time this week, that if anything happens to me now, there's no-one to help out.

Once you have reached the maximum height of the hill, the path undulates pleasantly, which my ankles are particularly grateful for. There are some wispy clouds in the sky and a bit of gentle mountain rain is falling, which results in a couple of rainbows forming. The walk takes me around some browning ferns and into a wood of chestnut trees. It is harvest time and I see people for the first time in a couple of hours. Men and women are scrabbling on the slopes, filling up sacks and we exchange smiled greetings. Nearby stand some donkeys looking indifferent as chestnut bags are strapped to their bodies.

A few minutes later, I wish I had a donkey as the pastoral beauty ends, the path turns viciously downhill and "The Bastard Scale" is immediately reintroduced. For all my efforts, I have walked an extra 3km and it has taken me an additional ninety minutes. I've enjoyed it, well the flat bits at least, but I can't deny that it physically hurts. My legs are in agony from the toes upwards and they now have to deal with dropping 300m. It is a delicate descent, dodging my way through the surface stones while my calves feel like they've had basketballs attached to the back of them.

The trees provide some shelter on a day that's warming up considerably, but the real enemy is the slope and not the weather. It's almost like tip-toeing, so small are the downward strides. I almost stumble into a café at the bottom of the hill in Trabedelo. My legs feel unable to deal with flat terrain, and it's a painful effort to go up to the bar. My tentative plan for today was rather optimistically to stay over at a place called O'Cebreiro, but that's 17km away and involves an ascent of over 700m. There's no chance I'm going to achieve that. The way I'm feeling at the moment, it's unclear if I'm going to make it out of my chair again. Over my orange juice, I look at my guide and realise that I've already racked up a similar distance today, with over half of it being taken up just

164

by getting to Villafranca. I barely noticed that bit, and it isn't going to be the part of today's stage that stays with me. Very few pilgrimage stories begin without a bit of physical discomfort.

As I'm not going to move for the best part of an hour, I weigh up the options on possible places to stay. I'm fortunate, as there is plenty of room for improvisation. The climb up to O'Cebreiro follows a road which links several villages. They all seem to merge into one another and nearly all of them have sleeping opportunities. I'll keep going until the body says no. I rather get the feeling that it isn't going to be that far.

From now on, I'll be walking along the main N-VI road, something the sensible pilgrims have been doing since Villafranca. A motorway has been built nearby which takes away a lot of the traffic but there are still a fair number of big lorries to deal with. All that separates them from us vulnerable walkers is an unattractive concrete barrier, about waist high. It looks solid enough but how much difference it will make when eighteen wheels worth of petrol tanker careers through it at 60kph is something I don't want to witness being put to the test. There's not a lot of it either. Very soon it's back to walking with only a white line separating pilgrims from traffic. This is accompanied by a familiar rising awareness in the senses and a loosening of the bowels. I know that in normal life this type of walk wouldn't bother me too much, but after spending so much time on quiet paths and roads, it becomes a very scary shock to the system. Once again, you're in the hands of those driving around you, and it's not a good sensation to have.

On the other side of the path is the Río Valcarce, which probably bubbles along the valley floor if you could hear it above the traffic. The modernity of the route takes away the feeling of tradition, but there are clues to the history of the area along the way. One of these is Vega de Valcarce, which is a prosperous, largely agricultural-looking place. On one side it's overlooked by the remains of an ancient Saracen castle while on the other you can see the huge concrete structures that prop up the motorway above. I'm attracted by the castle but decide that my body can't handle any lengthening to the day. I'd want to spend some time there to do it justice. That's the trouble with Saracen castles - they're very Moorish.

Vega de Valcarce has a *refugio* which describes itself as Brazilian. It's scruffy in appearance and resembles a neglected 1960s school building that's been taken over by squatters. Looking at it, you could be forgiven for not knowing if it is being done up or vandalised. It advertises Brazilian hospitality, atmosphere, and music, which makes me ponder if the girl from Ipanema serves behind the bar, the back garden's heavily deforested, and you get mugged on the way out. Pilgrims aren't a finicky bunch, but even with my body in the state it's in, I am not tempted to stay there and decide to press on a bit longer.

I finally stop in Ruitelán which is away from the main roads, in the sense that they are on bridges a significant distance above the village. Having said that, I can still hear the traffic noise, which I keep mistaking for thunder. The other dominant sound is the cowbells, which are constant and somewhat more soothing. I was hoping to walk on a bit further but the shoulders are starting to hurt quite significantly, which worries me a bit. The yellow arrows are also starting to point forebodingly uphill from now on. Even so, I stand outside for a few minutes before going in. It is not the most flamboyant or eccentric of places. It's basically a normal house that's been converted, and it doesn't look any different from any other building I can see in the vicinity. It also doesn't look particularly welcoming. As I'm standing there, debating whether to go on to the next village, the decision is made for me. I feel the discomfort in my shoulder again and decide that, regardless of the reception, I do need to rest now.

The opening door sets off some wind chimes, which summon the *hospitalero* to the signing-in desk. As well as explaining the curfew time which is the standard 10pm, I'm told that from now on I'm to enter and exit through a different door, which is at the side of the house. The door I've just walked through is only for pilgrims entering for the first time. He's very earnest about all this and as rules go, it's a trivial but unique one. I can't honestly say that the idea of hearing wind chimes every ten minutes appeals to me either.

There is only one other pilgrim here when I arrive – a German man whom I have never seen before called Marc. I set about the daily ritual of having a shower and washing the clothes I've just been walking in. Just as I am hanging them out to dry having walked through the appropriate door, I feel a tap on my shoulder and a familiar voice.

"Well hello Rudy, we keep bumping into each other!"

166

The bastard BC has found me again. I hadn't seen him since I left the Hi-di-Hi hut at Cacabelos this morning and, on a route with thirteen *refugios* on it, he's happened to walk into mine. I'm beginning to think I'm being stalked.

It may have looked unexciting from the outside and have an unusual door policy, but the hostel does more than provide the basics. There's an internet facility, a shared meal, and you can also have a massage. Nearly all the hostels have a visitors' book and the in-house food here comes highly recommended. To be honest, there isn't a choice to be had. There is a bar in Ruitelán where I have a leisurely afternoon beer, but I don't fancy a lonely evening there, even if it means avoiding BC. I'm also suffering a bit from *menú del dia* fatigue and my previous experiences of shared meals have been memorable. I am hoping for a few more people between now and the evening, because at the moment there are exactly three of us.

Before the meal, I decide to have a back massage. My shoulder ache has been around for about a week and, while it hasn't got any worse, it's still a discomfort. Apart from anything else, I've walked about 600km and think that for an extra €10, a general MOT will be worth it. The massage room is just off the smaller one which houses the computer. BC is installed there, bashing away at the keys with the air of somebody who might actually have friends. His head raises a little bit but not enough for me to see his facial reaction when I walk past him and am given the instruction to take my shirt off and lie down.

It's not the scented candles that worry me. Nor is it the new age music soundtrack that accompanies my massage. What really disturbs me is that the bloke who is pummelling my body out of my view is breathing really heavily, and I mean really heavily to the point of disturbing. There is also an unsettling rhythmic sound to it. You know when you get that feeling that something unpleasant is happening and you don't want to look and see what it is? Well, it is exactly like that, and it goes on for a long time. Meanwhile, I am rubbed, pressed and hit all over in systematic fashion with what feels like a nailbrush. After manipulating my back, the masseur plays around with my ears before twisting my head and neck to make sure I'm not an owl in disguise. The whole thing lasts about twenty agonising minutes, but I do feel absolutely wonderful afterwards.

That's the physical health sorted out but the mental health might take a bit of a kicking this evening.

Seven of us sit down for our evening meal: BC, Marc and I are joined by a jovial German couple, Hans and Gisela who are both retired, an athletic looking Frenchman called Phillippe, and yet another Canadian, this time a woman called Catherine. With the exception of BC, they are all new to me. We try to converse using each other's languages but we are soon dominated by the man who speaks fluent bollocks. We are joined at intervals by the chef who is a thickset man and looks like a cross between Ernest Borgnine and "The Hood" from Thunderbirds. The food is as good as the visitors' book suggests, starting with vegetable soup, followed by salad and pasta. I don't know if I am becoming more BC tolerant but it certainly is a good and happy evening. He raises the point that it's almost impossible to have a meal on the Camino unless there's a Canadian present.

There are nods of agreement and Hans laughs loudly. "Yes, that is so. But why are there so many Canadians on the Camino?"

Hans timed that brilliantly, BC has a mouthful of salad to contend with so Catherine jumps in. "We are here doing missionary work in Europe. We are here to show that not everyone from North America is all bad."

"Of course," declares BC, hastily swallowing some lettuce, "we have to deal all the time with you people thinking that we're Americans."

"You're lucky," I pipe up, "people keep thinking I'm German." It just came out and I regret it milliseconds afterwards. What follows is one of those moments when time seems to stand still. Happily, there's a big laugh from everyone - believe me, I checked - which does enough to cover my sigh of relief.

BC raises an interesting point, though. The number of Canadians I've met on the Camino so far must be around three figures now, but to the best of my knowledge, the only people I've met from the USA were the *hospitaleros* at Estella and two couples who were staying there that night. BC suggests that most Americans wouldn't know the Camino exists "unless they'd tried to bomb it".

It is strange to have regrets on a journey like this but, after evenings like this one and the ones at Estella, Grañon, and Tosantos earlier in the Camino, I feel I should have sought out more *refugios* that provide communal meals. Although I love walking on my own, there is a great joy to be had in swapping stories over food, and remembering that nobody knows or cares what you did in your life before. We are all long time walkers tonight, and it's a welcome and wonderful return to the here and now, with no thoughts about Santiago.

I don't know how you woke up this morning but I surfaced just before 7am to the sounds of *Ave Maria* being played at an ear-crunching level. Even so, BC manages to sleep through it, snoring away obliviously. I am one of the last to rise as everyone else is fully dressed by the time I get mobile; I rather get the feeling that BC might have woken everybody up before the hymn actually kicked in. I've obviously built up a tolerance. Hans is pointing at BC and smiling as if to indicate, "Isn't this funny?" He's lucky he has only had one experience of it; I've had to suffer for the best part of a fortnight. *Ave Maria* then segues neatly into *Nessun Dorma* - nobody sleeps. Ho bloody ho. It has the desired effect as BC finally opens his eyes to find six people staring at him, some in awe of his snoring ability and at least one with murder on his mind.

Breakfast is provided here and it's better than most I've had. It's still only bread and jam, but both are plentiful and the gang are in a chatty mood. The main talking points are the upcoming climb up to O' Cebreiro, and where to stay. There is a lot less flexibility today in choosing a hostel. I've mentally pencilled in staying in Triacastela. If every step is indeed a prayer there will be at least 30km's worth, with the first 9km involving a climb of 600m, but I feel like challenging myself. It will be tough because of the terrain, but it will be worth it for the sense of achievement. Oh, who am I trying to kid? I am doing it to put as much distance between me and BC as possible. I am convinced he's going to stop well before then.

I actually get on the road at about 7.30am. Apart from the correct door policy, another house rule is that we are not allowed to leave before 7am, which is certainly not unusual as *refugio* regulations go. The reason, in this case, is that the inhabitants of Ruitelán don't like the sound of walking poles on the street – a bit rich from a village that lies under two motorway bridges, but rules are rules, and in this case, a late-ish start isn't a bad idea.

Although the path is not on the main road anymore, it's still on a road, and it's an unlit one. It's dark and there are a few cars about, so it's a nervy beginning. I keep my torch handy to shine on myself when I hear an engine. It starts getting light just as I turn into the village of Herrerías; how I wish I had stayed here purely for the comic potential of the name. There's a hostel here too and it is chucking out time. I'm joined by about a dozen walkers and together we try to find our way out of Herrerías – try to get that image out of your head. After what has been a moderate walk uphill so far, things start to get serious now as we head up to the next village of La Faba, which is 3km away and about 200m higher.

There is an early warning sign of what's to come. So far, everything has been on a road but this pilgrim has learned to fear the worst when the route divides into one for walkers and one marked out for cyclists. It usually means that those committed to Shank's pony are about to do some mountaineering, and so it turns out here. Cyclists continue along the tarmac while the walking pilgrims head onto a rugged looking path. This develops into as wearisome a walk as I have encountered. It strays too close to the vertical for my liking, and finding a stable footing among the rocks is an awkward task. It isn't so much the gradient - yesterday's climb was far worse - but the roughness of the path that is doing the damage. Overhanging trees give a claustrophobic feel to it, and soon I am breathing as heavily as the guy who massaged me last night. I pass through La Faba, which means that O'Cebrerio is about an hour away, and involves walking up a one in ten gradient for all of it. The path is a lot better than before, but an ascent of 400m is still a demand on the legs which have done a fair amount of climbing over the last 48 hours. It still doesn't seem as painful as yesterday's way out of Villafranca, but it is a hell of a lot longer.

The path finally levels out just before O'Cebrerio and at 9.45am, after eighteen days in Castilla y León, I enter Galicia, the final region of the Camino. Those ugly but informative plastic signs that lie at the entrance of every settlement are now no more. Galicia's way of marking the Camino is putting up tombstone-like kilometre posts. The stone at this border states that there is 152.5km to go to reach Santiago. More immediately important, it's only about twenty minutes to a stopping point.

O'Cebrerio is a grey stone, picturesque place that looks like it could be part of Emmerdale. While the much smaller La Faba, which I passed earlier, is a functional farming village, there is a bit more of the decorative here. It is also the home of the Camino's oldest church. It was built in the ninth century and is another one notched up in dedication to Santa María in all her guises – in this case, Santa María la Real. There is a lot to thank a former parish priest here for, and there's a bust of him near the church. His name was Elias Valiña Sanpedro. He arrived in O'Cebrerio in 1959 and spent a lot of the next decade giving speeches around Europe on the importance and relevance of the Camino. He wrote books on the subject and was a driving force in rebuilding the church and some of the nearby buildings. It was also his idea to mark the route with the now familiar yellow arrows.

Not surprisingly for a town 1,330m above sea level, the views are dazzling and I am able to look back over the narrow valley I've been walking up for the last two days. I arrive in the village at the same time as Jonathan. British people have been a rarity over the past couple of weeks and we sit down to a hot chocolate together. He's an interesting character. He lives in a community in Lyme Regis, and is a strong advocate of that particular type of largely self-sustaining living. I listen attentively as he explains how everybody works for each other and how they provide opportunities to help people rehabilitate after prison or substance addiction. One of the things that this walk has told me is that nothing is achieved without help. We may walk individually but we are dependent on those who provide us with food and shelter. You become aware of small gestures and realise their importance. There have been dabbles with communal living along the way, and I've really enjoyed them and I can see why it makes sense, but it's just so far removed from the life I live, or at least lived. Even so, after forty minutes in his company, I don't know if he's mad for living like that, or I am mad because I don't.

When I emerge from the bar, the entire village is shrouded in an all-enveloping fog, which has brought visibility down to almost nothing at all. I hadn't expected this and due to a bit of random walking about before I stopped for a drink, I can't remember where I last saw an arrow. The chances of me seeing another one now are virtually nil. I have lost all sense of the geography of the village and walk around helplessly trying to remember how I got there in the first place. I come across the church again and find myself in the graveyard, which in the current climate could send a shiver down the spine of Vincent Price. For the first time on the Camino, I am forced to ask for directions and it's in the village and outside the church where the man who clarified the route lived. It is time to put some rusty Spanish into action, providing I can find anyone to approach. The first person I can distinguish turns out to be Japanese, and he is lost too. I end up going into a shop and suffering a nightmare familiar to all language learners. Asking questions may well be straightforward but trying to understand the answers is anything but.

I am directed downhill, though I am not entirely convinced I am going the right way. There is certainly no path and no clear Camino way-markings. I find myself walking along a roadside where visibility can be measured in centimetres, and it's definitely not quiet. All of a sudden, a walk in a misty churchyard feels like a really pleasant experience. I can hear cars through the fog and when they appear they seem to be travelling at alarming speeds, so they must only see me - if they see me at all - milliseconds before they shoot past. Each sound of a distant motor makes me lean back against the crash barriers as far as my body will go, and makes the heart beat a little bit faster. I can't see what's on the other side either. It's petrifying. At least I could witness the traffic yesterday, and on the way into León. Here the murkiness distorts every noise and it's disorientating. I don't know if cars are coming towards me, driving away, or on another road altogether. There are not enough moments of silence. Never before has my life seemed so tenuous. I just want this stage of the walk to be over, I want the fog to lift and I want to discover that I am heading in the right direction.

It is a long ten minutes of gently edging along the crash barriers before the wisps of fog thin out and the topography opens up. Optimistically, I can see a trail of about a dozen walkers in front and they are on a path rather than a road. Awkwardly, the nearest walker has the familiar hunched gait of BC. The walk along the road has shred my nerves and I'm not quite ready to talk to anyone. I slow down, have a lengthy water break, take in the surroundings, and wait for the heartbeat to return to normal.

With the mist disappearing, it feels like a curtain opening up on the surrounding hills and valleys. After the narrowness of the past couple of days, there are now great open vistas showcasing fields of lush green hills covered in trees, hedgerows and animals. The view stretches for miles across the mountain peaks where the only signs of human activity are the roads and the pylons. Of course, it's green for a reason – it rains a lot in Galicia. Santiago registers rainfall on two hundred and thirty days a year on average, but I sincerely hope that's the only thing it has in common with Manchester.

I catch up with BC at a drinking fountain. It's been quite an intense morning on the body and the nerves, and we both are suffering. His normally ruddy features have turned ashen. It's a few seconds before either of us speaks, and BC's voice has an unrecognisable hint of weary exhaustion to it. He points tiredly back up the road with one of his poles.

"I'll happily walk up any path the Camino throws at me. Any path or mountain pass. I'll do it in winter. Hell, I'll do it blindfolded. Anything, as long as I don't have to relive that last twenty minutes again."

We're both still shaking from the experience. He's thinking of stopping soon and I sort of fulfil a fantasy by leaving him in hospital. No, I don't knock him unconscious with a walking pole. It's just that that's the name of the place - well it's actually called Hospital de la Condensa - where we part ways.

You could be forgiven for thinking that a stage involving a mountain pass might provide the highest point of today's journey. I did right up until I stand at the bottom of the bonus hill of Alto do Paio. It's not even clear on my map that there's a slope to climb. It may only be marginally higher than O'Cebreiro, but I've descended a reasonable distance since then. I have been walking on a path which shadows the main road, and this new shift uphill is a violent one. There is no winding trail to follow; this is a full-on assault, which starts on tarmac and then downgrades on to a track. It's all the worse for being so totally unexpected, at least by me. It's not long but it's steep enough to hurt. I can feel myself turning purple as I reach the top. With one last ounce of breath, I get to the summit and shout "Bastard" loudly in a mixture of triumph and exhaustion. If the hill was a surprise, so too was the bar at the top of it. Every outside table is full, and every occupant stopped to look at who'd done the shouting. My face was pointing downwards the whole way, pushing so hard on my poles that I didn't even notice it. I can't blame that one on Caitlin.

This particular bar must do a roaring trade in revitalising the knackered pilgrim. I can't think of a better-situated hostelry anywhere else on the walk, and it's busy as a consequence. I was planning to stop, but a mixture of total embarrassment and lack of space have put paid to that. As I reconnect with the main road, a steady stream of cyclists whizz past, each one shouting "Buen Camino" as is the tradition. I can't even begin to reply and just make a pitiful wave, which they have no hope of seeing. I have a lengthy look back at the bar because there is something that doesn't seem right. The clientele is a bit more sharply dressed than the average pilgrim and it's obvious that none of them look as if they've walked up Alto do Poio. They are still smiling for a start. And they're capable of speech. They are certainly kitted out for walking, but they lack the broken-in feeling of the hardened Santiago-ist. There is a coach nearby which gives the game away. This appears to be the en-masse starting point for what I have decided to call "The Unleaded Pilgrim".

I had read about this phenomenon when I was doing my research into the Camino. Certain travel companies give you the opportunity to do the latter stages of the walk (you only have to walk the last 100km to get a *compostela*), and will transport your luggage for you. Not only that, the pilgrims who do it this way can rest easily in a hotel bed at the end of the day, and are spared the trials of basic communal living. Not for them the paucity of showers, the rows over washing line space, the morning ritual of banging your head on the bunk above, and a relentless Canadian who can bore the balls off a buffalo and then snore like one.

It is another attack of pilgrimage snobbery, and I get the feeling it might not be the last. Despite the tiredness, I decide that I can keep on to the next village, assuming there are no more surprise hills, and will stop there. Things do become easier and I finally have a path that is good and level, which is close - but not too close - to the road. It's very busy with unleaded pilgrims who shout enthusiastic "Buen Caminos" as I walk past. I respond in similar fashion but there's a part of me that wants to shout "And where did you start from? Where the bloody hell were you on the path up Monte Irago? Call yourself a pilgrim? I started on the other side of the sodding Pyrenees." The rants stay internal though, and I remember that some people I know had gone to Santiago this way, and they had given me some useful advice.

175

Two of these people were a married couple, Vin and Trish. A couple of months prior to starting the walk, I attended Trish's funeral. After the service, I was invited back to the house for a drink and discovered that a blue tile with the yellow shell image, the common Santiago sign, was embedded in the wall next to the front door. Later that afternoon, Vin asked me when I was going to Santiago. "You'll regret it if you don't go", he said, his eyes twinkling through the tears. He didn't know it, but the plans were already underway. The tile was another sign that I was heading in the right direction

Fonfría is a farming village set back slightly from the main road. What hits me straight away is the smell of cows, not just the cowpats but of the animals themselves. It isn't the smell you come across by walking past a farm in the UK. This is intense and it makes me stop in my tracks, and not just because I'm looking to see where to put my feet. Some may think of the sea or wine, but this is the smell I associate with Spain. It was the smell of the village where my dad grew up, and where I went on holidays. Even the scenery is similar, with small cowsheds being an integral part of the houses, and straw on the roads. I'm transported romantically back to childhood by the least romantic of smells, and I stand still with my eyes closed for a few seconds to contemplate, and breathe in the odour.

My thoughts are disturbed by a voice that is getting louder and louder.

"Sind sie Deutscher? Sind sie Deutscher?"

Here we go again. I am more annoyed to have my peace disrupted than have my nationality questioned. I'm just about to utter the words "No, I'm frigging not" when I look down on the elderly woman who owns the voice. She is straight out of central casting, and is wearing a shawl, underneath which is a face that has lived a bit and it hasn't been easy. She tugs at my sleeve and repeats her question.

"Sind sie Deutscher? Sind sie Deutscher?"

I feel like shouting, "I'm Spanish just like you, but I just don't have the vocabulary" but I don't because, well, I don't have the vocabulary. Or the grammar for that matter.

"Soy Ingles," I reply and she seems happy with that.

"English! English!" she enthuses and points to the plate she is carrying, "Pancakes! Pancakes!" She peels one from a stack of about

176

ten and hands it to me. Her English then takes a remarkable turn for the better.

"I make them for pilgrims. For a donation."

This is accompanied by a smile which makes me speculate who else uses Shane McGowan's dentist. It's not every day you are mugged by an old lady, and no self-respecting pilgrim is going to sell her short, are they? In fairness, the pancake is delicious and I don't mind reaching into my wallet for some change. Given her love of repeating words, if the bottom falls out of the pilgrim pancakes market she could always get a job naming pandas. I am tempted to loiter a bit longer to see what her gambit with the next couple of pilgrims is going to be. They are South Korean and I rather get the feeling she knows a few words of that language too. Tiredness gets the better of curiosity though, and there are some spaces that a pancake just cannot fill. It's time head off to the village bar for the traditional *bocadillo* and a reasonably lengthy rest.

Fonfría holds a strategic place in today's stage. Stop here and I have rattled off a very respectable 23km worth of really difficult walking. If I carry on, it means finishing off in Triacastela, which is a further 7km away and 600m lower down. I am convinced that Fonfría is the logical place for BC to call a halt and I decide to press onwards and downwards. As I head back onto the road, I feel a sense of guilt that my decision on where to sleep has been influenced by an uncertain dislike of another person, rather than walking in my own way and time. The last time I did this led to the uncomfortable trek into Astorga. If it wasn't for BC, I know I would have stayed in Fonfría but it's too late now. This feeling, along with my attitude to the unleaded pilgrims, points to me having an extremely uncharitable day. These thoughts dominate my mind as the Camino heads downhill. As well as the kilometre stones, there's another indication that the ultimate is now not too far away. There's a great, pale scar in the hills where quarrying is taking place. This is where the stone came from to build the cathedral at Santiago.

Despite its being named after three castles, none actually survive in Triacastela. It's an easy mix of old and new, with the main street being too narrow for any kind of wheeled transport so traffic is diverted around the outside. The oldness is in the detail and my guide tells me that there was once a pilgrimage prison here. I wonder how it compared to the current *refugio* in León. There is a positively decadent choice of five places to rest my weary legs here and I opt for the third one I come to, for absolutely no reason whatsoever. It is rather boring in comparison to yesterday's effort, and the only thing New Age about it is the design. It's clean, the main dormitory is light and spacious, and you can use the front door as much as you want. It's just off the main route and opposite a supermarket so I can stock up on chocolate easily. I am just happy to stop, as I'm exhausted. There is a computer with an internet connection near the reception and I log in to check my messages. I look up briefly and there is BC standing in the doorway, grinning.

"Hello Rudy. I've trusted your judgement so far so this has to be the right place to stay."

I am stunned. First of all, I didn't expect him to make it here and secondly he has a one in five chance of picking the right shelter, and he's bloody done it. What makes it even more galling is that I staggered in here about forty-five minutes ago, largely propped up by walking poles, and feeling more dead than alive; he looks like he has barely broken sweat. I'm at least twenty years younger than the bugger too. I'm beginning to think this is revenge for the afternoon's negative thoughts.

There's a temptation to head to a bar and stay in it until curfew, and they are not difficult to find. Hunger takes precedence over the shortcut to drunken oblivion, and I go into a restaurant and sit at one of the two tables that haven't been joined into a large L shape. The waiter explains that they have a coach party for Santiago here tonight, and once again, I find myself sniffing at and cursing the unleaded pilgrim, purely because they exist.

The waiter is sharply attentive and puts a bottle of red on the table within seconds of me sitting down, and before he has brought the menu. He clearly recognises what kind of day I've had, and knows a grumpy pilgrim when he sees one. There is a welcome change in the *menú del dia* too, to reflect the fact that a regional border has been crossed, and I take full advantage. I sample the local *Caldo Gallego* (cabbage and potato soup) which is excellent. The waiter further endears himself to me by leaving the serving bowl behind on the table, rather than filling my plate and then sodding off with it. This is followed by some acceptable veal, and I finish off with another new item to me, *Torta Santiago* - an almond flavoured cake decorated with sugar, and with the cross of St James imprinted on the top.

As I'm eating, the rest of the restaurant fills up with the great washed and dressed, and the noise level increases, though not unpleasantly. Thinking about it, the unleaded pilgrim doesn't look radically different to how we did on that first night back at Roncesvalles. Rationalising the events of today over a rather good meal, there has been a lot to be thankful for, and I now feel bad about my cranky behaviour and negative thoughts. I've survived a day of physical highs and lows, not to mention the terrifying negotiation of a busy road in thick fog. I've passed through the 30km barrier and, with an exhausted body and a full belly, I should be a match for BC's snoring tonight.

There's another happy ending to the evening. When I return to base, I see that there are only five beds taken out of thirty, so it should be a reasonably quiet one.

How wrong can you be? There was a South Korean couple in the bunk opposite to mine and they managed to co-ordinate their snoring in such a way that there was barely a quiet second all night. One of the buggers even managed to switch on the dormitory light at about 4am to look at his watch. Charity is in short supply this morning and BC is in a belligerent mood, having barely slept at all.

"Rudy, how can people snore like that?" He confides as we dress.

I look out for any hints of irony but there don't appear to be any. I shrug my shoulders sheepishly and put on my rucksack. I'm too tired to speak. As I'm leaving, BC smiles and says,

"Make sure you reserve a bed for me in Sarria!"

Sarria is today's obvious destination but I am not heading there yet. I'm off to the main street in Triacastela in search of breakfast. A lot of the bars and restaurants are surprisingly busy, and I detect the spending power of the unleaded pilgrim once again. I discover a subdued place where there is a solitary and vaguely familiar pilgrim sitting at the bar. I know he's a Spanish bloke in his mid-30s called Pepe, but I can't for the life of me remember where I first met him or when I last saw him. He's pleased to see me, and orders me breakfast while I go through the rigmarole of taking off my rucksack and carefully leaning my walking poles against the bar, only for them to fall down seconds later. We exchange a few pleasantries over orange juice and bread. Pepe's English is rather good, he having been to university in the USA. I explain that my father was Spanish and he slaps me on the back and smiles;

"I thought you had some Spanish blood in you. Welcome home!" he adds enthusiastically.

Maybe Pepe is being generous or just lying politely; after all, nobody in nearly forty years has singled me out as being Spanish by appearance, but it sounds sincere and has a strange effect on me. The barman takes an interest too, and my basic Spanish gets a bit of a work out as I try to explain my family history. It is a significant moment because it's just about the first time I tell the story without feeling slightly fraudulent about it.

When I was at school, I was in a class with an Italian boy called Alessandro and we were both used in lessons to illustrate how useful Latin was when it came to studying modern languages. We would be asked for translations of certain words to highlight their similarity with the words of Ancient Rome. The teacher even referred to us as "the foreigners". I felt uneasy about this; I was born in Liverpool but Alessandro was the genuine article. He came from Turin, English was his second language, and he looked the part as well. He had olive skin and jet-black hair. I had mousy hair and blue eyes. If someone had come into my class and was asked to find the person eligible to play for Spain, I would not have been in the top ten; and that's before they saw me play football.

The only time I normally am reminded of my heritage is when I get asked about my surname. I don't really go into much detail about my origins because it's invariably greeted with the sentence "You don't look Spanish". Occasionally, women would take it further by adding, "You don't look dark," and then adding wistfully that they liked "dark men". When I was at school, Alessandro was metaphorically beating the girls away with sticks. I hated him for it and wished I looked as foreign as he did. Outside of Latin lessons, I was just a British bloke with a funny name.

Here in Triacastela a couple of decades later, I actually start to feel Spanish, or at least not the imitation version I have been before. It's come at a significant date too; I look at my watch and take in the fact that it's exactly one month since I started the walk. I don't feel it enough to drink the coffee, and still cling on to my pilgrimage-long ritual of drinking hot chocolate because the British side of me believes that the tea here is rubbish. I slowly manage to string the odd sentence together, and am encouraged along the way by Pepe and the barman. As a result, breakfast takes longer than usual and I head back out at 8am which is the latest start so far.

Everything I have ever read about Galician weather is true this morning. There is low cloud and persistent rain. As I'm walking down the main street the street lamps switch off but there's no apparent change at all in the prevailing light. It remains implacably dark. It's neither cold nor windy but the weather decides whether I take the longer route to Sarria via the well-regarded monastery at

Samos, or the route that is about 2.5km shorter. I spend a bit of time at the T-junction weighing up the options and decide on plan B. I think the less time I spend in the rain the better, and I am conscious of the effects that yesterday's 30km plus effort might have on my body. 2.5km equates to about forty minutes.

It may be shorter but there is a familiar uphill start to the proceedings. For the first forty minutes, it's difficult to see anything because of the obstinate climate. The bits I can make out are green and lush, but most of my focus is on the walker kitted out in red in front of me. This is..

a) So I know where I'm going, and
b) To use him as bait for any wild dog that might jump out.

As I follow the mystery walker, doubts creep into my mind that maybe he isn't on the Camino at all, but these are assuaged on the odd occasions I see a yellow arrow sprayed on a tree or stone. I also speculate on the wisdom of following someone wearing red: look what that did for Donald Sutherland in the film *Don't Look Now*. Although there is a damp and gloomy feel to the weather, the rain is certainly not heavy enough to be unpleasant. There are some lung bursting climbs but they are short and I am coming to the conclusion that it wouldn't be the Camino without a bit of uphill. My path is interrupted by sheep for the first time since day one and the Pyrenees, and there's a small cattle-induced traffic jam as cows cross the road from one field to another under the watchful eye of a farmer.

Apart from the gradients involved, the other bit in the small print I didn't take into account when deciding which route to take was the availability of stopping points. Villages are few and far between (for "village" read "bar") this way and although the rain has stopped, a break will be greatly appreciated. On several occasions, the twisting path leads tantalisingly close to some promising-looking rooftops, but then it turns away suddenly and heads back towards the greenery just when you think you are reaching your goal. Ain't life just like that sometimes?

A bar finally materialises on the outskirts of a village called Furela, which is a long 10km into the walk, and thank God it's open. It's definitely a hot chocolate sort of day and, to my delight, they sell slabs of cake as well. The appreciation that I've been walking for an entire calendar month allows my mind to wander into the future. I work out that in five days' time I should finally arrive in Santiago and I think about what my feelings and reactions will be. Then I come to my senses and realise that I'm not living in the day anymore, and switch back immediately. Santiago is still as far away as it was when I was doing practice walks along the Thames Path. A lot can happen in the next 100km or so, and I return to contemplating my food and drink and feel happy just to be sitting down. I do eventually decide to carry on and pay the customary toilet visit before I leave. Rather strangely, instead of the usual symbols for toilets, the appropriate doors are decorated with a picture of either Elton John or Kylie Minogue.

Not for the first time in my twenty-four hours in Galicia, I leave a bar only to head out into a thick autumn fog. It's a joyful walk along an uncomplicated path rather than along a busy road and so it is all very ethereal rather than potentially life threatening. The mysterious red dressed route finder has disappeared so it's up to me to discover the yellow arrows now. The chances of getting lost aren't that great as there is only one way to go, and visibility improves with every step. The greyness that was all consuming when I left the bar eventually lifts and even through the intermittent rain, I enjoy every step of the walk to the point that I really wish I'd taken the longer route via Samos and its impressive sounding monastery.

You can see Sarria from a long way off. As I've mentioned, to get a *compostela* you have to walk a minimum of 100km and the town is an important part of the Camino as it's the last place you can start from and still achieve this. Because of its geographical significance, its pilgrimage roots go back for centuries but you wouldn't think so by looking at it. It is the biggest place since Ponferrada and gives no impression at all that it's a Camino town. The buildings are modern and functional rather than aesthetic and, from an urban point of view, it is the epitome of non-descript. It has a railway station and several big shops which fight for space alongside apartment blocks. It is also busy and there's constant movement in every direction, which is bewildering and slightly disorientating after a walking day of barely seeing anyone. It's not so much the volume of traffic that's befuddling but the noise. Even a solitary passing car is deafening in the built-up surroundings.

We pilgrims are swallowed up and made to look anonymous walking into a town which is enjoying a normal Saturday, but regroup when the Camino runs along   - the conveniently pedestrianised - Rúa Maior. This feels like the "Pilgrimage Quarter" where the ordinary citizens of Sarria are filtered out and where four of the town's six hostels are located. There's also a statue nearby of King Alfonso IX which looks like a Celtic chess piece and fits in nicely with the town's origins. He founded Sarria in the thirteenth century and also died here, en route to Santiago. At the bottom of the street is a shop that specialises in walking and camping equipment and sells multilingual guides to Santiago, as well as English language novels. It doesn't matter where you are in the world and in what culture, the moment you come across any place selling books published in English, it's a racing certainty that you'll always be able to pick up something by the unholy trinity of Jane Austen, Ken Follett and Joanna Trollope, and this is no exception. Not that I am in the mood for a novel anyway. If they really wanted to make a killing here, they should devote a shelf or two to the works of Paolo Coelho and self-help, and then reinvest the profits in old rope.

There is a café opposite my *refugio* and it's as loud as the town centre. I can count the people there on the fingers of two hands but everyone feels the need to bellow loudly. They appear to be locals rather than pilgrims and there are card games going on, but I find the noise really difficult to deal with. It's enough to drown out some Korean snoring. I don't know if this is a reaction to urban living, but everything sounds strident in Sarria. All it needs now is BC to arrive and I might head down to the camping shop to see if they have any earplugs.

I go for a wander away from the town centre to find out which direction I'll be heading in tomorrow morning. All the old parts seem to be in this area, with the commercial heart slipping further downhill as the town expanded. There's a ruined castle, heavily disguised as nature slowly takes possession of it, and a rather stark old convent building. The route then leaves Sarria by crossing over a medieval stone bridge. If you weren't on the Camino it's doubtful that you would notice these things are here, even though they're on a hill. There's a clear demarcation between the ancient and modern in Sarria, and the Pilgrimage Quarter has a very different look and feel to it.

It is big enough to absorb a fair number of pilgrims, and the unleaded variety has a very low profile here. It's only in the evening that we gather again on the Rúa Maior. Most pilgrims chose to eat their evening meal in the loud café. The decibel count is the same as earlier but it's full this time, so I travel the short distance across the road to another bar. It is so empty that it makes me deliberate what's wrong with it, but I needn't worry. It fulfils my two main criteria that I look for in somewhere to eat: I get a full bottle of wine and the waiter leaves the soup dish on the table. It's another excellent *Caldo Gallego* though it bears little resemblance to the one I had last night, even to the point of being a different colour. This is followed up by rabbit and, by the time my *flan* arrives, the bar has filled up with people who are here to watch the football on the big screen. I'm still having problems with the noise, and I retreat back to the safety of my *refugio*. For the third night running, I am staying in a place which is not even close to being half full. I withdraw to the silence of the back garden and look at the clouds as night falls. I think about how beautiful the sky looks, how lucky I am to be doing the walk, and wonder why the bloody hell my washing isn't dry yet despite hanging out for seven hours. As I get into my sleeping bag a few minutes later I calculate that 400km away back in Tosantos, somebody will be reading the prayers that I wrote twenty days ago.

Today's late start has nothing to do with *refugio* rules and a lot to do with sleeping in a virtually empty dormitory. There are no nocturnal disruptions, and I sleep straight through to about 7.30am. For the majority of the past month, I would have already rattled off about forty-five minutes of walking and be enjoying the gradual fading up of daylight around now. It's incredible what a Canadian-free 24 hours can do to the body. The thought puts a spring in my step, and I get dressed quickly and head to the bar next door for breakfast. It's only when I leave that I see BC stepping out of the noisy café, so the early stage of my walk is at a sprint to put some distance between us.

It is already daylight and it's another gentle, misty morning, but it's dry and looks like it's going to stay that way. It should be a good one too as it's a full return into the countryside along paths and lanes where any sign of motorised transport will be a major talking point. So it proves to be. The Camino winds its way around fields and along a country road where a succession of villages seem to merge into one another. Very few of them seem to have bars, but what they do possess are drinks machines. No self-respecting Galician hamlet, it appears, can survive without a large Coca-Cola dispenser propped up against a wall. In a Hardy-esque landscape of grey stone and endless green fields where nothing looks like it has changed for decades, they're gaudy and inappropriate. It feels like today's stage has an unwanted corporate sponsor.

There may not be many cars about but the pilgrimage traffic is significant. As well as the unleaded pilgrims, there are also the latecomers who joined at Sarria; their backpacks smaller, their boots cleaner, their smiles not hewn out of hardship. They couldn't be more identifiable if they had beamed down from another planet. They also haven't developed the "yellow arrow twitch" which is the instinctive knack of knowing where to look for the next direction pointer. This means they stop briefly and often, before casually strolling on again with renewed confidence. My ability to stroll anywhere disappeared up the Alto del Perdón, possibly along with my charity.

It is a good day to be out and Galicia's rising to the occasion. We ease snugly between farm buildings and pasture, before the horizon widens to reveal distant villages, far away hills and several hundred pilgrim heads bobbing up and down behind hedges and fences. There's a good reason for counting down the kilometre posts today as the stone marking 100km to go appears just before a place called Morgarde. The Camino path has changed a bit since the stone was laid down and the real distance to Santiago is actually around 109km. It may be inaccurate but it is still symbolic. It's also been severely vandalised by previous pilgrims who want to celebrate the proximity to their goal by writing all over it. It leaves me with mixed feelings too. I'm doubtful if entering the last 100km to Santiago is something to celebrate or not. I don't really know if I want to come off the Camino. I am used to its simplicity and, as the walk into Sarria yesterday proved, the thought of adjusting back to normal urban-based life is a difficult one to comprehend. It also shouldn't be a thought for today. It's time to snap back into the present. There is still an eighth of the journey to go.

Morgade does have a bar where I'm served by a server who bears a striking resemblance to the actress Emma Watson, albeit an unsmiling version. I am joined by two fellow pilgrims who have the weather-beaten look and the dirty boots which make me think that they haven't started their pilgrimage this morning. I'm greeted with the English variation of the opening gambit of "Are You German?" It's amazing what a good night's sleep can do as I'm not even tempted to reply using expletives. Nor do I draw on the deep well of Teutonic stereotyping that I have access to. It is a good job too as Wolfgang and Heiko come from Stuttgart. I don't understand why, if they were so sure I was German, they asked the question in English. Even after introductions, Wolfgang isn't going to the let the subject drop.

"But Rudy is a German name!" he declares.

I can't really argue with this, but for some reason I try. "It's actually short for Rudolph" is all I can muster and I know what's coming next as soon as the words leave my mouth.

"But that too is a German name!"

Not the way I bloody spell it, but it is pointless, not to mention tedious, to continue. There are other things to talk about, and the 100km stone has also put doubts into their minds about life after Santiago. They too, are part of a dwindling breed of pilgrims who started at Saint-Jean-Pied-de-Port and have led a Camino life for nearly five weeks. Our days revolve around finding food, water and shelter. We don't know huge amounts about each other's backgrounds so there's an equality between us. We are all pilgrims and that's all that's needed. It's a difficult thing to surrender and we talk about it at significant length. This is accompanied by the usual skirting around the issue of why we are doing the Camino in the first place. The discussion is halted abruptly as Wolfgang and Heiko are clearly walking to a timetable. As they are putting on their rucksacks they inform me that I "look more German than Spanish" and disappear off into the Galician countryside.

Apart from the 100km to go stone, and possibly connected to it, Morgade is also the site of a tiny stone chapel, which you walk past on your way out of the village. It's another odd bit of piety and is allegedly a place for pilgrims to leave messages for one another, though how they would find them is beyond me. It is chaotic to the point of defacement. The walls have been written on, and there is paper strewn all over the floor. It looks like it's been ransacked and then had all the furniture removed. Not for the first time today, I find myself cursing the pilgrims who have gone before. It has all the spirituality of a bus shelter, only without the smell of urine. Like the 100km to go stone and the rubbish strewn at the foot of the Alto del Perdón, it reflects a sour side to pilgrimage behaviour.

It is not difficult to spot Portomarín, my destination for today. After several hours of walking through grey villages, a comparatively big town comes into view on a facing hillside where every building, with the exception of the church, is a brilliant white. There is no thousand year pilgrimage legacy here as the town was rebuilt in the 1960s when the previous settlement was flooded to build a reservoir. The church is original though and was moved, stone by stone, to its current site. It still a long way off and you don't actually see the drained river until it's time to cross over it.

Portomarín has an odd feel to it. It looks pleasant enough but there is something unnatural and sinister about it. The colour makes it look out of place and, on this particular afternoon, the sun is bouncing off the buildings, which gives it the look of a Mediterranean holiday resort. The main street is colonnaded on both sides and slopes uphill to a square dominated by the transplanted church. Close up it looks very austere indeed compared to the rest of the town. As it is a Sunday, I look for mass times but discover that there is only one today and I've missed it by several hours. I feel the need for a bit of quietness and decide to sit inside and gather my thoughts. Sadly, a few minutes later a tour party comes in with a particularly vocal guide and, with the commentary and the endless photograph taking, my concentration evaporates and the moment is lost.

There are options for places to stay and I head towards the nearby municipal hostel, which is another one that looks like an old, neglected college with big windows and corridors. It's definitely open as I can hear echoing voices and the unmistakable sound of showers being used, but the reception is unmanned. I sit and wait for several minutes and shout every now and again, but nothing happens. While I wait, I notice how dirty the place is and, as nobody seems to be in a major rush to take my money, I go in search of somewhere else. I head back down the colonnaded road to a place where two *refugios* are sited. The one I go for is the most expensive I have stayed in since my memorable first night in back in Saint-Jean-Pied-de-Port. It's setting me back a whopping €9 (the municipal one would have been €3). It is big and airy and, like most of the rest of the town, it is dazzlingly white, especially as the sunbeams are radiating through the huge windows. The dormitory is about the length of two tennis courts and, with all the bunk beds in it, it looks like a cross between a Pink Floyd album cover and a hospital ward. White net curtains partition the room and it is clinically clean. Wolfgang and Heiko are here, so are Hans and Gisela from the night in Ruitelán, and there is also a group of about a dozen walkers from America whom I've never seen before.

Today's walk was about 22km and I feel in really good nick, which is a sign that I took my breaks at the right moment. I spend a lazy afternoon having a wander around. I go down to the Roman bridge and walk across it. There is another stone church here too, strikingly brown in a sea of white – the town's clearly colour-coded its religious buildings. It also appears to be yellow arrow-free. My attempts to find the way out for tomorrow morning take the best part

189

of an hour, which is when I finally realise that the Camino doesn't go through the town at all but just skirts the side of it. It is a bit too much activity for the heat, and I compensate by settling down at a café on the main square, with a large beer in my hand, and watch the world go by. There are lots of people out and, unlike a lot of the Camino stops I've passed through on a Sunday, most of the shops are open so there's a lot of bustle. There is still something oddly unsettling about the place, and if the Spanish want to make their own version of *The Prisoner*, this would be a shoe-in as the town to film it in. It's pleasant but there's something not quite right. I half-expect to feel a stranger's hand on my shoulder at any minute and hear the words, "No-one ever leaves Portomarín."

It is warm enough in the evening to eat outside. Having dined well over the past couple of nights, my luck runs out tonight and I choose badly. It seems that rationing is in place at this particular restaurant, as there appears to be a shortage of bread, wine, and good humour from the staff. What I lose out on in terms of eating, I gain in the form of company. The evening is salvaged by the arrival of two German pilgrims, Herbert and Jürgen, who share my table due to lack of places elsewhere. I have seen them a few times before and think they are the pair who started out behind me on the climb out of Villafranca. Jürgen looks a bit like Waldorf out of the Muppets, with a round head and a white moustache. He doesn't speak any English but Herbert, a tall thin dark haired man with a friendly smile, speaks a few words which is on a par with my German. We soon discover that we all speak fluent football and the evening progresses with discussions about the merits of David Beckham and Bastian Schweinsteiger and great players of the past. Their enthusiasm is infectious and even a re-living of the Euro '96 semi-final penalty shoot-out is well meant. There is plentiful laughter as we try to communicate, and the lack of enough food hardly matters at all. Overall, it has been a rather Germanic day and all the better for it.

The colours are lovely just after sunset and I watch darkness fall with a strong sense of contentment. Back in the *refugio*, there's the familiar voice of BC asking someone which country Zurich is in. He is a long way from me on the other side of the partition but his voice does have a significant carry. He then follows this up with a running commentary about his preparations for sleep.

"It's funny because I always take this boot off first, but when it comes to socks I always take this one off before the other."

How bleeding fascinating. It's a timely reminder that although he makes one hell of a racket when he's asleep, he can be considerably more tedious when he's awake. Even so, there is that jealousy again. He strikes up conversations wherever he goes with ease. For me, it's always at least an effort, and sometimes an ordeal. I am much better when somebody approaches me. He's probably been laughing at me for a fortnight.

Anyway, he is not the bête-noir of the evening. That title falls to one of the leaders of the American walking group. Most of them are in their twenties but he looks as if he must be near or past retirement age. He comes in at about a quarter past nine, staggeringly drunk and having been given the gift of talking bollocks in tongues. He approaches one of the women in his group who is lying on her bunk, and talks loudly and gratingly in what sounds like a clumsy attempt at trying to chat her up. A few of us were asleep but we are all awake now and focusing on this man and a very embarrassed member of his party. When she suggests he might be causing a disturbance, he replies by saying,

"We're in Germany. Who cares?"

Given the makeup of tonight's dormitory he's not too far wrong, but when it's pointed out to him that he's in Spain, his reply is "Same difference."

That was two nationalities out to get him straight away, and I will happily freelance. He may be found dangling under the Roman Bridge tomorrow with a lot of stones in his rucksack. Hans looks at me from his top bunk with his "Aren't this lot funny?" smile.

Just as the situation starts edging into tension, a couple more people from his walking group surface and they drag him off somewhere, presumably to save him from either an international kicking, or himself.

My dormitory actually overlooks the footbridge that marks the start of today's walking. Well, it did last night, but this morning it is steeped in a dark Galician mist and nothing is discernible through the window. When I get to it, I can't see the other side and don't know if I am following the Camino or leaving East Berlin. There is a real autumnal feeling in the air as I navigate my way through some woods by barely adequate torchlight, and deliberate if the fog is going to be a prelude to sunshine or rain.

Gradually the visibility increases, the world becomes brighter and the weather mirrors yesterday, with streaky white clouds high above and the potential for it to be warm to scorching. It is another largely leafy day, though the path does follow a minor road, which provides a steady climb towards today's high point, Sierra Ligonde. About halfway up, I catch up with Rod and Cassie, the two South Africans I first met in Los Arcos and last saw nearly a fortnight ago in Mansilla de las Mulas. Rod is suffering a bit with shin splints, which possibly explains why I have caught up with them. I remember them ploughing effortlessly through the mud on the way to Nájera, leaving me and several other pilgrims in their wake. They are both in excellent spirits though, and it's really good to see them. We stop in a village called Gonzar for a drink and a catch-up. I was under the impression they'd been a couple for ages but in fact they have only been together for three months, and one of those has been taken up with walking across Spain.

"We figure out that if we can survive this we can survive anything," Rod grins, while Cassie nods her head in agreement. And who said romance was dead?

They are certainly doing fine so far. Their attempt at doing the Camino on a budget and cooking their own food wherever possible is proving to be a problem in Galicia. Although many hostels have kitchen facilities here, they don't supply pots, pans and other utensils, and this has meant eating out more often than they'd like.

"We're not bothered today, though," says Cassie with enthusiasm. "I went shopping yesterday and found some grinnery bigots."

Obviously, my face betrays confusion so Cassie elaborates.

"I discovered a great bakery and bought some grinnery bigots".

It's only when she reaches down into the depths of her rucksack and pulls out a whole grain loaf that the Rand finally drops and I realise she means a granary baguette.

They are good company and have led interesting lives. Rod has worked in a variety of restaurants, while Cassie had a sabbatical from her job in magazine publishing to spend a year helping out at a baboon sanctuary. She loves her animals and dislikes the way that so many along the Camino have been chained up. I imagine in the case of dogs that it's to stop them ripping the faces off pilgrims, which many look capable of doing. When I mention this, she shakes her head and says it still isn't right. She also refers back to the bull (and cow) running at Viana which created a negative impression on her and, to be perfectly honest, with me as well.

The walking in some places is now starting to resemble a procession. Rod refers to unleaded pilgrims as "slugs" because they don't carry their belongings like us "snails" do. It's now almost an endless round of saying "Buen Camino" as the route gets remarkably crowded, and overtaking and being overtaken is very much the norm. It feels like a weekend day out rather than a typical Camino experience. We're no longer the same homogenous group who can swap stories about the mystical Cruz de Ferro, the prosaic nature of the Meseta, and the annoying bastards who kept us awake at night. We're overwhelmed by people wearing clean boots and fresh smiles, who've never had to fight for washing line space and will never know the difference between a day like today and the walk into Burgos.

It's about 12km of climbing to get to Sierra Ligonde, which is about 400m higher up than where we started, but because we're following a road and there are well spaced stopping points along the way, the climb barely registers. Just after going over the summit I see the ten or so members of the American walking group from yesterday. I try to think of something sarcastic to say to the leader who was drunk last night as I pass, but can't think of anything, and settle for a cheery and unironic "Buen Camino". If the Germans and the Spanish didn't beat him up, why should I? The woman involved in last night's incident doesn't look particularly happy, it has to be said.

I decide to stay in Palas de Rei - don't worry there aren't any more rhyming couplets. Unlike Portomarín, it keeps itself hidden until the suburbs suddenly jump out at you. I am the first in the queue for a rather unloved-looking building which has peeling paint and a dark aspect to it. As *refugios* go it won't be a new entry into any pilgrim's top ten. I am signed in warmly by the smiling female *hospitalero* who seems glad that somebody has finally arrived, and am directed to the brighter but still shabby looking dormitory.

In the limited experience I have of Galicia, Palas de Rei is unique, in that I can't find anything going for it all. Absolutely nothing. Despite its regal sounding name, it's as undeniably dull and unattractive place as I have stayed in and possibly walked through. And this is with the sunshine bouncing off it: God knows what it looks like when the clouds roll over. It is difficult to gauge how big or what shape it is and, to be honest, you're hardly better off when you can. The alleged centre of the place turns out to be where I'm staying. It's truly featureless and it's not aided by the fact that today is a public holiday, meaning a lot of it is closed. It is the type of place where the sun goes down and wonders why it bothered to come up in the first place.

Once again it's time to embrace doing nothing, but somehow this is more difficult to do in an urban setting. There's a bench which is placed in the downward meander of the main road. It is quiet because of the holiday but it's hard to relax, and time passes slowly and painfully. In a week's time, I'll probably be screaming to have a moment like this, but now I feel edgy. The only person I've seen walking around the place is BC but he's staying in the town's other hostel. I want to preserve a moment of peace and tranquillity and think about what the Camino means to me and what's been achieved but, try as I might, it's not going to come. This is not going to be a great pilgrimage moment, or indeed a great pilgrimage day.

When I get back to my dorm, there is a group of about half a dozen Spanish girls in their early 20s, all talking excitedly. They are dressed for a big night out and I would love to know where they're going to find one. I am also questioning why they've brought spangly dresses and posh shoes on the Camino. Unsurprisingly, they started in Sarria, a town that now resembles Las Vegas compared to here.

I did notice earlier on that there are a few bars open though none jump out at me as being particularly attractive to eat in. One of them will have to do, and I walk around looking for the least worst. This messing around means that by the time I come to a decision many of the places are full up. I manage eventually to find a spot to eat in when a waiter reluctantly opens an outhouse across the courtyard from the main part of a restaurant. I eat a very lonely meal as the only inhabitant in the extension. Meanwhile, across the yard, I can see into the main bar where BC and the two German women are smiling, laughing and generally enjoying themselves. There is an empty space on their table too. This has been a really ill thought out end to what has been the dullest day on the Camino. The end is in sight and I must try to make the most of the time ahead.

I am half expecting to have my sleep disturbed by the Spanish girls breaking in after missing the ten o'clock curfew but I hear absolutely nothing. I'd love to know where they ended up, bearing in mind that most of Spain is deciding to go out at roughly the same time that pilgrims are being bolted indoors. Perhaps there is a lively bar in Palas de Rei, perhaps it gets going early, and perhaps the Pope is Jewish.

Come the morning I can't get out of the place fast enough, though speed is greatly reduced by the complicated route out of town and the fact I am doing it in the dark. My first aim is to find somewhere to eat, and after about forty-five minutes of careful navigation, I make my way through the beaded doorway of a *refugio* in the hamlet of San Xulián do Camino. It is full of familiar noise and colour, as pilgrims are getting their things together and preparing to head out. To my delight, I see Herb and Brian who are coming to the end of their breakfast and ask me to join them. They stayed here last night and eulogise about its friendliness and the communal meal they had in the evening. Other pilgrims on the table concur, and there is a really different atmosphere here to the place I've just left. You can sense a communal, resolute pilgrimage buzz throughout the building and, although there's very little to San Xulián itself, somehow doing nothing here would have been a lot more pleasurable than an evening of sod all in Palas de Rei.

Although today's walking is mainly on pathways with the occasional detour down a country lane or two, there is a significant reminder that the end is in sight. Not too far away is the N-547 which will be crossed a couple of times today. It's a main road that leads all the way into Santiago, and even when you're not flirting with it you can still hear the sound of its muffled traffic in the distance. There is a lot of woodland to enjoy, where butterflies dance in front of you and chestnuts and acorns fall intermittently on the path. It's corn harvesting time, and the lanes and fields are full of tractors. Those *horreos,* the small shed-like buildings on stilts which every house in Galicia seems to have in their gardens, will be full soon.

It's more glorious sunshine with a gentle wind blowing through the trees. It is the sort of day that Enid Blyton would write books about if she edited out the swearing.

Despite the heavy agricultural feel to the region, the local food speciality is octopus, and as I'm passing through Melide I'm enticed into a bar by a bloke standing by an open window who's chucking a few into boiling water with unadulterated enthusiasm. He also has the patter and informs everyone walking past that this is the best place to eat octopus in the whole of the region. I have no way of testing this as I'm not a big fan of seafood. What I can tell you with some certainty is that this place sells the biggest chorizo *bocadillo* I've ever seen in my life. I think about taking it outside and getting a lorry to run over it a bit, so I can get it into my mouth. I opt instead to push down on it and my actions crack the plate it is resting on. It takes a long time and some extensive chewing to finish it. I have consumed *menú del dia*s in less time. I do feel a bit guilty for not trying the octopus, so on my way out, I ask the man at the window if I can try a bit. A couple of minutes later a tentacle is dismembered and a small ring is cut off for me. It almost takes as much chewing as the *bocadillo*. I can't say I hate it but it's doubtful how much I could manage; I certainly wouldn't eat it out of choice. In the words of all amateur food critics with limited vocabulary all over the world, it tastes of chicken, albeit one made out of rubber.

Melide is just about the geographical centre of Galicia, and it's also where the Camino Francés is joined by another route, the Camino Primitivo, which starts in the northern city of Oviedo. It also appears to be a pre-determined lunch break for many of the unleaded pilgrimage groups so it is almost impossible not to see someone wearing a backpack. I stop my wander around and sit for a few minutes in the church of Sancti Spiritus. It's quite warm outside and this is a good place to cool off and have a Camino moment. It's two days to Santiago and I feel glad to have made it this far. My genuine fear of not making it over the Pyrenees seems a long time ago and a world away.

Now that I am coming to the end of my walk, I think now of whether I've made the most of it; and what things I could have done differently. I ponder the places I didn't linger in and think how the experience would have been different if I had. I manage to snap out of this dangerous line of thought. Everybody's Camino is different and there is no magic formula to have a better one than anyone else. Whatever decisions I have made were the right ones and made for the right reasons; possibly with the exceptions of the 30km epics into Astorga and Triacastela, but even they had positive outcomes. Last night was as disconnected from the pilgrimage as I have ever felt, but there is a lesson there too; the Camino – be in it.

There are sudden guilt feelings about my more uncharitable thoughts towards BC and other pilgrims along the way. I think back to the iron cross at Monte Irago and all those petitions written on paper, stones and on the soles of shoes. I don't know what's made my fellow pilgrims make all this effort to go for a long walk but the chances are that some of them are dealing with unspoken tragedy. Ultimately, we all have the same goal, whether we started in Saint-Jean-Pied-de-Port, Sarria or Paris. We are all pilgrims and we're doing the walk in the way that's best for us. If I haven't lived the past few weeks as charitably as I could have done, I now make the decision to fully embrace the time that's left and definitely make sure that every step is a prayer over the next 72 hours.

Like most Galician towns I have encountered, Melide appears better when you're looking over your shoulder at it. Pleasant though it was, and it is several dozen notches above Palas de Rei, it's good to be away from the cars and the noise, and embracing nature again. Using my classification, this is the last long-distance day of walking. It's a bit of a rolling trek, partly explained by the fact that the path crosses over six different rivers, but all the major climbs and epic stages of the Camino are now over. There is a faint smell of eucalyptus in the air and it's an easy stage to enjoy. It is also a rather good day for place names: I walked through Casanova earlier in the day and am seriously tempted to follow a sign to Villantime, which sounds like a gangster-run television programme. I don't want to deviate too much from the path, as the plan is to be settled in the picturesque haven at Ribadiso da Baixo by early afternoon and spend the rest of the warm daylight hours with my feet in the river, enjoying the sights, sounds and smells of the countryside.

What is it about the best-laid plans? Or in my case, the casually laid plans? When I get to Ribadiso the *refugio* is closed, for today at least. It is a shame as the place wins the prize for the best-looking hostel on the entire Camino. It is not particularly old but is a carefully built stone reconstruction of an older pilgrimage hospital, and it's beautifully in tune with its surroundings. It looks absolutely gorgeous, like an elegant farmhouse, and I was really looking forward to staying somewhere quiet and more scenic. Having completed a healthy 26.5km today I don't particularly want to carry on walking.

The bar next door is open so I sit outside with a beer and get my guide out to study my options. The solution is straightforward in that I have to press on to the town of Arzúa. There are several possibilities there so at least one should be open. The bad news is that is that it is 3km away, it's all uphill and it means taking in another slice of urban Galicia. I don't know anything about the place but I suspect it won't come close to being as tranquil and pleasing as here. There is a huge reluctance to put the backpack on once again and leave the banks of the Río Iso and its rather lovely bar, particularly when the body thinks it's time to stop.

Arzúa is another place that won't be finding itself on the lids of biscuit tins, though it's just about an improvement from yesterday's stopover. It is a bit different to Palas de Rei in that it has two distinct parts to it. There is a new ugly part, which stretches along its main street, but if you look just beyond that you can find the old ugly part as well. Architecture has not been kind here, and I am fast coming to the conclusion that Galicia doesn't do towns particularly well. I have walked through several villages today which you would happily put on a postcard, but when things get even slightly urban they get significantly unattractive.

The hostels are all on the main road which heads into Santiago and are clustered at the entrance to the town. There is nothing charming about any of them, and in that respect, they match the character of the rest of the place. If anything they have a look of hotels about them, and they are about as far removed from the charm of the closed hostel at Ribadiso as you can get. Mine has only been open a couple of years and you can tell. Unlike other hostels, this place actually smells new and feels a little characterless. Still, at least it has doors on the shower cubicles. There are no catering facilities but you could probably eat off the floor if you wanted to; it really does look that clean. It is pleasant enough and it's another place where you don't need a crowbar to prize a space open between bunks.

As usual, I check my route out for tomorrow morning and then take up my usual afternoon position in a bar. Given the noise and the dust of Arzúa and the fact that a main road goes right through its middle, it isn't the most pleasant place to have an outdoor drink. I still have one though; it tastes particularly good and feels well deserved. It has been a prayerful, if unintentional 30km plus day, and the sun is shining again. Things improve still further with the arrival of the ever cheerful Brian and Herb. After this morning's brief chat comparing hostels, it is time for a proper catch-up. We haven't met up since León and the tone of the late afternoon becomes more and more celebratory and considerably less sober.

Herb has suffered from shin splints but Brian and I have remained unscathed. The worst pilgrim complaint I can come up with is the bit of muscle pain in my shoulder.

"But it's not a pilgrimage without suffering," Herb argues with the familiar friendly glint in his eye.

"My torture's been mental", I reply and regale a few stories about my encounters with BC, who I'm guessing must be in Arzúa too.

Their version is a man they mentioned back in the evening at Agés; Luck the British man whom I've heard about a few times – Rod and Cassie talked about him yesterday – but I've gone through the entire Camino without our paths having crossed. I can count the number of British people I've met on one hand and he certainly isn't one of them. Brian suggests we have had an inter-country annoying person swap although both BC and Luck, we decide, are harmless.

We adjourn across the road to a restaurant, which has a comprehensive *menú del dia*. As a form of celebration, we decide on a greatest hits package which involves us choosing the things we've eaten the most over the past few weeks. Possibly for the last time ever I consume meatballs followed by pork and chips, and some *flan*, exactly the same course-for-course as Herb, as we talk about pilgrimage highlights and drink more and more.

Their highlight was crossing over Monte Irago very early in the morning under a full moon. "I'm not a believer Rudy," Brian adds confidentially while scratching his beard "but there was something magical about it. I felt something." He almost looks embarrassed to say it.

I have to think about my best bits. In terms of the walking, coming through the cloud line in the Pyrenees on day 1 is up there, but I talk about the moment of total peace and contentment during my evening in Castrojeriz. Now it's my time to feel slightly embarrassed about trying to explain something that really doesn't make an awful lot of sense to anyone else.

"We've all had moments, Rudy. Lots of them and maybe we'll be the only ones who'll be able to understand and share them." Brian continues wisely, if drunkenly.

The mood changes when they jokingly ask if I've got engaged to Carrie, and I look at my watch and notice that her mother and aunt were due to fly back to Canada a couple of days ago. I will never know if they made it to Santiago or not. We swap pilgrimage and *refugio* stories amid much laughter and only decide to leave when there is no more space left on the table for another empty wine bottle.

It is strange how fate has a way of sneaking up on you. There may be just a couple of days of flat walking to go, but trouble can be closer than you think. In my case, it happened on the drunken sway back to my bed after last night's rather joyous meal. I was fortunate to be opposite my hostel when I felt my stomach loosening rapidly, and a pleasantly drunken amble became a frantic dash to the toilet. Sickness came on quickly and it was clear that this wasn't an ordinary stomach upset. In the space of about ninety seconds, I'd gone from being alcoholically content to thinking I was going to have that John Hurt *Alien* moment. I actually sprinted across the road, through my hostel and straight to the bathroom. When I got there, my body was so unsettled that I didn't know which end to evacuate first. What happened was that I had to do both, which made me feel like a dog chasing his own tail. I threw up with such spectacular violence that I could feel the muscles in my neck expanding to the size of a tree. The vomiting physically hurt to a degree I'd never encountered before. If that wasn't bad enough, there was also simultaneous diarrhoea, and the sense that my whole body was erupting in pain. It was a difficult few minutes of constantly turning round as my stomach contents queued to leave my body via the fastest means possible.

If only it had ended there and then, but this was only the prelude. I went back to my bunk and tried to settle down, but after a couple of minutes the stomach pains returned and I had to negotiate my way out of my sleeping bag - never easy when you're in a hurry and drunk - and head to the bathroom again for more audible illness and tangible agony. And so began the pattern of the night, with me legging it across the dorm at regular intervals to the bathroom and not knowing which end of my body to see to first. There were at least half a dozen panic-led visits, and it got to the stage where it would have made more sense if I'd just brought my sleeping bag into the toilet and tried to sleep there. Every return to bed had me rolling around in a fever-induced delirium, waiting for my insides to erupt again. Luckily, the hostel, although large, had fewer than ten pilgrims in it, and only one of them was in my curtained off section. Attempts at sleep were futile; my body was making disturbing noises, my neck muscles were still throbbing and my mind was rambling and feverish. For the first time ever in a dormitory, I found myself shivering and, despite fishing several blankets from a nearby pile, nothing seemed to change. This was easily the most uncomfortable and viciously ill night of my life. My body did eventually quieten down, but it was a long time coming. I managed to sleep from about 5am to 6am but that was the sum total of kippage.

I feel extremely woozy when I wake up and I go through the motions (an unfortunate word given the night I have just had) of getting ready for the day's walk, but I know I'm not up to it at all. I am a mixture of dizziness, exhaustion and irrationality, and the sensible part of my brain is telling me to stay in Arzúa. I have no idea what the rules are for staying additional nights in *refugios* are but it will be a tough *hospitalero* who would turn me down in my hour of need.

I decide to head out but only to next door where Herb and Brian are staying, and which has a café open for breakfast. Even that short distance feels like an ordeal. I'm not hiding my state particularly well, as they both comment on how pallid and tired I look when I join them. They are both in good shape so I assume the food from last night wasn't to blame. I spare them the gory details of the last nine hours but they can guess at the agony and won't get even close to the reality.

Herb returns to a theme of last night's meal, which now feels a very long time ago indeed. "As I said Rudy, it's not a pilgrimage without suffering."

He then catches the look in my eye and back-pedals carefully, "But I guess you didn't really want to hear that right now."

I gaze at what is available and curse the fact that when I finally arrive in a place which can put on a substantial breakfast I'm too bloody ill to take advantage of it. The only thing that looks vaguely manageable is dry toast, and even that turns out to be a struggle. Apart from the general gut rumblings, I can also feel a huge pressure building up in one of my ears. If I go head down on the table now I am not going to wake up for hours. My friends are concerned and I try to make light of my predicament, despite the overwhelming evidence to the contrary. I let Herb and Brian go on and I stay in the café a bit longer to see if I feel any better. Looking back at yesterday, I consider that I may have drunk some dodgy water, so I use the opportunity to clean out my bottles completely and refill them from the available taps. When I do get out of my chair, it is with all the grace of Bambi trying to learn to walk.

My walking poles are a necessity just to keep me upright as I walk gingerly down Arzúa's main street. It's painfully slow going and I'm aware of just how many other pilgrims are walking past me. If the illness doesn't get me, the energy expounded by saying "Buen Camino" just might. I manage about 2km, just enough to take me outside the town and back on a rural track. The effort in getting this far has taken a lot out of me and I have to sit down and rest. It's the first time I have to take such a break, and the sad thing is it really is badly needed. This is, without doubt, the lowest ebb of my Camino. I feel totally drained of all energy and morale, and really wish I'd done the sensible thing and stayed in my hostel. Turning back doesn't feel like an option now as it just seems so far away.

Just as I try to stand again, leaning heavily on my sticks, my stomach decides to give up what little I had managed to eat for breakfast, and I ruthlessly and loudly pebbledash some ferns. This happens just as BC comes around a corner behind me. On another day, the two events might have been linked but certainly not today. He is with the two German women again and they rush towards me. His concern is genuine and he searches in his rucksack for dried fruit and instructs the women to give up what they have.

"I swear by dried fruit for an upset stomach. It never lets you down," he pronounces and puts his arm around me.

I can't be certain of the medical veracity of what he's just said, but the arm around the shoulder means a lot. After a fair amount of rooting around in her rucksack, one of the girls finds some dried berries and gives all her supply to me but with a warning.

"They make your mouth go red," she says with a very concerned look on her face.

As if I'm bothered. I don't care if they turn my body fluorescent green and make me grow antlers. I take a few straight away and just hope to God that I can keep them down. My helpers want to stay with me for a bit longer, but it would be unfair to hold them back. I am not exactly going to be pleasant company. Mind you, that could have easily been said on a couple of other days on the Camino. I thank them with what little energy I have and wave them on. BC looks over his shoulder as he walks away and shouts,

"If you're not in Santiago in two days we're coming to look for you."

I am too full of self-pity to respond and I can't help thinking that I've been a bit off-hand with their very welcome and measured help.

I sit down for a bit longer and swallow some more dried berries and apricots with a little water, and take a few tentative steps forward. I definitely feel better and can keep going in the right direction, which is more than I could a quarter of an hour ago. I stop again about thirty minutes later but this time manage to do it in a village café. I can't face the prospect of food but the idea of a sit-down and a hot drink has a massive appeal. It is also an excuse to get my guidebook out and have a look at the possibilities for today's stage – something I hadn't thought about in my dazed and confused state this morning.

It is not a bad day if you are stupid enough to be ill and walking. The route is generally flat and uncomplicated, with a good selection of strategically placed cafés along the way - I can feel that there's going to be a lot of resting today. The only downside, and it's a serious one, is that the first option of an overnight stop is Santa Irene, which would mean a walking day of 18km. This would rival my shortest day on the Camino so far, and it's considerably less than I walked yesterday but right now it really does seem like a hell of a long way.

I pay absolutely no attention to what is going on around me as I walk. My face is pointing downwards and the only thing I become aware of is that the sun has come out after a fairly chilly morning. I stop again after a further 4km in Calle where I draw the attention of Jürgen and Herbert, who are worried by my appearance and walk over to ask how I am. Apparently, I have very pale skin and a bright red mouth. They were not planning to stop here until they saw me, but they sit at my table and encourage me not to move anymore today, with Herbert announcing, "You must rest!"

They are all for trying to arrange for a taxi to take me somewhere, but I refuse and tell them I'm alright; easily the least convincing sentence I've ever uttered in my whole life.

They are not fobbed off that easily, and they stay with me for twenty minutes before heading reluctantly on. I barely know the two German women, and Jürgen and Herbert - of course, I know BC a little better - but their genuine concern to help has really affected me. They may well all be laughing at my expense somewhere along the route, but I very seriously doubt it. It is simple help for a fellow pilgrim, given without question and not seeking reward. If I ever doubted the Camino spirit before, I certainly don't now.

The rest of the morning turns into a real foot slog. I am no longer feeling the urge to throw up, but every step induces pain that seems to reverberate around my body. This is accompanied by a loss of concentration, which means that toes keep getting stubbed and my wits are hardly about me as we crisscross the busy N-547 road. It is just as well that some of the crossings are by a subway, as I'm doubtful as to how well I can judge the speed of oncoming traffic. I'm aware that other pilgrims are stopping to have picnics in the warm Autumn sunshine but all I'm thinking about is getting to my next stopping point, ticking off the landmarks as I go. It is agonisingly slow going and my legs feel as if they are wading through treacle. I didn't have much energy to begin with this morning but now the needle is well and truly in the red zone.

Another thing I notice is something I don't really want to see at all. Just as I feel I am on the brink of collapse, there is another roadside memorial to a pilgrim who died on route to Santiago. I don't want to be reminded of someone popping their clogs twenty-four hours away from reaching their goal, but it stays in my head as my footsteps become shorter and the sun beats down ruthlessly with greater and greater intensity.

It is a lengthy and painful 7km between Calle and the next café at Brea, which is just off the main route of the Camino. In that time, I haven't passed a single water fountain, or at least haven't noticed one, and both my water bottles only have droplets in them. It is about midday when I almost fall through the door of a café, with the aim of not leaving it for at least half an hour and probably longer. I order an orange juice and promptly fall asleep with my head resting on my table. The waiter wakes me up about an hour later and asks me if I'm alright. I feel like I am welded to the floor. If every step of the Camino is indeed a prayer, my feet have turned agnostic. I don't want to go anywhere; it's not the illness that's finally got to me, it's the absolute exhaustion. It may be the lack of sleep from last night, yesterday's lengthy walk, or the accumulated wear and tear on the body after covering 775km in five weeks, or more likely all of the above that has finally caught up with me. Fatigue has drowned me in one huge wave and left me beached in this café. I also belatedly realise that I am hungover as well. The day isn't over either.

I am told that Santa Irene is still 3km away. That is comfortably less than an hour's walk on a normal day but this is a long way from being one of those. With water bottles refilled, I step outside into the afternoon heat. I still feel bloody awful and not even slightly revived by the brief sleep. Despite my vow to walk the entire distance, I can't help thinking that if someone offers me a lift right now I'll take it.

Never before have the kilometre posts felt so widely spaced. I'm still stubbing my toes and tripping over my walking poles, and the dusty pathway is echoing to the sound of some good old Anglo-Saxon profanities that have never been used on flat terrain before. Just when I am thinking that I'm going to keel over on my poles, the *refugio* comes into view and I make a dive for it. I am too worn out to be relieved.

Sweat is falling down my face in raging torrents, my eyes are bulging and my mouth looks like I've been chewing broken bottles, but the *hospitalero* doesn't appear to notice. I'm greeted with a friendliness I'm unsure I deserve. She is also very apologetic,

"I'm afraid that we do not have any opportunities for you to eat here."

I don't care if there isn't a bloody roof, just give me a bed. There is a further delay because I try to buy a €5 bed with a €50 note and the *hospitalero* doesn't have change. All I want to do is sleep and I am tempted to tell her not to worry about it and keep the change. In my current state, I certainly won't regard it as a waste of money. As it happens, a Dutch pilgrim comes through the door and after a bit of note swapping with her, I pay the appropriate cash and I'm directed upstairs to the dormitories. It is 2.30pm on what has felt like one of the longest days of my life. I am devoid of energy, enthusiasm and pretty much everything else. Every part of my body is throbbing and aching, and there is no way on the sodding planet that I'm moving from my bed until tomorrow morning.

15th October: Stage 34 - Santa Irene to Santiago de Compostela

I didn't even undress before getting into my sleeping bag and I wake up after fourteen hours of largely uninterrupted sleep. During that time, I am only intermittently aware of anything going on in the dormitory. I vaguely remember hearing Spanish voices when I was drifting off but that's about it. Of Santa Irene the place, I can tell you absolutely nothing, apart from the fact that this particular hostel is on a bend of the N547. I know this because on the odd occasion my eyes did have the energy to open during the night (and there weren't many), my dormitory lit up like the closing scene of *Close Encounters of the Third Kind* every time a lorry or a bus went past.

I don't feel brilliant but at least I'm in a fit state to walk and maybe even enjoy it, which is a vast improvement on yesterday when I felt like Keith Richards, warmed up. I am still a bit lethargic but quite able to face the world, and I get up and out early enough to enjoy the last moments of morning darkness. There is a waning crescent of a moon but the rest of its outline can easily be made out. It is joined by a good scattering of other heavenly bodies, which is appropriate for the day I should finally make it to St James of the Field of Stars. All being well (I'm not taking anything for granted now), this is my last morning on the Camino and I'm sure I should be excited or sad. To be honest, I feel exactly the same as I have done on every morning I've been walking; I enjoy the moment and don't really think about any destination, even if it's the ultimate one. After yesterday's experience, I'm just happy to be able to put one foot in front of the other without feeling pain, and to be able to take notice of my surroundings again. Anyway, I have a more immediate target to think about than Santiago.

The early part of today's route leads away from the road and along a sizeable woodland path. I'm glad it's wide as my torch battery gives out just as I enter it, and there is just enough moonlight to make out where I'm going. Apart from avoiding branches, all my thoughts this morning have been about BC and the German women. I really want to thank them for their help yesterday: it was their words as much as their actions that have stayed with me over the last day. I find my way out of the woods and a couple of tunnels lead me back and forth under the road before I finally reach Arca do Pino. This would be the logical place for pilgrims to stay over before Santiago, as there are two big *refugios* here. Right on cue, BC and the German women walk out of a café just as I am walking in. They are all smiles and are really pleased to see me. Apparently, I was talked about last night with real concern. The strange thing is that I am happy to see them too. Genuinely happy. As I've often thought in the past few weeks, you may do the walking on your own but you need an awful lot of people to help you along the way - in the Camino as in life; I'm just noticing it a lot more now. I give them all a huge hug but I am not prepared for the next bit at all. I find myself crying. Not a lot, but enough to feel embarrassed, as I thank them for their help yesterday. They ask me how I'm feeling and to be honest at this moment I feel absolutely euphoric; still a bit queasy as well, but the joy of seeing them again drowns out that sensation. We vow to meet up in Santiago and I promise that I will be buying the drinks. Even saying that doesn't make the city feel close. Arriving there seems just as remote today as it has ever done.

I enter the café, have a hot chocolate and then enjoy some bread, the first non-dried fruit related thing I have managed to keep down in 24 hours. Another pilgrim I vaguely know joins me and we exchange pleasantries. When I go up to the bar to pay the bill I am charged an unusually large amount for the very little I've consumed. The waiter then explains that he thought I was with the other walker and put his breakfast on there too. He is just about to issue a new receipt when I suddenly remember the mysterious beer arriving on my table when I was in León, bought under the misapprehension that I was Irish. Here's a chance to pass on some fortune to someone else which I promised myself I'd do, and I feel happy doing it.

I head back onto the Camino just as the sky becomes more day than night, and it's another walk through woods, with its familiar and heavy scent of eucalyptus. At least I can see where I'm going now. I am facing ahead rather than looking downwards, and I'm in a position to enjoy it. There is an increasing sensation of personal celebration; not because the end of the walk is nigh, but purely because I am not in the same state as I was in yesterday. Jubilation builds on joy and happiness as I think about my helpers and the fact that I'm still going. I am walking in fledgling sunshine where stubbed toes can be laughed off, and I'm quite likely to hug anyone who thinks I'm German. Even the main road starts to look attractive. This private world of positivity lasts right up until I reach the village of Amenal. Here my walking activates a talking advertisement for a guesthouse in Santiago. In such a quiet place, the shock is unsettling. The locals must love it. I give them something else to cheer about milliseconds later when "Fuck me!" echoes through the parish at a considerably louder volume. Possibly not the language to use when approaching a shrine but very much in keeping with the previous five weeks. On the way out of Villafranca, I think I broke the world record for the number of times the word "bastard" has been uttered in an hour-long period. There was a lot of swearing that night at Terradillos, not to mention my uncharitable thoughts every time BC hove into view.

Being scared shitless in the middle of nowhere by a speaking sign is enough to burst my intimate rapture bubble and bring me down to normal pilgrimage levels. I'm back to the here and now. Another village has the now traditional Galician abomination of a vending machine propped up against a dry stone wall. The normal words have been removed and the Coca-Cola swoosh now represents the map of the Camino complete with place names. It's laughably vile but it's a reminder that a past life is fast approaching. The traffic is getting louder and the walk becomes stealthily more urban. It also starts to become an exercise in ticking off the landmarks along the way.

The Camino skirts the edges of Santiago's airport, and once again the wire fencing marking the boundary is filled with improvised crosses made from twigs. I slow down and look at them as I pass, hundreds of them of varying sizes, materials, and frailty. There is a similar barrier which separates the Camino from the main road, and that too is filled up. I have never been sure if these crosses are meditative or decorative. I've never been tempted to add to them, and there's a fear here that if I take a step back and scan the entire structure, they may have been ordered to spell "Coca-Cola".

I stop for a drink in Lavacolla. It may sound like another soft drink but it's another traditional stop on the Camino; it's where the pilgrims of yore used to wash in the local river before they entered Santiago. There is a reasonable chance that this tradition started because of a mistranslation. Apparently, Lavacolla comes from the Galician for "full of scree" but an early monk translated it as "wash your genitalia." At least that is what he said when the police came looking for him. I'm not here to wash anything. I'm after more hot chocolate at a bit of a sit-down. It is a busy place and there are backpacks everywhere, but there's no sense of excitement among the pilgrims, no sense of goal achievement or approaching triumph. This could be any café on any stage of the pilgrimage and the only thing that distinguishes it is the occasional sound of a plane taking off or landing nearby.

The walk continues down small roads and lanes; the milestones appearing with what appears to be stunning frequency. The next landmark to tick off is the local television station and then it feels like no time at all until the arrival at Monte del Gozo. Traditionally this is where pilgrims catch their first glimpse of the towers of the cathedral, assuming the Galician weather isn't playing up. Its name means "hill of pleasure", and this is based on the idea of being able at last to see the final destination. It's one of the most talked and written about places on the Camino, but it often comes with a warning in books and articles as it tends to provoke extreme emotions. For some, it is the happiness of seeing the goal of their walk. For others, there is an incredible sadness to be had in nearing the end of the pilgrimage and the thought of adjustment afterwards. Tears are commonplace and it is easy to understand both emotions.

Although it is a beautiful day, it's difficult to spot the cathedral due to some vicious tree planting, but it is in view. It's an occasion that cries out for some kind of feeling; a sense of achievement, of euphoria, or unhappiness. I have only a sense of neutrality, accompanied by the leftovers of yesterday's nausea. I stay for a few minutes, looking ahead to my target and waiting for a surge of emotion to sweep over me, but nothing is going to come. I am enjoying the view as I have any other view along the Camino, but I can't manufacture a feeling of either elation or melancholy. I remain strictly dispassionate. To be honest I was a lot happier to see the *refugio* at Santa Irene yesterday afternoon.

The significance of Monte de Gozo has led to some redesigning - that is the polite way of putting it - which may account for my lack of feeling. Pope John Paul II came here in 1993 and the hill was remodelled to provide a place to put up a monument to commemorate the visit. It is a hideous and totally unnecessary steel ball. I'm guessing the vast majority of people who come here are pilgrims, and I suspect none of us cares it's there. It's just as much an aberration as the drinks machine I saw earlier but this was publically funded with the idea of enhancing the Camino. In that, it fails brilliantly.

The revamping didn't end there. Lower down the hill on the Santiago side, a site was cleared to build a huge hostel that resembles a holiday camp, albeit an austere one. There are spaces here for several hundred pilgrims; bear in mind that most of the places I've stayed in cater for around forty and the largest one in Astorga had one hundred and fifty beds. There is a sizeable demand for people who want to stay here a night, allowing them a triumphal march into the city the following morning in time for the pilgrims' mass at the cathedral. I know a couple of the unleaded pilgrimage groups stop here. You can't disguise the ugliness of the entire site – and by the look of it no attempts were made – but whatever sense of history that still remains is smothered by artificially imposed modernity. The feeling I have is one of anti-climax, and that has nothing to do with finally seeing Santiago.

What all my reading about Monte de Gozo has not prepared me for is the fact that the city begins 300m away, at the bottom of the hill. I was expecting some sort of gentle shift from the rural to the urban to allow some gathering of thoughts and reflection, but I am going to have to deal with road junctions and traffic in a matter of minutes. The adjustment is going to be rapid and all consuming. The steel memorial ball marks an abrupt, unpleasant and unexpected change of gear. The urban sprawl has enveloped a historic centre of worship and we pilgrims are going to be absorbed into it. We are now going to be outnumbered.

I forget how grim walking to a city centre can be. Thankfully, it's not as tedious as the way into Burgos, or as dangerous as trying to get into León, but it's as far removed from the Galicia I've mostly enjoyed over the past few days. It is a big jump in scale from the towns as well. There are buses and lorries and people in suits talking into mobile phones. Normal life for many, but alien to a pilgrim: we are from another age and life, and this is not our world at all. The Camino passes an exhibition centre on the way in with a sculpture showing the names of famous people who have done the pilgrimage.

Shortly afterwards I stop off in a bar which is gearing up for the lunchtime trade. There is nothing here to suggest that this a regular pilgrim haunt. People are wearing ties for a start, and the only backpack on display is mine. The orange juice is superb though and it comes with friendly conversation from the barman who encourages me to stay and have lunch. Looking around, this would be the poshest place I have eaten at on the entire walk, but I am not quite ready to sacrifice my pilgrimage status yet, even though the barman is adamant that walkers stop here all the time. The longer I stay, the more I feel I don't belong and the more I want what has become familiar. I want to be with my own again; the scruffy lot who are used to sharing dormitories and surviving on one meal a day, the ones who know all about the size of the Meseta because they've walked across it, the people who can sniff out unmarked village shops, and can spot sprayed yellow arrows in fog.

For some reason, part of the fringes of Santiago remind me of Guildford, but it does get better. It is only when I am nearing its centre that I realise that I don't actually know where I'm going. Unlike other days, I have three possible destinations: finding somewhere to sleep, going to the cathedral, or seeking out the pilgrimage bureau. I am not used to facing decisions like this and I am so caught out by it that I stand still for a few seconds, which become minutes before settling on what to do. I come to the conclusion that the last day should be like the others, and my first priority should be finding a bed for the night. This involves turning left away from the heart of the city and heading towards the rather imposing Seminario Menor de Santiago which is situated on a small hill. It is a massive place with shares its pilgrimage shelter status with being a school. I get there just after it opens and find myself standing behind the Hungarian bloke whom I walked with on the way to Pamplona. He has actually done an additional three-day walk to Finisterre and came back to Santiago this morning. He wants to stay for another night and, by the look of him, he is more than capable of walking all the way back to Saint-Jean-Pied-de-Port.

This is a far more formal signing in. Gone is the simple form filling on a table before getting your *credencial* stamped. This involves queuing up at a reception desk and it has a formulaic and impersonal quality to it, which makes it more hotel than hostel. Unlike other *refugios*, you can stay here for three nights, and I

213

decide to do just that. I am aware that I'm not 100% after yesterday and want to fully recover. I am also curious to see who else is here and who's going to make it into the city over the next couple of days.

The dormitories are upstairs and they look like Victorian hospital wards. There are no bunks but rows and rows of simple beds with a bedside locker situated next to them. The space between each bed looks like it's been measured to the millimetre and repeated for the entire room, giving it a meticulous sense of order. Sunlight is pouring through large windows but it still has a severe ambience to it. There is enough space here for two hundred people to sleep, making it the largest abode I've stayed in.

Even though it is the last day, I stick to the usual shower and clothes washing routine before I head towards the Cathedral and the city centre. It is a walk down one slope and back up a facing one to get there with an easy transition from the new to the old. I find myself wandering through the narrow medieval streets and taking in a few of the shops. Inevitably, a few are selling Camino t-shirts, one of which has various destinations printed on it separated by yellow arrows. One of the places mentioned is Samos which I missed by taking a different route to Sarria, and for a brief couple of seconds I look at it and have a strange feeling of guilt as if I've taken an illegal short cut. I also see the t-shirt that I saw on my first day at St Jean with the bandaged foot on the front and the slogan "No Pain No Glory". I smile looking at it now and think back to how worried I was at the beginning. My feet have survived the journey remarkably intact. It is just my insides that have suffered and, given what happened to me, that really wouldn't make an attractive t-shirt.

It's a casual amble, which involves taking mental notes of bars and restaurants for potential use later, but my immediate aim is to find the Pilgrimage Office and receive my *compostela* – my certificate to show I've completed the Camino. It is not too far from the Cathedral itself and there are several people ahead of me in the queue. I wait patiently with my *credencial* and study its impressive and colourful collection of stamps from *refugios*, bars and churches. One of my friends who did the last 200km of the walk as an unleaded pilgrim praised the warmth of welcome that he received from the *hospitaleros* here. They asked with an air of genuine concern about his physical state, and whether he had somewhere to stay. When I reach the desk I just get a rather impersonal form to fill in, before having my name written in Latin in the appropriate space on the *compostela*. It is certainly not unfriendly, but it does feel a bit clinical. This isn't an ending and it doesn't feel like one.

The Camino can only finish in one place and I walk the short distance to Praza do Obradoiro, the main square of the city and stare at the façade of the cathedral and its towers. I am not alone in doing this. There are groups of people with their tour guides and a lot of cyclists are having their photos taken in front of the most popular view of the cathedral with its gothic towers and staircases. There are group hugs among backpackers and high-fives being displayed. There are smiles of achievement in all directions. I am anonymous among the tourist activity and I don't recognise anybody. My backpack is back in the dormitory and, at this moment, I feel a bit naked without it. I want people to know I walked 800km to get here and didn't just step off a plane. I want to tell people that the red specks on my boots are from La Rioja and that I have been over the Pyrenees, crossed the Meseta and been violently ill in Arzúa. That I have survived the distance, the weather and the snoring. But there's no-one to tell and, at this moment, no-one to celebrate with. It's not anti-climactic because it doesn't quite feel like the end, but it is low key.

Everything looks beautiful and inviting in the late afternoon sunshine but there is a huge part of me that doesn't want to go into the cathedral at all. That would mean the end of the pilgrimage and I am still somehow not ready for that. I stay in the square just staring at the buildings around me for about half an hour before deciding to take the plunge and go through the main door. It's still fairly busy inside and I'm distracted by guided tours and the cameras, and even though there's enough space for all of us, I know it's not supposed to finish like this. I can see the statue of St James above the altar but I stay just inside the doorway and say a silent prayer before walking out again.

I head back in the narrow streets of the old part of the city and my vague wandering is disturbed about ten minutes later when I hear my name being shouted. Herbert and Jürgen are sitting on an outside table of a café with a bottle of wine between them. Looking at them, it's probably not their first. I pull a chair over while they try to grab the waiter's attention with no success whatsoever. I shout a confident "jefe!" and the waiter reacts as if somebody's put some voltage through him. I can't resist a self-gratifying "Yes" and a look up to the heavens in celebration. If my dad is up there feeling proud he probably loses this sentiment seconds later when I ask for a wine glass in Italian.

They seem delighted to see me; particularly as the last time we ran into each other I was trying and failing not to look ill. It is hard to believe that was only yesterday morning. The sickness is brushed over with some fractured German and a couple of gestures. The fact is that yesterday doesn't really matter anymore. We are in Santiago di Compostela – we've made it. They laugh at my description of where I am staying and contrast it with where they are. They have holed up at the Hospital de los Reyes Cátolicos which is on the same square as the cathedral and has the reputation of being possibly the oldest hotel in the world. It's now one of the most expensive Paradors in Spain but, like the one in León, it was originally designed for pilgrims. I am guessing there are no queues for the showers or shortages of washing line space. They can probably take their walking boots right up to the side of their bed and leave by whichever door they want whenever they want.

I should point out that that is where I'll be dining there this evening too, but my experience is going to be considerably different to theirs. The place has a tradition of inviting the first ten pilgrims who show up with their *compostela*s at the appropriate times to a meal, whether it be breakfast, lunch or dinner. It sounds great until you get to the small print. The meals are at unusual times compared with the rest of the hotel and you don't get to eat in the main dining room, so there'll be no throwing of bread rolls in Herbert and Jürgen's direction. The Parador goes to great lengths to minimise the luxury of dining there to the extent that it feels like the most token of gestures. Even so, it's part of the Camino experience and if anyone had offered me a free meal over the past five weeks, I'd have taken it enthusiastically and blessed the person who had made the invitation.

I head towards the hotel at 6.25pm for a meal that is served at 7. Needless to say, the hotel doesn't want scruffy walkers who have accumulated several weeks of mud and dust anywhere near the main entrance, and you're directed to wait in the doorway to its underground car park. This is situated on a road leading down from the main square and out of the sight of anyone who may be looking in awe, either at the cathedral or the Parador. When I get there the only two people already waiting are the German women who have spent a lot of the last couple of weeks walking with BC. Oddly and sadly, BC isn't here on the one dining occasion I would really like to see him. They ask me how I am feeling and, much to my embarrassment, I realise I don't know their names. I manage to thank them properly for their help yesterday and discover that they are called Klara and Monika, and are on a gap year before university. I like the symmetry of starting the pilgrimage with a Monika (the woman on the train to St Jean whom I didn't see again) and my last walking day with one. For the rest of their gap year, they have some charity work lined up in Africa which starts after Christmas. They have made it to Santiago unscathed, as has the next person to join us, an athletic and happy looking German woman in her twenties who is new to me.

I was expecting the notion of a free meal would be a popular one but there are only seven of us in line when the appropriate hour comes. In keeping with the surroundings, a roughly dressed member of staff appears out of nowhere and checks our *compostela*s to make sure they're less than three days old. He is offhand, clearly irritated, and makes the encounter feel as if we are taking part in a drug deal. He then points us back up the street to the hotel reception while he disappears through the back of the car park and meets us there. We are then ushered through the reception and courtyards of the Parador at great speed - it is easily the fastest I've walked on the entire Camino - and finally shown into a pokey room with mismatched furniture, and dirty tablecloths which were probably white at some stage. It is then a march upstairs to the kitchens and a wait in line with a tray while an unenthusiastic chef places various courses on it with a fair amount of impatience, followed by a return to our dining room. Everything about the experience says that we are an inconvenience. After weeks of people being happy to see us, or at least giving that impression, we are all a bit shocked by the unfriendliness, but we are receiving charity and rise above it. In fact, it is a good icebreaker, bringing laughter to the event, and the meal takes place in an atmosphere of good fun and an unspoken but tangible sense of achievement in getting here.

217

The major topic of conversation is no longer about previous experiences along the way, but whether to continue the walk or not. The Camino can be extended by another three days to finish at the Atlantic Ocean at Finisterre - world's end - and the athletic German woman is heading there tomorrow. My other German friends are staying here for another day and are looking at taking a bus to a place called Muxia and having a one day walk to Finisterre from there. It may sound odd to be thinking about where to go next when we've only just got here but it's understandable to have the need to keep walking. It is going to be difficult to adjust to normal life after this, and if you can "warm down" by a having a few days of extra walking, I can see how that would help. I know I am not going to do it, but the temptation is there.

The company, like on most Camino meals when you are thrown together, is superb. I would love to tell you how delicious the food is but this would be a complete lie. None of us knows what the meat of the main course is, and we can't safely rule out roadkill. It might be pork, but if bets are being taken, the wallet is staying firmly in the pocket. As meals go it is about as remarkable as the surroundings and quite possibly the worst one of the entire pilgrimage, but you certainly can't argue about the price.

Afterwards, Klara and Monika lead me to a café where we meet up with BC for a drink. He is heading off to Finisterre tomorrow morning and our paths will never cross again. We all have a beer which is quite definitely triumphant. I forget the days and nights when I cursed him for inanity and snoring, when I would plan a day's walking to avoid him. All I see is the man who helped me yesterday. I have thought a lot today about what he and the German women did and I have deliberated about what I would have done if the situation was reversed. I certainly would have helped - there is no doubt about that - but whether I would have done it with such compassion and concern is doubtful. Taking the piss out of him afterwards behind his back would have been a more likely course of action. Somehow, buying him a beer doesn't feel like enough. Of course, he might have taken the piss behind my back too, but I don't think so. He is a better man than that. BC's treating himself to a night in a hotel, but he's going to bed early. There is warmth in the goodbyes but I think we all know that the friendships we make here are not necessarily going to continue. They are a special moment in a special time, but I know I won't forget BC or Klara and Monika.

There is the luxury of a midnight curfew which is two hours longer than we're used to. The German girls and I order more beers and we're joined by other pilgrims. Amidst all the laughing and joking, there is a French woman who is quiet to the point of sadness.

She is heading back to France tomorrow and can't come to terms with the fact that she can get a direct train to the French border. "I just want to walk back", she laments and we all know exactly what she means.

We're also spotted by a rather boisterous Pepe and some of his friends. He pats me violently on the back and says,

"We made it!" and then adds, "Do you feel Spanish?"

I look down over my Irish rugby jersey to where my blue England cricket hat is resting on my knees. I don't really feel Spanish at all (though I probably will when the next international football tournament gets underway) and haven't done for the entire journey. It is still a foreign country, though I know a lot more about it now I've walked across it. It doesn't seem to matter somehow. What the journey has done has brought alive the memories of my father, the man I lost at the age of 14. I saw his car in Carrión de los Condes, ate soup with him in Mansilla de las Mulas and smelled childhood holidays in Fonfría. Some may see these signs as evidence that I have been guided along the way. I am too sensible and rational for that. Of course I am, I think.

Klara and Monika have no idea of my Spanish background and Monika looks at me over her glasses,

"At first, we thought you were German".

It brings out a few laughs including a genuine one from me. We're on for the evening which several beers later eventually leads to a rather drunken uphill scramble to get back to our hostel before the midnight curfew which we make with a couple of minutes to spare.

It is a novelty to wake up and not think about walking, but old habits die hard and I am up at 6am. I'm not alone either but soon a collective "why bother?" ripples through the dormitory and we all drift off again. It doesn't make a huge difference as we all are all up and about ninety minutes later with some people packing their rucksacks to head back to their own countries and their normal lives.

The only appointment I have is at the Cathedral for the pilgrims' mass. This is at midday and, after another exploratory trip around the streets of Santiago, I get there an hour early to get a seat in the transept. This will put me in pole position for the swinging of the *Botafumeiro*. This is the great silver incense burner which looks not unlike the FA Cup. It rests in front of the altar suspended on a 35-metre long rope, and at a given time, half a dozen people pull on the other end allowing it to swing over the congregation. It is something of a tourist attraction now but it originally served the practical purpose of disguising the smell of arriving pilgrims. It is not used at every pilgrims' mass and there is some ambiguity as to when it's employed. There's a rumour that a lot depends on how many coach parties are in town and how much their groups are willing to spend to witness it but I have no idea how true this is. All I know from other pilgrims is that it was certainly swung yesterday. It is in position though, so that's a good sign, and it seems that there are enough tourist groups around to fill up the cathedral.

It is difficult to spot fellow pilgrims now, even at mass. We have all merged in with the great well-washed. There are a few with backpacks who have just arrived, but everybody seems reasonably well groomed compared to normal. We are starting to shake off our pilgrimage identity. I am sitting with a group who has travelled here from Italy by plane, and the woman next to me is very excited that I'm a genuine foot pilgrim and I'm asked by several of the group to pose for photos. One woman wants to take a photo of my feet but I politely refuse. My mother warned me about women like that. I am actually sitting in a row reserved for their tour but hadn't noticed. Just before the service begins, their group leader approaches and asks me to move. My new friends aren't having this at all and I get the feeling that I've just been adopted.

"He's a real pilgrim. He walked 800km to get here and he needs to sit down. He can stay here," argues one formidable looking woman a couple of seats down. There is vocal general agreement all around her, though this could be because she looks considerably scarier than the rep does.

The leader knows that he can't take on a bench full of Italian women without

a)   creating a scene, and
b)   any chance of winning,

so he decides wisely to walk away and not pursue the argument any further.

Most of the mass passes by in a bit of a blur. During the sermon, the priest reads out the nationalities of the pilgrims who have arrived in the past 24 hours but we are all waiting for the *Botafumeiro* moment and it comes near the end. Six men emerge in robes and pull on a rope and the silver incense burner starts to move, gradually at first but soon the arcs get bigger and it rises up towards the ceiling, filling this part of the Cathedral with bluish smoke. "Oohs" and "ahhs" emanate from an animated congregation who behave as if they are watching a firework display. The *Botafumeiro* descends at an alarming speed and, while it doesn't hit anyone, it feels as if it comes closer than it should. The rope pullers don't exactly look as if they are in complete control of it either, but they expertly slow down the pace, the swinging gradually stops, and the applause is thunderous.

Even after the mass when most of the congregation has left, the cathedral still feels too busy and impersonal to finish the pilgrimage formally. Even trying to sit down quietly is proving difficult because of the sounds of photographs being taken and historical explanations being given – the continuous noise of tourism. I keep trying to pick a moment to head towards the statue of St James but it is not even close to feeling right. It shouldn't end having to push through crowds and listen to guided tours. I feel sure I will recognise the right moment when it arrives, but after twenty minutes of sitting there and waiting, I get up and leave.

The rest of the day is spent sauntering around Santiago. I pick up a couple of English language novels and also feel the need for some time on my own which I can't get in the cathedral, so I sit in a park for a couple of hours before heading back to the town centre. I decide to act on the policy that was so successful yesterday, which is just to wander about and see who I bump into. This results in something of a delightful "café crawl". It starts with a drink with Michael and we're soon joined by Jim and Sue. The last time we were together like this was at Carrión two and a half weeks ago. We have a couple of beers and arrange to meet up later for dinner. I also meet Jan and Andrew who have made it after walking together every day for over a month. I really want to ask what the future holds for them but it just feels like too personal a question. Jan is flying back to Scotland from Madrid in a couple of days, while Andrew is heading back to Australia on the same day via Paris. They make no comment on what is going to happen next and I hope it is not the end for them. I am willing to bet that there will be no sadder parting on the Camino this year. Rod and Cassie are also here, as too are Brian and Herb, and it becomes a very drunken and joyous afternoon indeed.

I return to the cathedral in the early evening. In one of the side chapels, there is a meeting every day for pilgrims to share some of the experiences of their journey. Michael is already in situ, translating the stories of others from Spanish into German, English and French. It's not one of the most publicised activities of the Camino, which is possibly why there are only about twenty of us in attendance, most of whom are strangers to me.

One man gets up and starts off by saying "I don't know if any of you recognise me". I do; the bugger's snoring kept me awake in Rabanal. I inwardly curse my lack of charity, sit back, and devote my full attention to his words. There are tears in his eyes as he talks about all the goodwill he received along the journey, which is enough to make me feel guilty. It turns out he's a doctor, and while he talks about helping pilgrims on the way it's very clear that he feels that he's received a lot more than he's given.

Others get up to talk, with one or two thanking the doctor for his help in times of illness. There are other tales; of pain, smiles and tears, all accompanied by the frequent nods and laughter of recognition. It is a shame BC isn't here because he would have loved it. He was a great believer in the Camino spirit, liked to talk, and enjoyed an audience.

I intended to keep quiet and listen to everyone else but I suddenly decide that if BC can't be here in person, he really should be here in anecdote. I stand up right at the end of the session and tell my tale of getting ill in Arzúa and receiving BC's help when I was at my absolute weakest, despite my previous attitude towards him. It feels like a confession. There can't be that many times the word "bastard" has been said down a microphone in the cathedral at Santiago, when I briefly forget that I'm in a house of God and not walking up a hill. Nobody says anything, or more importantly, appears to wince. When it is all over we exit into a deserted cathedral.

My mind is full of the people I haven't seen; I know Olivia was here yesterday as I bumped into her occasional walking partner, Nita, at the pilgrims' mass, but alas we never had a catch-up. I don't know what's happened to Bernard and his famous bottle of wine, and the other Francophones from that delightful night in Calzadilla; I've no idea if Carrie and the in-laws made it here, or know the fate of Marco or Valerio, Tony the retired pilot and his wife Margaret, even the tedious Caitlin. I'll never find out and it doesn't feel right somehow. I hope they all arrived and that their reasons for doing the Camino are fulfilled. I also think back to the tragedies that affected my friends this year. Without them, I wouldn't have come here.

I don't have any interest in statues and relics. I don't like too much emphasis being placed on the mystic, but I do need an ending. Behind the main altar of the cathedral is a statue of St James. If the truth be known I find it hideous, but it represents the reason why I'm here. At the side of the altar, we all wait in line to climb some steps which will take us behind the statue. The traditional thing to do is to hug him from behind which is something I'd normally baulk at, but I find myself embracing it for all I'm worth. For some reason, the words of the woman I met at the British branch of the Confraternity of St James come back to me, "I wish I was going to Santiago for the first time again." They make perfect sense now.

It is then a descent below the statue to where some bones which may, or more likely may not, belong to the man himself are kept in a silver casket. I don't think it matters if they're genuine or not. It's not what they are but what they represent. This is where the Camino ends for all of us but in my case, the pilgrimage is continuing. For me the easy bit has just finished; things are now about to get uncertain.

I got here last night and, after nearly six weeks of only using my legs, I had the luxury of experiencing two coach journeys. In seven hours they covered about half the distance of my Camino but in the opposite direction. It is a warm morning and the sun is shining over the green hills. There is a dog barking nearby as I walk up a short brick path to an unlocked iron gate. Opening it isn't straightforward; it has to be lifted up slightly to release properly. I struggle with it for a few seconds before successfully navigating my way through the entrance to the enclosed field within. I've never been here before, but have thought a lot about what it would be like when I did. Even so, this moment is not how I imagined it to be. I look around for a few brief seconds, even though I know the exact place to find what I am looking for. There are nine places marked in the stone wall and my eyes focus on the middle one. It is the date that I notice first; September 10th, the day I started my Camino. This isn't a coincidence. Neither is the name engraved above it: Rodolfo Noriega. I don't know what to say - there's nothing I can say - but I can feel tears welling up inside me. Destination reached. Pilgrimage achieved.

ACKNOWLEDGEMENTS

Writing this book has taken a lot longer than it should have done, but it wouldn't have seen the light of day at all without the encouraging words from Tracy Maylath, Jo Street, and Paul Waters, who managed to say the right things at exactly the right time. Tracy also managed to read through previous versions of this story as did Seamus Graham, Fiona Dick, Neil Hatfield, Paul Ryan, Ed Snape, Trish Ebrell, Susana Raby, James Wickham, Mary Theresa McGrellis, Matt Drake, Jim Kerr, Lynda Ryalls, Nick Ryalls, Jason Pealin, and Sally Beswick. I'd like to thank them for their comments and advice. I'd also like to thank Sophie B. Hawkins for her album *Whaler,* which was played in the background when a lot of this was being written. To Jason, Margriet, Sally, and Ted whose personal losses helped me make my mind up to do the Camino, and finally to my dad who made me Spanish.

ABOUT THE AUTHOR

Rudy Noriega was born in Liverpool in 1970. He is a freelance radio producer and broadcast journalist. He has worked on programmes for BBC Radio 2, Radio 5 Live, Radio Sweden International and Radio Ara in Luxembourg. You can occasionally hear him on the air but only when he's doing a voiceover as a world leader, a Kremlin spokesman or an international terrorist. His hobbies include pub quizzes, darts and not surprisingly, walking.

He writes the blogs, www.thingslearnedthisweek.blogspot.com and www.planeboattrain.blogspot.com .

He lives in the West Midlands.

You can leave any comments on the Grumpy Pilgrim Facebook page:

https://www.facebook.com/thegrumpypilgrim/

Printed in Great Britain
by Amazon

42792902R00133